Journey of Soul

HAROLD KLEMP

Mahanta Transcripts
Book 1

ECKANKAR
Minneapolis
www.Eckankar.org

Journey of Soul, Mahanta Transcripts, Book 1

Copyright © 1988 ECKANKAR

Printed in USA

Compiled by Joan Klemp and Anne Pezdirc
Edited by Anthony Moore and Mary Carroll Moore
Illustrations by Signy Cohen
Author photo (spine and page 295) by Art Galbraith
Fourth printing—2019

MAHANTA

This book has been authored by and published under the supervision of the Mahanta, the Living ECK Master, Sri Harold Klemp. It is the Word of ECK.

Library of Congress Cataloging-in-Publication Data

Klemp, Harold.
    Journey of soul / Harold Klemp.
        p. cm.
    Includes index.
    ISBN 978-1-57043-234-7 (pbk. : alk. paper)
    1. Spiritual life—Eckankar (Organization) 2. Eckankar (Organiza-tion)—Doctrines. I. Title.
    BP605.E3K56 2007
    299'.93—dc22
                                                         2007000155

CONTENTS

Foreword ix

The Altar of Blinding Light 1
The Meeting • The Altar • The Return

1. The New Living ECK Master 7
Into the Heart of God • Paul Twitchell's Mission • What
Eckankar Offers • The New Master Announced • 1970
ECK-Vidya Foretells Mastership • Invitation to Master-
ship • In Presenting the Message of ECK

2. The Line Was Busy 17
Spirit Wants to Lead Us to Truth • The Importance of
Taking Your Time in ECK • The Line Was Busy • What
Gives Life to Presenting ECK? • The Living ECK Master
Is a Wayshower • That Still Small Voice • Always One
More Step • A Message to Garcia • The Sound and Light
of ECK

3. The Acorn Planter 33
The Sound of ECK • Planting Seeds • The Acorn Planter

4. The Journey of Soul 43
Life's Lessons • Soul's Journey • Responsibilities and Spiri-
tual Unfoldment • Healings via Spirit • Losing the Fear of
Death • Giving Space to Others • Experiences of Soul • The
Darshan • ECK Spiritual Aides • Being Vehicles for ECK

5. The Secret Path to Heaven 61
The Cycles of Life • Where Is Heaven? • The Path to Self-
Mastership • Storytellers of the Cheyenne • The Secret
Path beyond Soul Travel • The Protection of the ECK

6. The Law of Silence 73
Is ECK Real? • What Is the Sound? • How the Law of
Silence Works • Karma's Delayed Fuse • The Greater

Disciplines • Is ECK Truth? • Finding the Path of ECK •
Becoming a Co-worker with God • Our Mission in Life

7. Child in the Wilderness 89
    Past Lives • The Call of Soul • The Source of Our Problems
    • The Wayshowers

8. Spiritual Liberation 99
    The Light and Sound of God • The Purifying of Soul •
    Healing and Karma • What Is Illusion? • How to Be a
    Vehicle for ECK • Recognizing Spiritual Experiences •
    Overcoming the Fear of Death • Lessons in Charity • How
    the Master Gives Love • Interpreting Dreams • Climbing
    the Mountain to God

9. The Liberation of Soul 117
    A Key to Life • How to Figure It Out • Shedding Guilt •
    Cause and Effect • Insight on Healing

10. The Divine Knowledge 129
    What True Detachment Means • Being Involved in Life
    • Contact with Divine Spirit • The Path of Direct Experi-
    ence • A Life of Action • Facing Responsibilities • Inflow
    and Outflow • No Worship in ECK • The Key to Liberation

11. The Enigma of ECK 143
    A Nudge from Spirit • The ECK Masters' Role in History •
    The Culture of ECK • The Spiritual Laws • Stepping-
    Stones • The Reality of ECK • Self-Mastery

12. The Knack of Self-Reliance 159
    Children's Day • Children and Discipline • Immobility
    Traps • The Plus Factor • Awakening Your Self-Reliance
    • How to Talk about ECK • Keeping a Good Thing Going
    • A Firm Foundation • Mixed Blessing

13. The Nature of Soul 173
    Creating Your Own World as Soul • Children in ECK • The
    Spiritual Consciousness of the Child • The Foundation of
    the Light and Sound • Proof of the Existence of Soul? •
    Motivation • Touched by the ECK

14. Eckankar, the Crossroads of Life 187
    The Right Way to Pray • One More Step • There Is Always
    an Answer • Soul at the Crossroads • The Voice of God •
    Studying the ECK-Vidya • The Waters of Immortality •
    Embrace Life with Responsibility • How Come You Are

Always Calm? • Meetings with the Vairagi Masters • The
Point of Self-Mastery

15. **Eckankar, the Great Adventure** 203
Effect of the Sound on the Light • Communicating with God
• Three Basics in ECK • If He's Real, You'd Know • An
Openness of Heart • Speaking Soul to Soul • ECK Foo Yung
• A Little Message • Fitting in the Spiritual Exercises •
What Is the Purpose of Soul? • The Blue Light Special

16. **The Secrets of ECK** 219
The ECK Provides • How Spirit Comes into Our Life •
What Is the Key? • The Heart of the Teachings • Living in
the Presence of God • Opening the Door of Soul

17. **Questions and Answers** 229
One-on-One • Freedom for Soul • Sex and Eckankar •
Finding a Balance • ECK and Drugs Don't Mix • Violation
of the Spiritual Law • Teaching Small Children about
ECK • Practicing Detachment • Entering the Inner Temple
• Your Key to the Spiritual Worlds

18. **The Practical Wisdom of ECK** 243
Bringing Mastership into Our Life • Shining the Light of
Soul on Fear • The Power that Fear Can Have

19. **ECK Consciousness Five** 249
The ECK Spiritual Aide Program • The Spiritual Heritage
of Soul • Surrender to God • The Protection of the ECK

20. **Consciousness Five** 255
Following Two Paths • The Outer and Inner Master •
Help from Spirit • In the Nearness of Your Heart

21. **The Breath of Life** 263
Moving toward Self-Mastery • The Purpose of the Negative
Power • Working with Common Courtesy • The Divine
Laws • Keeping in Shape Spiritually • The Balance of the
Sound • Meeting the ECK Masters • What Makes ECK
Real? • The Controversy over Abortion • Living the Golden
Rule

22. **The Master Power** 279
ECK, the Master Power • The Protection of Spirit • Con-
tacting the Master Power • How the Secret Word Works
• Who Is My Inner Master? • What to Seek First • Contact

with the Light and Sound • Why Can't a Woman Become the Living ECK Master? • The Importance of the Monthly Initiate Report • Requests for Healing • Turning It over to Spirit • Fixing It Yourself

About the Author 295

Next Steps in Spiritual Exploration 297

Glossary 301

Index 305

FOREWORD

The teachings of ECK define the nature of Soul. You are Soul, a particle of God sent into the worlds (including earth) to gain spiritual experience.

The goal in ECK is spiritual freedom in this lifetime, after which you become a Co-worker with God, both here and in the next world. Karma and reincarnation are primary beliefs.

Key to the ECK teachings is the Mahanta, the Living ECK Master. He has the special ability to act as both the Inner and Outer Master for ECK students. The prophet of Eckankar, he is given respect but is not worshipped. He teaches the sacred name of God, HU. When sung just a few minutes each day, HU will lift you spiritually into the Light and Sound of God—the ECK (Holy Spirit). This easy spiritual exercise and others will purify you. You are then able to accept the full love of God in this lifetime.

Sri Harold Klemp is the Mahanta, the Living ECK Master today. Author of many books, discourses, and articles, he teaches the ins and outs of the spiritual life. His teachings lift people and help them recognize and understand their own experiences in the Light and Sound of God. Many of his talks are available to you on audio and video recordings.

Journey of Soul, Mahanta Transcripts, Book 1, contains his historic talks from 1981 to 1982. May they serve to uplift you to a greater vision of life.

THE ALTAR OF BLINDING LIGHT

ruly, when you begin consciously to participate in this Life Stream, there is in you a well of water ever springing up, sufficient to supply the whole world.

—The Tiger's Fang

The world I was to visit shortly was that of Divine Being. It demanded perfect loyalty to the Sugmad and the ECK. It required total commitment, before the gates to a hidden spring were opened for me to experience and enjoy—to fill myself with the divine Light and Sound of ECK.

Eventually I would return with the love and blessings of the Living ECK Master, the Nine Silent Ones, and the Order of the Vairagi.

THE MEETING

The Living ECK Master called a meeting on the Inner Planes. About twelve ECK couples attended, plus a number of single ECKists. He had business with everyone on the list gathered in the open meeting room. The first couple on the list called before the small assembly was to be initiated by the Master. Since their initiation had required a verbal affirmation from my wife and me, we endorsed them.

"As long as you and your wife are still up," the Master said, "Let's do our matter with you too, right away."

This was a surprise, since we were scheduled last on the consultation list. Walking to the front of the group of Higher Initiates, we faced them. The Master sat off to our right and said, "Now we have to consider whether they have earned their place in the spiritual worlds." He instructed everyone to contemplate, to look into the inner vision. "When you look to the Mahanta, what do you see?" he asked the Higher Initiates.

My last gaze swept around the group. Several of them avoided my eyes. I thought, *Well, I'm not always seeing eye to eye with some of them. And now my wife and I find ourselves on trial. They are our judges.* I slipped into contemplation, deeper and deeper into the inner worlds, my wife beside me.

"Open your eyes," she said excitedly. "Oh, Harold, open your eyes." But with that her words were drowned out by the beautiful music of the ECK, the Holy Spirit. I opened my eyelids with difficulty, finding myself a newborn babe slipping into a strange new heaven. "Keep going," whispered someone in encouragement. Struggling, I moved out of the womb of the lower worlds into this new and higher but unknown world of divine truth, infinite love, and justice.

> I moved out of the womb of the lower worlds into this new and higher but unknown world of divine truth, infinite love, and justice.

Slowly, I crawled out and emerged into the new land. The fear of slipping back into the womb of security lay behind. I had made it. Instinctively I inched forward on my belly toward an altar of blinding Light. Here glistened the Light of God.

"What, how dare you come here, you, you pallid thing," challenged a voice from the golden mist surrounding the pillar of Light.

"I have earned the right," I snapped in defiance. "I have earned the right."

"Oh, did you now," retorted the voice with discernment.

"Yes, I did," I shouted. "I worked and slaved for this opportunity through all my varied lifetimes."

"Well, go then and see what reward you've earned," laughed the deep, melodious voice.

I worked and slaved for this opportunity through all my varied lifetimes.

The Altar

I now crawled into the altar of pure, brilliant, shattering Light that streamed from above, and was snatched upward to heights beyond my wildest dreams. "And so, do you serve the ECK, the Sugmad?" demanded the unknown inquisitor, as I continued to soar upward through the many subtle worlds of Divine Being.

"Yes," I said, giving my oath. "I give divine love to the ECK and the Sugmad."

"And compassion and tolerance to all your fellow creatures?"

"Yes, to the Sugmad, the ECK, and all divine creatures."

"Do you hold back in your love and service to Sugmad, in your loyalty?"

By now I was flashing into the very heart of God. Yet, paradoxically, I tenaciously clutched my narrow attitudes and self-righteousness out of fear of losing myself in the immense Ocean of Love and Mercy.

Then I surrendered all to the Sugmad.

Turning loose every vestige of self-service, of self-love, I spun free of my clinging, lower nature and soared more freely than before, reaching beyond the limits of my imagination. I gave up all, crying to God while being swept inward to the Divine Being.

THE RETURN

After what seemed a long interval, I slowly returned. "You may open your eyes and return now," spoke a firm, high-pitched voice. "It's over. You're done." Before me stood a white-robed man, who had invisibly accompanied me in carrying out this mission. I recognized his presence. He reminded me of Fubbi Quantz, the ECK Master in charge of the Katsupari Monastery in Tibet. The Living ECK Master sat beside him smiling.

"Thank you," I said to the white-robed figure.

"I shall thank you," he replied.

"That was an extraordinary experience," I further thanked the Master, as my wife stood beside me.

"You were right all along in your understanding of what's been happening on the physical plane at the Eckankar International Office," said the Master, commenting upon a situation that had troubled me. "And this proves it to you." The Master went to the door to step into the vast worlds of God to travel as he chose.

The other people had long gone. My wife and I took our leave to puzzle about the divine mystery that had touched us.

This excerpt, from a personal letter by Harold Klemp, was read by the Living ECK Master at the 1981 World Wide of ECK in Anaheim, California. He read it to introduce his successor, Sri Harold Klemp, the 973rd Mahanta, the Living ECK Master.

In a private meeting in Anaheim, California, on the night of October 22, 1981, Sri Harold Klemp received a blue carnation from his predecessor, symbolic of the completion of the ancient inner and outer ritual of the passing of the Rod of ECK Power. He had already accepted the Rod of ECK Power as the 973rd Mahanta, the Living ECK Master at midnight on October 22 in the Valley of Tirmer in northern Tibet, during an inner ceremony.

1

THE NEW LIVING ECK MASTER

I wondered how to approach this subject this evening. My little girl just turned eight, and as you know, children are sometimes tuned in to the ECK more than we are as adults.

She gave me permission to say this. She said, "Just know that you're talking to each person, one at a time, about the ECK and about the Sugmad."

This was yesterday, and I must not have had the full understanding of it, because she came to me again today and said, "Now remember, Daddy, a person doesn't know how the one sitting next to him feels and how he thinks. So it's you talking to one person at a time." And, of course, this is speaking directly to Soul.

INTO THE HEART OF GOD

It must have been a year and a half or two years ago that I had written and put away the letter that was just read about the altar of blinding light. I kept it in my dream notebook and thought this was something very quiet and very private.

In *The Tiger's Fang*, you may recall how Rebazar Tarzs took Paul Twitchell through the God

Worlds of ECK, beginning in the lower planes and going upward into the heart of God. After they had gone to the Sugmad and returned, they met another spiritual traveler, Shamus-i-Tabriz, who said to Rebazar Tarzs something on the order of, "Ah, he has been to Sugmad. He has become the Anami?"

Rebazar said, "Yes," and Shamus-i-Tabriz, having had the experience himself, said, "I can see by his light that he has much to learn. But there is time."

PAUL TWITCHELL'S MISSION

One of the biggest things Paul Twitchell did for us was to show us what a spiritual Master is really like. This was a difficult task because the spiritual light had grown very dim.

The message of ECK was to be brought out again into the mainstream of life.

The Order of the Vairagi determined that the message of ECK was to be brought out again into the mainstream of life, so Paul Twitchell was brought forward as the Mahanta, the Living ECK Master in 1965. He came out with the ECK message and presented it simply, through his writings and his lectures.

One thing he had in mind when presenting this message of ECK was to let the uninitiated know about it through a book; to let the people know about the Sound and Light of the ECK, of Divine Spirit.

Paul, through his writings, provided tools for us. We could give someone a book such as *The Tiger's Fang* or leave it on a park bench or in a Laundromat. Or we could put up a poster that told somebody where to find more information about the Sugmad and about the Divine Spirit, the Audible Life Current.

WHAT ECKANKAR OFFERS

Eckankar has much to offer to the people of these spiritual times, because it gives the gospel of liberation—of spiritual liberation.

The orthodox religions—and this is not a criticism but an observation—have gone to the social gospel, which is all right. But we look to spiritual liberation, and one who is interested in finding Self-Realization and God-Realization can do this.

Throughout history the Living ECK Masters have set out a series of spiritual exercises—and there are a whole series of them—whereby an individual may unfold himself into the state of knowing who and what he is, what his mission is in life.

This is Self-Realization, and then on to God-Realization.

There is Light and Love in this path such as I have never experienced in any of the other teachings where I had searched before finding this. And many of you have found the same.

An individual may unfold himself into the state of knowing who and what he is, what his mission is in life.

THE NEW MASTER ANNOUNCED

October 22 is the spiritual New Year for Eckankar, and last evening, several of the Higher Initiates were called together for the announcement of the new Living ECK Master. They had all seated themselves when Patti Simpson, whom some of you know, came in and saw two slips of paper on the sofa which said, Reserved.

She ended up sitting on the floor with somebody else, and she wondered, *Why am I sitting on the floor, with those two yellow pieces of paper sitting on the sofa?* The seats were reserved for my wife and me.

There has always been a Living ECK Master at all times on this earth planet and in all the other universes, both on the physical plane and in the higher worlds that are described in *The Tiger's Fang*, all the way up into the pure positive God Worlds.

Fubbi Quantz was a seeker who had this thirst for God-Realization. He was studying at a monastery, and life had put him against the rock where he couldn't see his way out. So he made a decision: I'm going to go up to the mountain. He probably figured that the mountain peak was as good a place as any to resolve the situation.

He got up to the mountain peak, and he said, in effect, "God, why have you forsaken me?"

After a little while, he heard a voice that said something like, "My son, I haven't forsaken you. I have been with you through the ages." I don't have the exact words, but the lightning flashed and the thunder rolled, and from that point on he knew the meaning of the words *I am always with you.*

He had the experience of Sugmad. He had been to the Anami, to the Ocean of Love and Mercy.

He went back down to the monastery, and the abbot who was in charge knew and understood what he had experienced and left him alone. Fubbi Quantz went into his cell and contemplated for quite some time, at the end of which he came out and took up his mission, his responsibilities as the Mahanta, the Living ECK Master.

What I'm saying here is that it may seem easy and sometimes it may seem hard as we walk the path of our own God Worlds. The Living ECK Master is there as the Wayshower but also, even more, to assist us in our own efforts.

It may seem easy and sometimes it may seem hard as we walk the path of our own God Worlds.

1970 ECK-VIDYA FORETELLS MASTERSHIP

In 1970 at the Fourth World Wide Seminar, while Paul Twitchell was the Mahanta, the Living ECK Master, I was sitting in the audience when the ECK-Vidya opened for me. The words came—very slowly and distinctly—that there would be another Living ECK Master, and then after that would be my turn.

I sat back and, of course, felt really secure, because you feel safe when you know there's another one ahead of you. I started to chuckle to myself. I thought, *Boy, this is really something, how the ECK and the Mahanta, the Living ECK Master will bring out whatever one needs to know in his life, sometimes very clearly by words and most often by a feeling or a knowingness, or whatever.*

We were all sitting at tables, and I started chuckling out loud and didn't really pay particular attention to anyone else. All of a sudden I noticed that people were giving me funny looks as I sat there laughing. *Why is he laughing to himself?*

I decided I'd better knock this off. This is one of the little secrets I had better hide if I want to sit here for the whole lecture. So I had to keep this to myself.

The next year Darwin Gross stepped in, and I still felt pretty safe. The ECK or the Mahanta, the Living ECK Master will give you direction, and you know it. Yet when I went to Las Vegas that time, I hoped something hadn't been moved up or that any plans hadn't been changed. And when Darwin was announced, I applauded as hard as anyone. I was really very happy. I gave him my whole support, and it was heartfelt support.

The Living ECK Master in every age has been a hard worker. To earn the gift, one must work for it. One must earn it in the true coin whether it's for the First Initiation, the Second, the Fifth, or on up. We must earn it in some manner, in a way that suits us.

INVITATION TO MASTERSHIP

The time had come last year when I was approached by the Living ECK Master; by the Order

The Mahanta, the Living ECK Master will bring out whatever one needs to know in his life, sometimes very clearly by words and most often by a feeling or a knowingness.

of the Vairagi; and by the Silent Ones, the Council of the Nine. I was asked if I would take this position, and of course I said yes, because I felt strong enough.

I figured from the inner experiences over the years that had given this same knowledge again and again by the Inner Master, at that temple within myself, that I was strong enough. And when I said yes, it knocked me for a loop and I went flipping over backward a couple of times.

It reminds me a little bit of Milarepa's master, Marpa. Some of his disciples said to him, "Can we help you carry some of the load?" First he said no, but they insisted that they wanted to, so he directed some of his spiritual load at a heavy oak door. He said, "A little bit will be put there," and the oak door split.

Each individual is given, or earns, his share of the Sound and Light of ECK and the blessings.

They stood and looked and said something like, "Oh-ho!" And from that point on, they realized that each individual is given, or earns, his share of the Sound and Light of ECK and the blessings. I found this out too. It was too much.

There was a meeting up in the Himalayan mountains last year where the ECK Masters Fubbi Quantz, Rebazar Tarzs, Lai Tsi, Gopal Das, Peddar Zaskq, and others were walking along this dirt road, and I was with them. They looked over the situation, and they were very. . . understanding, I guess is the word, and let me off the hook for another year, until there was enough strength to make this possible.

IN PRESENTING THE MESSAGE OF ECK

The point I made earlier was that in presenting the message of ECK we can let the uninitiated know about the Sound and Light of ECK through a book. A second point is to keep the ECK message simple. One of the ways that was passed along to keep the

ECK message simple is, before a talk or before any ECK function, to declare oneself a vehicle for the Sugmad, the ECK, and the Mahanta. Then go do it. Don't think twice about it.

There will be a difference in the way you give the talk or speak with another individual. There will be a difference. And this is a real help and a real aid that I have used myself—to declare myself a vehicle for the Sugmad, for the ECK, and for the Mahanta.

Several of us participated a couple of years ago in a TV show. We who were being interviewed felt we were doing very well. But it turned out that if we had put more attention in our presentation of ECK on the temple within us, it would have been more helpful to the un-initiated who viewed this program a number of times—three, four, and five times—on a Christian network station. Since then, I've realized that to keep the ECK message simple, a primary point to bring out is to go to that temple within you. But don't stop there; go on. Go to that temple within you, but don't linger there.

Go to that temple within you, but don't linger there.

It is a real privilege to be with you this evening and to work with you in presenting the message of ECK to the uninitiated. Paul Twitchell brought out the ECK writings and the ECK books as a foundation, and this direction will continue.

The initiates of ECK have become stronger, so that now it has become possible to take a new step. There are many Souls that are ready to hear this ancient gospel. We are ready, in a gentle way, to reach out with the books of ECK, with our own being, to present it so that they may make up their own minds without any pressure.

The Living ECK Master will not influence any-one in his decisions, whether it is what direction he should take on the spiritual path, in his health mat-ters, or his personal problems. There is assistance given from the Inner Master for each individual. This help and this love come directly from the ECK, and each of you has direct access to it.

In the Light and Sound of ECK, may the blessings be.

First Talk, World Wide of ECK, Anaheim, California, Friday, October 23, 1981

I knew, using the creative faculty, there was a way we could get to sit down, talk, and work this out. I went across the street to the phone booth by the grocery store and called home.

2
THE LINE WAS BUSY

he ECK culture is coming out in the music. Music has a way of getting through where talks, and sometimes even books, come through in second place. It gets through to us in a gentle way, and especially if there's a catchy tune or a haunting melody, we will carry it with us and hum it, sometimes absentmindedly. Of course, it is the positive tunes we like to carry with us.

SPIRIT WANTS TO LEAD US TO TRUTH

There are many times in ECK, as the greater flow of Spirit comes through, that we would like to keep doing what we've always done. We would like to keep our habits and our routines. But when the ECK, this Divine Spirit in the form of the Light and Sound, touches the life of the truth seeker, It begins to bring changes. They'll be gentle at first, and they may always be gentle, depending upon how quickly we can give up our old ways and let go.

Spirit wants to lead us to Truth, to Self-Realization and God-Realization, and the way to do this is to remove those karmic conditions which have stood between us and the spiritual goal that we see in the example of the Living ECK Master and in the Higher Initiates. As far as understanding it in a mental way,

Many times, as the greater flow of Spirit comes through, we would like to keep doing what we've always done, our habits and our routines.

it's completely beyond us until we are able to experience that reality ourselves, such as reaching the Soul Plane and becoming established there, as in Self-Realization.

The Greeks said, Know thyself. We hear these words spoken so often today, yet one wonders if the people who use them truly know what they mean. It's like a parrot saying, "Know thyself, know thyself, know thyself."

Last night we were able to meet, many of us, and shake hands. This was a new experience for me. I said, "Well, a second baseman on the softball team who can hop off the stage with a little help ought to be able to shake hands with friends for a few hours." We started about 9:30 and went to 10:30. I had no sense of time. Then about a quarter after eleven or so, I felt sudden fatigue.

Then something happened, something I hadn't felt before. There was tremendous energy and the love coming from all of you—it almost took me by surprise. I began to feel better.

Just a few minutes later, one of the Eckankar staff members came up and said, "You know, you have two more nights." There were several of you standing in that area, maybe two hundred, and we had started out with about thirty-five hundred. I decided somehow we'd keep going until we could say, Well, we did the best we could.

The staff members who were standing by said, "We'll stick around. If you can do it, we can do it."

I was feeling better, really good, very strong. So good, in fact, that I said to the staff members who were standing by, helping to keep everything flowing, "You guys can work in shifts if you want to. I'm feeling pretty good, so you just come and go as you please." They said, "We'll stick around. If you can do it, we can do it."

So we met and said hello to the rest of you. Then

as I started walking out, still feeling pretty strong, I noticed my legs felt kind of wobbly.

A week ago Thursday we played in a softball tournament. This was the playoff, and on this night, if you won, you had to play again. It was just our luck to win, because we all wanted to go home. We had other things to do. We had to play several games until a quarter to seven. After that game the umpire said, "You guys won. Come back at nine o'clock." Of course, we didn't live right on the ball field. Most of us lived miles away, but we said, "All right, we'll do that."

We came back at nine o'clock and, as luck would have it, we won again. Some of the boys wanted to go home, but when it came time to play another game, they were just like those of you who waited last night and decided to stick it out. We played that game and we did well. And we won in spirit; I'll have to say that. I won't say what the score was, but it was respectable.

So I was feeling pretty good last night. Except for the rubbery legs as I walked away, I was feeling strong. I went back to the room and slept well.

The Order of the Vairagi, the ECK Masters, work together. They help out, and for those of you who have the eyes to see, you will see the ECK Masters. Sometimes you aren't able to see them, but they're there. The ECK Masters work in harmony and in love because of their love for the Sugmad. They are Co-workers with God.

There is a lot of help for you and for the person sitting in this chair from Lai Tsi, Gopal Das, Peddar Zaskq, Rebazar Tarzs, Fubbi Quantz, Yaubl Sacabi, Shamus-i-Tabriz, and a couple of hundred more besides. There is harmony and goodwill that exists between the ECK Masters as they work together to present the message of ECK in all the worlds.

The Order of the Vairagi, the ECK Masters, work together.

When you have a question, go to that temple within you. Read in *The Shariyat-Ki-Sugmad*, in *The Spiritual Notebook*; take this seed of information into contemplation, and find out for yourself. This way, once you get an answer, you will have it. It will be firm and solid. You will have it and know, and no one, nor anything, will ever be able to take it away from you, because you have found and discovered this for yourself.

This is where you will find that the teachings of ECK stand apart from any of the other religious teachings. You experience it for yourself. There is no attempt to influence anyone to follow this path. You realize that you have to know for yourself.

The teachings of ECK stand apart from any other religious teachings. You experience it for yourself.

THE IMPORTANCE OF TAKING YOUR TIME IN ECK

A friend was telling me about a very good music teacher who said, "You know, I never try to convince anyone to be a musician, because there are going to be days when the note doesn't come out quite as sweet and pretty." If this happens a couple of days in a row, the real musician is able to take the experience of the sour note and know that it's a step to the harmonious note that may be just a week away, a year away.

When the times get rough, the person who has been encouraged or convinced to step on the path of Eckankar might say, "Maybe I should have thought about it a little longer, read one of the ECK books, taken my time." Read one of the ECK books. Look it over, digest it, soak it up, take your time.

Several people came by to say hello last night and said, "I'm not in ECK, but my spouse is." I said, "There's no hurry. Take your time." In a family, if one person is following ECK, it's a kindness not to inflict it upon the spouse if that individual is not interested, because the family is important—the harmony and goodwill with your close ones. To let others have their freedom reflects the harmony and goodwill that is within. Sometimes, of course, we have to make our choices.

To let others have their freedom reflects the harmony and goodwill that is within.

I found it very easy to give space to others, but when I got home at the end of a hard day at work after giving everybody their own space, it wasn't easy to do the same for my family.

You've come a long way when you can give it to your family, knowing they may have had a hard day too. Whenever some situation comes up within our families, we can find a way of harmony. If things are emotional on one side and one spouse says, "I'd like to talk about it," and the other one says, "Not now," respect that. There's always tomorrow. Just say, "OK, we have an appointment to talk about this."

I have to mention something here about the Area Mahdis. These are the ECK leaders. We work with them to coordinate activities, and they work very hard. Their personal life is sometimes stretched to the limits, and they have to work very hard at creating this harmony. They learn a lot of creativity, the use of the creative imagination, and they do this with the Spiritual Exercises of ECK and tuning in to this Divine Spirit, the ECK.

THE LINE WAS BUSY

My wife was the Area Mahdis for many years, and honestly, if that phone didn't ring every minute—I see a friend of mine here; she's nodding her head. She's been an Area Mahdis and knows, as do others of you. Yet they're the coordinators who willingly take on this job. But it's a great job, and it's absolutely necessary for presenting the message of ECK. Every time I'd walk in the door, my wife would be on the phone. If I wanted to talk with her, she'd be on the phone.

When she was off the phone, we'd start to talk and the phone would ring. I'd say, "Oh, man, how am I going to take any more of this?" I wondered about Alexander Graham Bell and what he had created. As with all creations from the inner planes, he must have meant well.

I wanted to say to my wife, "Hey, I want a little attention. I want somebody to say I'm important. I'd like a little hug."

I knew, using the ECK principles in my daily life, there was a way we could work this out.

So one night I figured it out. I got a dime. It was 9:00 or 9:30 at night, and as I went out the front door, I smiled and waved to her. I knew, using the creative faculty, using the ECK principles in my daily life, there was a way we could get to sit down, talk, and work this out. I went across the street to the phone booth by the grocery store and called home. The line was busy. But I knew she had to come up for air, so I waited. And the next time I called, she answered.

She said, "Hello," and I said, "Hello, this is Mr. Klemp. Could I arrange for an appointment sometime within the next couple of days?" She started laughing and couldn't talk, so I hung up and walked home. She said she didn't feel like talking that night; her sides hurt.

We made an appointment and finally sat down and talked about the situation: how she could work with those who wanted to help, instead of trying to do it all herself.

As she looked around, she found that there was somebody who wanted to do the ECK newsletter. "I'll have to approve it," she said, "but I don't have to write all the articles, just one." Then she asked some of the other ECKists, "Is there anybody who would like to sit the ECK Center so someone will be there if somebody comes in off the street or calls?" Sure enough, there was somebody. It was almost a miracle; it was worth the dime.

Gradually she was able to shift much of the responsibility to those who wanted to help. Then, of course, if you're an Area Mahdis or an ECK leader—which means anyone, whether you're putting out a book or whether you're teaching an ECK Satsang class—there comes a time a person will say, "Well, I've done enough; I'd like to do something else."

We need to be flexible and recognize that the law of ECK will have some way and someone to step in.

WHAT GIVES LIFE TO PRESENTING ECK?

Several years ago, there was a lady who learned a very good principle when she worked for a national organization, in one of the social programs. She had said, "I'd like to volunteer to help here."

After she worked for a while, she was offered the position as head of this large and influential organization. The person who took her on said, "Now do what you can, if you want to, and enjoy it. Learn from it and grow until the day comes that you want to step aside and maybe do something else. If you can, let me have some notice so that we can make plans for a smooth transition.

Do what you can, and enjoy it. Learn from it and grow.

You're doing it because you want to, the person ahead of you did it because she wanted to, and the person who will take your place must do it because she wants to."

This is what gives life to presenting the message of ECK. It's when you individually really want to do it and are growing. To take it one step further, maybe somebody else is just waiting and needs the experience. So there is this freedom to work and do and grow, and yet the responsibility and the opportunity to say, "Now I'd like to try something new or rest awhile," and make it a smooth transition.

Every so often we feel the need to rest and step aside from the spiritual path of ECK or whatever path we're following, and it should be done without any fear or guilt, knowing that our spiritual unfoldment is between the Inner Master and ourselves only.

It does not involve anyone else telling us we are going to hell, or anything else; we are not doing or looking at someone else's idea of worshipping God. It must be our own way. And if we want to step aside, we must be able to do so freely.

There is always a second chance on this path of ECK. There are those who have stepped aside in this lifetime and in past lifetimes. Many of us have been down this road in past lifetimes. We've said, "I have gotten as much of the Sound and Light of ECK as I feel I want this time." The decision when to take it up again is ours alone, and we may approach the Living ECK Master and ask when this can be done. Sometimes he may say, "Wait awhile. Wait another half year. Let's look it over and make absolutely sure."

The Living ECK Master is a Wayshower. He'll assist, but he won't do it for you.

The Living ECK Master Is a Wayshower

The Living ECK Master is a Wayshower. He'll assist, but he won't do it for you.

On our softball team, every so often they'd say, "Hey, we need a coach." So I'd run over to third base or first base and stand there. Then a teammate would hit the ball, come running, stand on base or something, and you're supposed to tell him what to do.

When the ball's hit out there, and he's running from second to third, the ball is out behind him and sometimes he can't see. The coach at third base is supposed to say, "Come on, run like crazy!" And when he gets closer, if the throw is close and he's going to be out, you'll say, "Slide." Other times the coach might say, "Stand up, take it easy," or "Go home," or whatever. The coach is supposed to have all the answers, and the player is supposed to look to him.

Well, often the ballplayer will run, or maybe not; in a league like ours sometimes you listen to the coach, sometimes not. It depends on how you feel. One guy might do it, while the next guy is kind of impartial to the coach. If the batter hits the ball at the plate and it goes in the outfield and you're the first-base coach, you're supposed to tell him what to do. You say, "Stop!"—he stops. Then the outfielder throws the ball, and it goes flying wild. Time is too short to tell your runner to go, so he thinks on his own, which is fine, and he takes off running like crazy for the next base. You're standing there very proud of yourself as a coach because you know you haven't done anything. He's done it himself. He almost gets to second base, and he stops, turns around, and comes running back. He's caught in the rundown, of course, and can only say, "Augh!" He's tagged out, and then all the players come off the bench and say, "Who's our coach?" And you say, "Well, the rules won't let me go out there and push him to second base."

Sometimes I was the one baserunning; and I'd miss the signal, run on my own, and get tagged out. Then everybody would look at the coach and say, "Did you tell him to run?" And he'd say something like, "Aiyiiiyiyiyi!" It gets really funny.

It's like that on the path of ECK too. The Living

Your runner's tagged out, and then all the players say, "Who's our coach?" And you say, "Well, the rules won't let me go out there and push him to second base." It's like that on the path of ECK too.

ECK Master will assist you, give you clues that there is a temple within you; there are the Spiritual Exercises of ECK. These exercises are to be found in the ECK books. The Easy Way technique is found in *In My Soul I Am Free*.[1] *ECKANKAR—The Key to Secret Worlds* has several other spiritual exercises. Try these. Read the books. Don't hurry. Check them out yourself at home. You may have a great inner experience while you're checking it out, though chances are you won't at first.

THAT STILL SMALL VOICE

The ECK often works in a gentle, quiet way. It is sometimes known as that still small voice. It'll give a nudge. So many people who claim they have a guide that tells them word-for-word what to do here and there are nothing more than puppets.

The Living ECK Master will meet with you on the inner planes, sometimes give suggestions, but he will not give you step-by-step directions so that you become a walking zombie. He is interested in the individual who is looking for Self-Realization and God-Realization, to become a Master in his own right. Puppets don't become Masters. He'll help; he'll assist you in your own efforts. Sometimes you'll say, "Oops, I missed the signal from the coach." But don't worry about it. There's always another inning, another game.

Sometimes I'd have the feeling that I had failed a test. Other times, three or four weeks or months would pass before I'd realize that way back there I had failed a test. But what was nice was that the day after I

The ECK often works in a gentle, quiet way. It is sometimes known as that still small voice.

1. This book by Brad Steiger is currently out of print. The Easy Way technique is also in *The Spiritual Exercises of ECK* by Harold Klemp.

failed it, I didn't know it so it didn't bother me a bit. I just went on with my life. By the time I came to the point of realizing I had probably missed a signal back there somewhere, I had regained the ground I had lost. I now had the understanding, and I had even gone beyond where I had been at that point.

So there is always the plus factor, there is always this one more step.

ALWAYS ONE MORE STEP

The Inner Master, the Living ECK Master, will always lead you one more step. If you're thinking of becoming perfect, there's always one more step. Even Paul Twitchell, since he went into the other worlds, is moving on to bigger and greater opportunities.

The Inner Master, the Living ECK Master, will always lead you one more step.

About a year ago an ECKist came up to me and said, "Gee whiz, I sure wish I could find a person who would carry the message to Garcia."

It sounded intriguing, and some of you may know the story behind the message to Garcia. I said, "What do you mean, Walter?" He said, "To find a person who takes that extra step no matter what he does." An example is Brother Lawrence, the Carmelite monk, who cleaned the pots and pans. Paul often spoke of him. He did this, the most humble task, as well as he could, and each time he did it a little better.

The ECKists are this way—you are—and that's why you're here. The cream of the crop of every religious teaching is here. You looked through the teachings of the world and wanted to find the way to the Sugmad. You looked everywhere, and you became the best in your field. You became the missionaries either in this lifetime or a past lifetime; the zealots who, in your yearning to find God, tried everything to find the direct path to God. You looked.

The ECKists are the cream of the crop because they're looking, they're taking that one more step. They know—you know—that there is always one more step.

The orthodox religions have been promising a certain heaven to you, and you've come to the point of saying, "Well, do I want to hang around for all eternity in the spiritual worlds just resting and soaking up love?" That's where Soul started, remember, and Sugmad said Soul is not unfolding, It's not giving, and so the lower worlds were created.

Sugmad said Soul is not unfolding, It's not giving, and so the lower worlds were created.

We came down here and began to learn. We had to learn to give. And we looked and met the Master, the Living ECK Master, sometime in the past—again and again. Sometimes we recognized him, sometimes not. But we're here again and we have another opportunity. We may say later, "Well, I'd like a break." Take a break. When you want to come back, let's talk about it. We want those in ECK who know the spiritual goal of God-Realization is what they are looking for, and they want to learn the spiritual laws of ECK that take one there.

A Message to Garcia

A Message to Garcia. This story was written in 1899 and published in a small-time newspaper.[2] At the time, the Spanish-American War was under way. At dinner one night the editor's son said, "You know, Dad, the real hero of this whole episode of history was a man called Rowan." He said, "What do you mean?" His son then told this story:

2. The story, *A Message to Garcia*, was originally written by Elbert Hubbard in the March 1899 edition of the *Philistine*, and by 1913 over forty million copies had been printed and distributed by various sources.

President McKinley was trying to get in touch with the leader of the insurgents, General Garcia, who was down in Cuba. At the time, there was no way the mail could get to General Garcia. The president wanted to gain his support for his own reasons, which we won't get into here; that's another principle. One of his aides said, "There's no way we can get a message to General Garcia. We can't do it by telegraph or by mail. But there is one person who can do this if it's humanly possible, and his name is Rowan."

Rowan was given the message from President McKinley. He took the letter, put it in an oilskin pouch, and tied it over his heart; then he got into a small open boat. Four nights later he landed in Cuba, crept into the jungle, and he wasn't seen again for over two weeks. But by the time he came out on the other side of the island where a boat picked him up and brought him back, he had delivered the message. There's a story behind that too, of the hardships he went through.

This man worked with the Law of Attitudes. He knew there was a way. He carried with him this corrected set of images that allowed for success, and that's how it's done. He went at it, and despite every obstacle that came up, he carried this message to Garcia.

When we do the Spiritual Exercises of ECK, we contact Divine Spirit. This opens us up to the creative imagination.

You can read about this in *The Flute of God*, where several of these laws are discussed. There is never a contest between the imagination, which is ruled by Spirit when one does the Spiritual Exercises of ECK, and the mind. The imagination will always win. Willpower will always take second chair to the imagination. In ECK, in meeting our daily life, we learn how to work with the ECK coming through; we get nudges from the

When we do the Spiritual Exercises of ECK, we contact Divine Spirit. This opens us up to the creative imagination.

Inner Master to help us begin learning how to create our own worlds the way a Master would.

There's an old saying: "Would you rather fish or cut bait?" The ECKist would rather fish. Cutting bait is for the guy who does the dirty work while the guy who's fishing has all the fun. The master or slave.

We get nudges from the Inner Master to help us begin learning how to create our own worlds the way a Master would.

THE SOUND AND LIGHT OF ECK

You have taken a big step toward self-mastery by stepping onto the path of ECK. As you receive more of the Sound and Light of ECK, you get greater responsibility along with the greater freedom. You see the Light and you hear the Sound, which are the ways that this Divine ECK can be experienced.

There is very little mention in the Christian Bible of the two aspects of Divine Spirit, the Sound and the Light. John says, "In the beginning was the Word," and "the Word was made flesh." And it doesn't say very much beside that. In another place it says, "The wind bloweth where it listeth," and to the effect that where it comes from and where it goes, no one knows.

This is the Sound of ECK. There are scattered references that still exist in man's scriptures, but those of you who have read *The Shariyat-Ki-Sugmad*, The Way of the Eternal—the ECKists' Bible—know that this is without equal. It also speaks of the Light in the Christian Bible with reference to Paul, who was Saul of Tarsus at the time. He was on the road to Damascus when he saw the Light. At the Pentecost, the apostles saw the flames and they heard the sound of a rushing wind. These are very low aspects of the ECK Sound. They're usually a starting point for the ECKist, and he goes far beyond them.

Each one of the planes of God throughout the lower worlds has a color and a distinctive sound, so that when you do the spiritual exercises you may hear or see this. Maybe not every night, maybe not every two weeks; maybe once a month, maybe once a year. You will perhaps hear the sound of the flute of God or you may hear the buzzing of bees. This is the Sound of ECK uplifting you in your spiritual consciousness, bringing you closer to that liberation, spiritual liberation, toward self-mastery, toward the position of being an ECK Master yourself. And that's why we're here. This is our goal.

This little flower has been sitting up in the room since October 22, and I thought it would be nice to bring it out here. Every time the Rod of ECK Power is passed, there is a revitalization throughout all the God Worlds. This is why we celebrate the ECK New Year on October 22. It is a very special time for those who have the ears to hear and the spiritual eyes to see.

It's a pleasure being with you who have chosen to step onto this path of ECK in this lifetime.

We might take about fifteen minutes now to shake hands. There's another meeting soon, and I won't be able to meet very many of you tonight, but I'd like to say it's a pleasure being with you who have chosen to step onto this path of ECK in this lifetime, the way many have before you and the way many will in the ages to come.

World Wide of ECK, Anaheim, California,
Saturday, October 24, 1981

"Probably ten or fifteen good trees will grow out of these hundred acorns," he said.

3
THE
ACORN PLANTER

*S*omebody asked me the other night if I was going to do anything with music. Well, I could whistle—off-key. I used to sing to myself in the camera room, but only when I was in the second room, with a double door, sure that no one could overhear.

But I like to sing, and I have to sing—to myself. It gives a balance. I'll hum, I'll sing, and when things start getting really fast and I wonder where can I find that balance within again, all of a sudden a little song will pop up. It may not necessarily be what we call an ECK song, but it's a happy one, harmonious; it will come bubbling up, and I'll go humming along.

When I worked in a printing company in Texas, I was very careful about anyone overhearing my singing because of something that happened in first grade. As I worked with many of the different pressmen, the graphic-arts people, and the customers, I would hum and sing to myself as I walked along. When I left that company, one of the men came up to me and said, "You know, I really liked the humming and happy sounds you made." And I didn't even know I was doing it.

If our children are allowed to sing and hum, or if they want to play an instrument, that's fine. In

When things start getting really fast and I wonder where to find that balance within again, all of a sudden a little song will pop up.

33

the first grade, I attended a little two-room country schoolhouse. We used one room mainly. There were twenty-four kids and one teacher who also gave us singing instruction. I would really sing, and I sang with my whole heart. One day I must have really been sensational, because he asked if I would please not sing anymore. I was only six years old, and that crushed me.

If that teacher had had any insight, he would have let it be and just let me sing, and I would have learned my own way. Maybe I would have even learned to sing the way other people felt I should sing. But here's a point: It's not important what anyone else feels about your voice. I don't know if it was karma for him, but he had a son about three or four years younger than I was who didn't begin school until a couple of years later, and his son sang just as well as I did. And he enjoyed himself just as much as I did too.

In singing, the subtle sounds of ECK are able to get through.

In singing, the subtle sounds of ECK are able to get through. In many ways, music is more effective than a talk.

Something else that is very effective is painting. Some of the ECKists in England had an art display; they put their paintings in an exhibition at a shopping mall or something—I'm not quite sure where they held it. Below each painting, they put a short quote from one of the ECK books, which that painting reflected. They set out a box of books so that when people came to the art show, they looked at the paintings, read the quotes from the ECK books, and then helped themselves to a book.

The paintings led them to a book, and there wasn't anybody pushing them. We have the paintings and we have wonderful artists. There are different ways of reaching out with the message of ECK that are very effective.

THE SOUND OF ECK

I was about two years old when I heard the Sound of ECK. The reason I was thinking of this is that I was just in the children's room a little while ago, and the little ones are such a clear expression of the ECK. It's a lot of fun being with them.

One little fellow had a little red racing car, and he said, "Want to see it go? Come on, I'll show you." Then he led me to where there was a clear area on the floor and demonstrated with a *whoosh*. He was so proud and happy. His brother, who was just a little bit taller than he was, came up and said, "You know, I spent nearly all my money at this seminar on my little brother." It seemed to be some kind of achievement in giving.

The little ones have this love, and we're like them. Some of us are quiet, some of us are more outgoing. Some of the little fellows, wanting to seem manly, would shake hands in a grown-up fashion. They were about so tall. I asked one little one, "How old are you?" He couldn't talk and started to hold up the fingers like this. He ended up with two, sometimes three. At first I said, "Three?" Then I held up two fingers and he lit up, just like the Light of ECK. That was the right number of years for him. He couldn't get his fingers working to pass it along, but he could let me know that was it. Wonderful individuals—Souls on the path of ECK.

So as a child I heard the Sound of ECK. We lived in a country farmhouse, and we all slept in the same room. I was about two, and my brother was four at the time. When I'd hear this high humming sound at night, I would ask my parents about it. There were telephone wires right outside the house. They could never hear the sound, but they said it must be the wires. I often wondered why they couldn't hear it,

As a child I heard the Sound of ECK. I'd hear this high humming sound at night.

because it was so very, very loud to me. It was the Sound of ECK.

You can do without the Light, because It is knowledge; but you cannot do without the Sound, for It sustains all life. My parents were not taught, as children, about these sounds; and so they couldn't help me. As I heard the Sound again and again and was told, "There's nothing; it's just your imagination," the Sound gradually dimmed.

You can do without the Light, because It is knowledge; but you cannot do without the Sound, for It sustains all life.

As I grew older and went to school, I was faced with school education and the teacher saying, "Please don't sing." Gradually, it closes in on a child, and the inner is shut out, until we are given the opportunity again to come in contact with the teachings of ECK and become reacquainted with the Sound of ECK, and the Light. Now we have the opportunity to recapture what we've had in another lifetime or in this lifetime as children. But for a while it was closed out, muffled out.

As I would fall asleep when I was about two or three, it was the strangest thing: I'd shut my eyes, and all of a sudden the Sound would come in and things would begin to whirl. I was caught up in the vortex of the ECK.

It began to swirl and swirl, and at first I didn't quite know what to make of it, so I sought reassurance from my parents that this was OK. I couldn't talk at two or express myself at three and barely had enough words at four, but there wasn't time to listen to a child anyway. It's cold in winter up in the Midwest—they had to get the house warm, had to get the wood in the furnace and the cookstove, and had to have the house heated up for my older brother and my dad when they came in from chores. Sometimes parents are so busy with everyday work that they forget that a child can have the experience even if not the words. And the words really aren't all that important.

We make it. We get there. We're here today.

As one goes higher on the path of ECK, the Sound will become fainter and fainter. At one time I wondered if something was wrong. My wife and I had moved to Costa Mesa, California, with its wonderful ocean breeze—natural air conditioning. Every so often we would both hear this really high peeping sound.

It wasn't the sound of the flute. We heard the sound of the flute and some of the other sounds later. But it was very, very high-pitched, and sometimes we'd hear it when we'd be just sitting there eating. We had very little money; the baby was coming, and we were putting all the money aside, trying to save up for the hospital expenses. Sometimes we'd sit at the table wondering if life was really worth it. We had barely enough food to get by, and we had to get good food for my wife, because a mother-to-be needs nourishment. And then we would hear this high sound; and as high as it was, it got even higher. Then for a period, after a couple of years, it was gone.

As you unfold, you will hear the sounds of ECK which uplift one in the spiritual state of consciousness.

As one goes higher on the path of ECK, the Sound will become fainter and fainter.

PLANTING SEEDS

There are those who have God-Realization as their goal. They look to the temple within themselves, and they will get there. There are others who are not in such a hurry, and there is no hurry; when the time is right, it comes too. Eckankar is an individual path. We go at our own pace, at our own speed.

The purpose of the teachings of ECK is to give us the freedom to choose our own way in our life. Freedom of choice. The other great aid or goal of Eckankar for the individual who wants the help is the preservation of individuality. We do not become one with God. We maintain our distinctness, our individuality, as Co-workers with God.

About a month ago or so, I read a book that had a very intriguing story. I don't recall the author, but the title, if I remember correctly, was *The Man Who Planted Trees.*[1] A very small book, very simple. The reason I mention it is that the effect—or the opportunity—that one gives, as a vehicle for the ECK, by leaving a book is quiet.

You may put out a book today and never know if anyone ever picked it up or if anyone was helped by it. If you're working in an area, you may put out ECK books for a year or two and notice very little growth in numbers of members, but this isn't important. Sometimes it takes a year or two for the individual to pick up the book. But he has been touched by the ECK and a seed has been planted, to germinate in its own good time, at that individual's own pace.

We do not become one with God. We maintain our distinctness, our individuality, as Co-workers with God.

THE ACORN PLANTER

The story involved a young man around the turn of the century, about 1900, who went hiking in a region of France where the land was barren and desolate. He went further than he had planned. When he ran out of water, he figured this was going to be the end, but still he kept walking. After a day or two, off in the distance he could see what looked like either sheep or goats. He couldn't believe it when he saw that there was also a man way out in this great wilderness. The man took him into his well-built little house, gave him water, and invited him to stay overnight. The hiker couldn't help wondering how

1. This story, which French author Jean Gionesco let fall into public domain, has been told many times and translated into many languages around the world.

this man could survive in such a remote place where there was no one else around.

The hiker regained some of his strength over the next few hours, and as they passed the rest of that afternoon, the other man sat at the table sorting a stack of acorns. He would check each acorn very carefully, look it over, and put all the good ones on one stack and the rest on another stack. He kept this up until he had a pile of one hundred good acorns. These he put into a little bag without saying one word about what he was doing.

The next morning he left the house early. The hiker stayed inside for a while. But he didn't have anything to do, so he decided to go out and look for his host. He found him poking holes in the ground with a long rod, planting one of the perfect acorns into each hole.

"What are you doing?" the hiker asked.

"Planting acorns," he said. "Out of the one hundred I'm planting, probably fifty won't germinate. Of the ones that do, probably twenty-five will go the way of the insects and several others will be blemished. Probably ten or fifteen good trees will grow out of these hundred acorns."

Near the little house was a small forest which seemed out of place. The hiker thought how foolish it was that the man stayed out here in the middle of nowhere, just planting these acorns.

A few years passed, World War I came, and the hiker spent some time in the service. When the war was over, he needed some peace and quiet, so he went back out in the wilderness to see if he could find this man. When he found his way back, he almost didn't recognize the place. It was now a big forest with trees everywhere.

"What are you doing?" the hiker asked. "Planting acorns," he said.

This land had once been fertile when the Romans were in France. There were still some old fish hooks in the dry streambeds and other evidence that this had once been a thriving area. Now all of a sudden, with the planting of the trees, the springs began to well up again, and with them came weeds and flowers. And with the flowers—well, the hiker found an unusual thing.

The man had gotten rid of most of his animals, keeping only a few goats for milk and cheese, because they were eating up the trees. He had set up hives, and he now kept bees. From the flowers the bees cross-pollinated the whole area.

The hiker returned a few years later, and this time he found a huge forest. In the meantime, people had come in and tried to log the area, but it was too far inland. It wasn't economical; it was too expensive. The closest village was a couple of miles away. It had been inhabited by people reminiscent of those mentioned in *The Tiger's Fang* by Paul Twitchell—that little village where Rebazar Tarzs had taken Paul to an inn and they drank goat's milk. The people, the consciousness, described by Paul were just like those in this village.

Every day he went out and planted one hundred acorns.

But after a while there was a change. Young couples moved up from the coast and had families. The hiker hardly recognized the town.

The acorn planter never even realized others lived at one end of this huge forest, and he didn't care. Every day he went out and planted one hundred acorns, and the entire land was revitalized. During his third visit, by which time the man was around eighty years old, the hiker said to him, "But how are you going to enjoy the fruits of your labor?"

"It doesn't matter," said the old man. "I'm just planting trees; I'm enjoying the trees right now, and

I like doing the work."

You know, it's a funny thing, but sometime later scientists were sent in, and these educated men could not figure out how this forest had sprung up when there had been no forest fifty years earlier.

They never found the acorn planter. He was off in another end of the forest, still planting trees.

Pretty soon forest rangers were brought in to protect the forest. It got to be really funny. They finally found the old man's little house and said to him, "Well, to protect this forest, you shouldn't light any fires!" The old man didn't say anything. He wasn't attached to the forest. It wasn't his. The hiker happened to be a close friend of the forest ranger and told him the story. The forest ranger said, "Ah, I see," and he gave the word: "Don't ever bother this man. Leave him alone and give him his freedom to do whatever he wants, to go wherever he wants."

Putting out the ECK books, whether it's *ECKANKAR—The Key to Secret Worlds* or *The Spiritual Notebook*, is like planting acorns. We're not interested in social changes, but that the opportunity is given for that Soul who is ready to hear the message of ECK, to learn about the Sugmad.

We're not interested in social changes, but that the opportunity is given for that Soul who is ready to hear the message of ECK.

It has been a joy being with you this weekend. These are great and adventurous times. It's the great adventure where we can work together, presenting the ECK message in a way that's comfortable for us if we want to declare ourselves as vehicles for the Sugmad, the ECK, or the Mahanta.

The love of the ECK is with you on your journey homeward. My love is always with you.

World Wide of ECK, Anaheim, California,
Sunday, October 25, 1981

As Soul, we go through lifetime after lifetime, getting experience, learning how to get along, until one day our vision grows and we see the Blue Light of the Mahanta.

4

THE JOURNEY OF SOUL

t's good to see you. I guess you're all used to the Gulf Freeway. I used to live and work here in Houston about ten years ago, and the Gulf Freeway is exactly the same now as it was then. It looks like they put another lane in since I was here. I thought that might make driving a little easier. But tonight as we were coming in, it started to rain just a little bit; and that was enough to slow the traffic. I like to be on time, but sometimes you find these things come up that help to develop patience.

The title of my talk is "The Journey of Soul," and all I can say is that I wouldn't recommend the Gulf Freeway.

LIFE'S LESSONS

As we move along, we have to recognize that once we set a goal and say, "This is where I want to be and when I want to be there," whether it's God-Realization or Self-Realization, then all the things that happen in between are life's lessons.

Sometimes we know exactly where we are going, but it just may take a little longer than we planned, and we can react in several ways. We can get upset—and this is usually how we do it for the first ten

Once we set a goal, then all the things that happen in between are life's lessons.

43

thousand or twenty thousand lives. But all of a sudden it just sinks in that this is what we learned from that experience, and finally we realize it doesn't pay to get upset anymore. We begin to know that we can take it easy, we can make our plans, and we can go on. Then if something comes up, we know it's there as a lesson, there for a reason, and it's a way for us to grow.

One of the events on the agenda during a trip to the South Pacific last fall, right after the World Wide of ECK, was a training session. As I left to go down to the meeting room, I looked at my watch and said, "All right, we're starting out to arrive in plenty of time." But outside my door were two ECKists who had traveled from another country, and they wanted to say good-bye. I hadn't planned on anybody waiting outside my door wanting to say good-bye for five or ten minutes, but I finally got there and the meeting had been started by someone else.

As we plan our ECK activities, such as introductory lectures and Satsangs, we set a time and plan to start on time; and we do the best we can. Unexpected delays can come up, but it's very important to use that as our goal—to start on time.

One of the things that Soul runs into in Its journey is procrastination.

One of the things that Soul runs into in Its journey is procrastination. It's a phase of attachment, one of the five passions of the mind. We run into this. Some mornings you don't want to get up, and when the alarm goes off, what do you do? You reach over and automatically shut it off. Later you wake up and say it never rang. But you know the alarm went off, really. And you know your boss won't believe you, so you're smart enough not to bring it up. Yet this is the little thing we carry in us as our own excuse—the alarm didn't ring. How did it get turned off? Well, who knows. Miracles happen.

SOUL'S JOURNEY

The journey of Soul takes It back home again. Soul has already made one journey. You have made one journey. You've made it from the spiritual worlds, and your trip here wasn't exactly on a red carpet. It was more or less like the bottom dropping out.

All of us as Soul made by God had our experience in the spiritual planes, resting, enjoying bliss, having a really good time. And God looked at us and said, "They are Soul having a good time, but they are not learning anything." So the lower worlds, the ones we live in, were created so Soul could gain experience.

Soul is also known as the Jivatma. It is a spark of God, or I should say we are a spark of God. We take on this physical body, and we come here to get our experiences.

We have a dim memory of an existence outside of eternity, when the bottom dropped out. In a way Soul, all these Souls, you and I, fell through the different planes. Some of us stayed on the Mental Plane, some went to the Causal, some to the Astral, and some down to the Physical.

In our first human incarnation, many of us came as a male. We were given karma by the negative power we know as Satan, who was just working under the auspices of God to give us experience. This negative power was told, "Here is Soul, a pupil. Put It in your classroom. Give this Soul lessons until It is ready to take Its place as a Co-worker in the God Worlds of ECK." And the negative power—the Kal Niranjan, or Satan—being the most negative entity around, just said, "Fine, wonderful. I'll do my best!"

So we woke up in the first body with our beginning karma. We were given our baggage, a suitcase full of karma, and when we opened it up, everything went wrong.

The lower worlds, the ones we live in, were created so that Soul could gain experience.

We were on our way. If somebody looked at us cross-eyed, we punched him out or hit him with a club. That, of course, set off a chain reaction—the guy we hit wasn't as big as we were, so he'd take a club and pound somebody smaller. This kept on until we were well on our way with the karma. Soul was on Its way.

The Kal Niranjan was sitting up there somewhere pulling the strings and having a good laugh, because that is the job of this negative power: to give us every experience in life, to push us here, push us there, stretch us and stretch us through lifetime after lifetime until finally we start developing the insight that penetrates those clouds upon which this negative power, this Kal Niranjan, is sitting. We eventually get a glimpse, for the first time, and we say, "Hey, that guy's laughing at me!"

For the first number of lives we spent here, we were too busy looking down at the ground and wondering, "What am I doing here? What is this all about?" But gradually, as we spent enough time here in the pains and sorrows, the joys and happiness of life, we became a little bit more the experienced Soul, and our vision raised a little bit more. One day we looked high enough to see this Kal Niranjan, the negative power, sitting there; and we said, "Oh, so this is where I've been getting my negative thoughts from. This is where the five passions of the mind—anger, lust, attachment, greed, and vanity—have come from. OK!"

And Soul began to learn.

As the vision grew a little more, Soul eventually came to know that there was a way out of this world. All It could see at this point was who was playing the trick. It took a little bit longer of being aware that there was a way out before Soul realized that a little further up was someone else, looking over the shoulder of the Kal Niranjan and waiting; it

This is where the five passions of the mind—anger, lust, attachment, greed, and vanity—have come from.

was that which we know in ECK as the Blue Light, or the Mahanta.

Some of you, some of the ECKists, saw the Blue Light before you came onto the path of ECK. This Light leads Soul to the temple within ourselves.

This is the source of divine inspiration and creativity. One thing that Soul has as a divine spark of God is the imagination. We use the imagination in the Spiritual Exercises of ECK which are in the ECK discourses. We use these spiritual exercises to learn how to go inwardly and do something, to meet the Inner Master, to go to that temple within ourselves and begin receiving insight into the things that come up in our everyday life.

So often when someone has a sickness, or for some other reason, they will ask to know the future. I could do as Paul did for a little while—he'd give a one-year reading from the ECK-Vidya, the ancient science of prophecy; but then what was Soul going to do for the year after? It was covered for year one; what was It going to do for year two? Paul stopped giving ECK-Vidya readings, so what was Soul going to do now?

Well, It had to do something. It kept on with the spiritual exercises. It tried one contemplative technique after another, experimented, used that imaginative faculty.

RESPONSIBILITIES AND SPIRITUAL UNFOLDMENT

We are often of the opinion that we have to give up everything for the Master. We do put our inner life in the hands of the Inner Master, but this doesn't mean your house, your family, your TV set—especially if there's a good "Rockford" show on. You want to be careful not to be careless with the things you give up.

We use the Spiritual Exercises of ECK to go to that temple within ourselves and begin receiving insight into the things that come up in our everyday life.

Long ago in ancient Egypt there were mystery schools, and some of the mystery schools had temples. It was considered a good move in those days to go into the religious life even though it involved very long training, the pay was poor, and at best you might be accepted as a worker in the temple.

Most of the people who made the approach were taken in. The priest would say, "Why, sure. Come on in. If you want to be a monk or priest here, OK; we've got a little training for you." And they'd go through training for probably five or ten years, in some cases longer, and then all of a sudden one day the priest would say, "You can go back out into the world now. Just go on out there and live life. We'll call you when we need you, when there's an opening here." So the guy would kind of stagger out of there, because actually he had meant to devote his whole life to the temple and this left him out in the cold.

It took him a little while to get a career or a business going, but after a couple of years he got the swing of it and started moving. Pretty soon he got married; a little later he had a family. The business was going well, he's got himself a wife and family, and he has a lot of friends. Soon they're going to need somebody to run for government office, and he's just the person—an upstanding individual with a good background as a community leader—so he gets elected to a government position. Then the word comes: "It's now time for you to go back to the temple."

When we come into this world and take on responsibilities, this is where we find our spiritual unfoldment.

In those days there was no choice. When you took a vow to give things up to the Master or to God, that literally meant you gave up everything. And they were wrong. They were absolutely wrong.

When we come into this world and take on responsibilities, this is where we find our spiritual unfoldment. If we think we'll find it by giving up our responsibilities, that is not the way. There is no quick way. Maybe you don't get along with your wife, so you decide it's time to go and join a religious order. You leave thinking you've solved that problem and it's all taken care of, you've given your life to God, and may everything else be taken care of. This is shirking our responsibility; this isn't the way.

Brother Lawrence—Paul has spoken of him— was a Carmelite monk in Paris around 1666. He was the monk whose duty it was to wash the pots and pans. Many of you have spent some time in the service, and if you were an airman basic, or a private, you spent your time in KP.

Brother Lawrence found a way to practice the presence of God while washing the pots and pans, doing even the very lowly jobs. The people around him couldn't really understand how he could be so happy while doing the dirty work. It was because he saw God in everything he did.

I used to do the pots and pans too, but it was for a different reason. The mess sergeant didn't holler at you when you worked in pots and pans because that was considered to be the absolute dirtiest job. As long as you got the grease off and got the dishes clean, he wouldn't holler at you. You'd work from maybe 5:30 in the morning until about 6:30 at night; but you worked hard, and the time went fast. Nobody bothered you— as long as you got the grease off the pots and pans. That's all you had to do. And another thing—you didn't have to get there as early for pots and pans. Nobody else wanted it, so you didn't have to show up at 4:00 or 4:30 to be at the head of the line. It started at 5:30. It was very nice because I didn't have to get up so early and I was my own man. Other people would come by and say, "How can you do it?"

Once in a while I had the bad fortune to get the

Brother Lawrence found a way to practice the presence of God while washing the pots and pans, doing even the very lowly jobs.

dessert line, which everybody else liked because there was no work to it. You put out the salads. You went into the big cooler where they had all these salads, you brought out the salads, set them on the serving line, and you just stood behind the counter with the tray in front of you.

When you got a little bit low on Jell-O, you'd make another trip back to the cooler, get yourself another tray of Jell-O, and take it back out. Of course, while you were in there you helped yourself to a couple of olives. You looked around first to see where everybody was, then you'd help yourself and wipe it off your mouth before you went back out so the evidence wouldn't show.

This was just Soul getting experience, learning how to get along.

It was learning there is an easy way and there's a hard way, and you can find your heaven in somebody else's hell—and you do. You'll learn to live in a way that no one else can, because through the Spiritual Exercises of ECK the consciousness has been raised so that you could live in a hut and feel as if you were living in a palace.

There have been many kings who were so impoverished in Spirit that they couldn't wait until spring so they could mount up all their men and go across the borders to attack the next kingdom, because they just had to have that land. They had so much wealth, but they'd never have enough. It was a poverty of Spirit.

In ECK I'm not able to promise you that if you step on the path, from this moment on your life is going to be sweet and easy, or that it's going to be like skating in $110 roller skates—the good kind, not the kind I have that clatter and make noise on the sidewalk and hardly roll. I can't promise you that. It doesn't work that way. But we do get the insight; we get the insight to find what we can do to make our life better than it was yesterday.

There is an easy way and there's a hard way, and you can find your heaven in somebody else's hell.

HEALINGS VIA SPIRIT

If we have a health condition or a sickness and we've gone to all the doctors, tried everything, and exhausted every physical means of curing this ailment, then we can always come back and ask the ECK and write to the Living ECK Master. Just a note will do, such as: This is my condition. I've tried everything. If it's the will of Spirit, I'd like a little help.

I may answer you or I may not, but it doesn't matter. I myself do not heal, nor did Paul Twitchell. Each of us acts only as a vehicle for Spirit. We let Spirit do what It will, in the time and way that It sees as right, which is best for our spiritual unfoldment.

I met two ladies on a plane who said they were going to a psychic healer in the Philippines. They both had a serious illness. "He is a very good healer," one of the ladies said. "We go back to him every year." They went to the healer expecting him to do the work for them, and the psychic healing would last less than a year. Every year they'd save up all their money so they could take this trip to the Philippines. There wasn't much pleasure in it for them—they had just enough money to get there, no time to stay, no time to enjoy themselves, only enough time to have the psychic healer work on them. It lasted almost a year. The next year they'd clean out their savings and do the whole thing again. And they swore by this man.

If Spirit heals an individual—whether it's in your purse, your health, or your emotional well-being—or if Spirit gives you a boost into the pure positive God Worlds, you'll find it's a healing which will last. Of course, I can't say it will last forever.

We were talking about the case of the Wandering Jew this afternoon. It is a fictional story of a legendary character who said something he shouldn't have

We get the insight to find what we can do to make our life better than it was yesterday.

at the time of the crucifixion in Christian biblical history, so he was cursed to walk the earth for two thousand years. Well, it's like a Soul going through life for two thousand years. It was very difficult at first, but as he went further and started to pick up the knack, he began to enjoy it.

When you get a spiritual healing, you don't necessarily end up living to be two thousand years old. There's a natural time when our mission is done here, and we leave the physical plane. It's a fact of living.

LOSING THE FEAR OF DEATH

You can lose the fear of death. You are then able to enjoy this life and to live it fully.

The Spiritual Exercises of ECK eventually bring us to the point where the veil that stands between the physical and the other planes becomes very thin; and as it does, you can see through it. You can lose the fear of death; and in doing this, you are then able to enjoy this life and to live it fully. Most people, no matter how successful they appear, have this gnawing fear of death. And just about two steps in front of it is its relative called loneliness, which is the fear and the wondering: Is there really anyone walking by my side? Is there such a thing as Soul forever?

In ECK we find that the Master is always with us. The Mahanta is always with us even though we may not always recognize his presence.

In the book *In My Soul I Am Free* there is a spiritual exercise called the Easy Way.[1] It's a good technique to mention to those who are just finding out about ECK and reading the ECK books. Give them this technique. Suggest they read and see if this path of ECK works for them. It may not. They can check it out; they can test it.

---

1. See footnote on page 26.

GIVING SPACE TO OTHERS

We are each an individual. We are all at different levels of unfoldment, each one of us—not in the sense of higher or lower, because there is no one who can look at you and say, "Oh, you are higher than so-and-so" or "you are lower." It doesn't work that way. That's a misuse of power when we try to do this. We just look at each other and accept each other as Soul working together in love and harmony as much as we can. And if you can't stand the person, what I used to do was just turn around and walk away. That took a little more courage.

At first I'd sit there and hem and haw while thinking of an excuse to get away from someone. I'd pretend I heard my phone ringing, or something like this, and maybe go in the house, shut the door, and lock it. Later you get more courage, you become stronger in ECK. You realize that you don't have to apologize to anyone for just being; that if you are willing to give another person his state of consciousness, you have at least the right to expect the same for yourself. It's not asking a lot. You're not asking the other person to wash your kitchen floors or scrub the toilet bowl. You are only saying, Let me have my space. Is that asking too much? You know, it's a very small thing; and yet it's surprising how few people besides the ECKists are willing to do this.

If you are willing to give another person his state of consciousness, you have at least the right to expect the same for yourself.

You find your religion, and you say, If it's good enough for me, it's good enough for everybody. You find vitamins—good enough for me, good enough for everybody. You become this flag-waving, wild-eyed fanatic for your particular thing that has worked for you, without understanding that it may not work for the fellow next to you.

He may not even care. It may have gotten rid of your dandruff; so you think, Hey, that guy's got

dandruff and maybe he ought to know about this—
it will get rid of his. Maybe he likes his dandruff.
Maybe it never bothered him. Maybe he's had a leg
problem for the last ten years, all his attention is on
getting his leg back in shape, and the last thing on
his mind is that case of dandruff. It's way down there
on his priority list, and when you mention it to him—
I have this excellent cure—he isn't interested. So
leave him alone.

We have the path of ECK, and if somebody else
isn't interested, leave him alone. He's not ready.
Whether it's the path of Eckankar, Christianity or
any of its branches, Hinduism, anything—if anyone
pushes it upon someone else, it's going to come back.

As sure as we put the chains of our belief upon
another, it isn't very much later that we find the same
chains are placed upon ourselves.

The person may say, "Yeah, I'd like to go to your
meeting, but I don't have a ride." So you say, "I'll give
you a ride," and you think he's going to get to heaven
because you're doing this. Then pretty soon he says,
"Well, I'm not going to be home, but I still need a ride.
I'm going to be two or three miles away at a friend's,
but could you drop by and pick me up?" Soon you find
out you're paying dearly for pushing somebody into
something he wasn't ready for. And eventually, despite your efforts, the guy starts arriving late or doesn't
show up at all.

EXPERIENCES OF SOUL

At some point we have the opportunity to come in contact again with the Living ECK Master.

I'd like to mention that you and I—Soul—are
here getting our experience. At some point we have
the opportunity to come in contact again with the
Living ECK Master. You don't have to believe everything I say. Read the ECK books. Read *The Tiger's*

Fang. You may even want to read *The Wind of Change*—it's lighter. Read the books and see if it works for you. You may not get a spectacular vision, but try it.

Someone told me this afternoon, "I read *The Tiger's Fang* and expected to have exactly the same experiences Paul Twitchell did, but I didn't. And after eight years I finally came to understand that I was having my own experiences. Some of them were like Paul's, but a lot weren't and many were quite different." The Living ECK Master is able to take you to your own mastership if you are sincerely interested in reaching into the two aspects of Divine Spirit which are known as the Light and the Sound. These are two parts of Divine Spirit that few religions know about.

Divine Spirit, the ECK—sometimes known as the Holy Ghost or Comforter—can be heard as Sound. It is heard as a flute on the Soul Plane. You may hear It as a buzzing of bees on another plane. You may hear It as an orchestra or as a chorus during your contemplation and at work. You may hear It often, or only once every year, but don't expect to hear It every minute of every day. It would drown out your work so that you couldn't hear anything else, and you'd become totally ineffective in your day-to-day life. This is not the purpose of ECK. It is to help you enhance your own efforts toward God-Realization.

You have to take the first step, then the Living ECK Master can help you. But he won't pull you where you don't want to go. He doesn't want to. It's against the spiritual law. It would be like when you've got a child and you want to go shopping and get things done quickly. As you're going through the store, the child stops. You look around for him and say, "Where are you?" Then you go a little farther, he

The purpose of ECK is to help you enhance your own efforts toward God-Realization.

stops again, you look around. You're trying to move on, and a half-hour shopping trip turns out to be a one-hour shopping trip.

The Living ECK Master will go with you, if you want to go, and give you the experiences which are necessary for your spiritual unfoldment.

The Darshan

As time goes along, you are becoming stronger in ECK. You are developing the spiritual stamina to realize that you must look to the Inner Master, that the Darshan can come from the Inner Master or it can come from the stage. It isn't necessary to shake hands. Sometimes it's possible and sometimes it's not. We can still see each other on the inner.

Some years ago there was a master who had written and talked for twenty years, and finally he said, "That's it." He took a vow of silence. From that point on, he would sit on a little platform in the middle of the room and not say a word. His disciples would troop in, sit down, just look at him for a couple of hours, and they'd get the Darshan. After about two or three hours, they would simply get up and leave. That man had had it; he wouldn't say one word. He had talked for twenty years, and he figured that was enough. He wasn't going to put himself out anymore.

The ECK Masters help you make that connection with the Inner Master.

Well, the ECK Masters have to keep working, have to keep doing something, helping out in some way; but mostly it's to help you make that connection with the Inner Master, where you have this linkup and where you have this knowingness.

ECK Spiritual Aides

The ECK Spiritual Aide program is just beginning, and there's a donation requested. I mention this because if we want something, somehow we must give something. The ECK Spiritual Aide doesn't heal but acts as a listening post concerning your spiritual situation. This is going to be one way that Eckankar will be able to provide a great service to the community at large.

Someone may say, "I'm sick. What should I do? Heal me." I may know a way to heal, I may know something about that person's condition; but I'm not licensed, and although it may sound funny, I don't dare say anything. But as I sit there, Spirit works. And if the person stays open, he will be led to the doctor or to the vitamin that can help, or he will get a direct feeling of what is needed at that particular time.

The ECK Spiritual Aides, if any of you are interested in this service, will have consultations tomorrow, as many as can be handled. It's merely a service; it's a way for the ECK to work more directly if you feel the need. Some of you are able to get the help directly, yourself, but it's a service that you are all welcome to look into as time goes on.

BEING VEHICLES FOR ECK

I would like to thank you for being vehicles for the ECK. That doesn't mean you have to do something all the time. Just being in the grocery store and being aware that at that moment you are a vehicle for the ECK is a way of giving. It may mean putting out a poster or leaving a book inconspicuously so no one knows you've done it. Not cluttering the area—that's not necessary—but one here, one there; we can do that.

As we get more in ECK, we have to give more.

We can begin giving of this love in this way, to let it flow through. As we get more in ECK, we have to give more.

Our mind is a little slow. We still have our old practices and habits at the First Initiation. When we get the Second, we have more Sound and Light, but maybe we haven't given more. And that doesn't necessarily mean giving out the ECK message. It may mean going out and playing a game of ball or bowling or sewing or something.

We have to do a little bit more to use this energy that's coming through. This will help us to avoid a lot of problems.

The point is, somehow we have to do a little bit more to use this energy that's coming through. This will help us to avoid a lot of the physical problems, a lot of the emotional conflicts, things going wrong at the office. It's just a little tip.

I don't know how best to say it, but when you get more ECK flowing through, you have to flow with It. It will lead you, and you have to go with It.

If you're willing to do that, there is never any need to have hardships around an initiation. Some, a very few, feel that when they have an initiation, things get hard. A lot of ECKists don't experience this. It doesn't have to be difficult.

*Houston Regional Seminar, Houston, Texas,
March 13, 1982*

The lady felt this very definitely was help from the Inner Master, but she had to use her own common sense too: When you see a taxicab with the door open, get in!

5

THE SECRET
PATH TO HEAVEN

The secret path to heaven is not really so secret. You all know the way. We do the spiritual exercises, and we step into the inner worlds, which until now have been a big mystery to us. As we looked into other paths before we came to ECK, we knew there must be a better way, so we looked and looked. Perhaps the God we worshipped was a materialistic God who did not give the answers we wanted. Maybe we were just asking at the wrong time, or looking to God only when we needed help.

THE CYCLES OF LIFE

It's an interesting point that when economic times get hard, people turn to God. There's nothing wrong with this, but it makes you wonder if man has made God into his own image. When times are hard, you look to God; when times are good, you go out and have a good time.

We're having quite a revival of religion again today, and this is not new, especially to anyone who is a student of history. You will find that every time our country feels a pinch in the wallet, interest in God goes up. This happened back in the 1870s, at the turn of the century around 1900, in the 1930s, and we're in it again today.

Back in the 1870s, a man named Robert Ingersoll was the great agnostic of the day. This means he expressed the view I don't know if there is a God. He was leaving it an open question. But he had a lot of fun, especially in this time of revival, challenging the different religious leaders: Prove to me there is a God. At one point he said that when people stop praying, they'll start preying—on their neighbors and everybody else.

Religions and religious teachings give us someplace we can go to find comfort and help when we need it.

When times are hard, religions and religious teachings give us someplace we can go to find comfort and help when we need it. When the stock market goes up, over a long period of time, then the need for God gradually goes down. An ECKist has gone through these cycles for many lifetimes. The cycle goes up, your emotions go up; it goes down, you go down.

In the story of Job from the Christian Bible, he goes through what we call the dark night of Soul. He had his family, his possessions, everything; then all of a sudden, these were all taken from him. His neighbors thought he must have been very bad because God was punishing him. Job was very casual about it, in a way, except for the sorrow. When everything that has meant anything to an individual is taken away, and he doesn't know what it means and can't understand it, sometimes it can bring him within an inch of taking his own life. But Job knew better and continued to love God. He sat in the sackcloth and the ashes on his head with everybody saying, "Oh, Job, you must've really done it." But he said something to this effect: "I am learning something.

God is giving me the opportunity to learn something." He didn't know why it was happening, he didn't understand the reason, but he kept his face to God. And eventually, Job got everything back again, very slowly.

Life goes up, life goes down, up and down like a sound wave; and with our emotions we go up and down. And right through the middle of these ups and downs runs a stable spiritual force known as Eckankar. This does not mean that Eckankar will take away your troubles; it does not necessarily mean that you will have fewer aches and pains. But you will understand them, and you will develop an insight as to why you are having to go through this.

Right through the middle of these ups and downs runs a stable spiritual force known as Eckankar.

As you get this insight, as the ECK comes through, you also learn that most of the troubles you have caused can be averted. You are the one who is in control of your own universe. It may take a little while to work through this stream of negative karma that has been created—and most of it has been created in this lifetime, not in another. It takes a little while. As you do the spiritual exercises, this karma, this stream or river, begins to dry up. It doesn't happen overnight.

After doing the Spiritual Exercises of ECK for just two or three weeks, someone will write in and say, "I must be doing something wrong. I'm not having any experiences. My life seems to be worse than before." If you're going to study to be a doctor—and it's a profession worthy of putting your whole attention into for an entire lifetime—how many would expect to become a doctor or be good enough to do intricate surgery after only two weeks? It takes longer for some. Others have done the groundwork in other lifetimes, and they pick it up faster.

WHERE IS HEAVEN?

I'd like to comment about the secret path to heaven. A few weeks ago we went to Houston for an ECK regional seminar, and a number of the ECKists came. We had made plans: the hotel was here, the ECK seminar was being held over there, and connecting the two was the Gulf Freeway. I used to work in Houston ten years ago, and this freeway was notorious at the time for being impassable. There was no way to get from one end of it to the other. It was clogged, there was heavy traffic, and you just could not get through. So before the evening talk, we had taken a drive up there, and it looked pretty good. They had added an extra lane, and I said, "Well, this looks like it's going to be OK."

Still, we allowed plenty of time to get to the talk that night. Then, sure enough, a light rain hit; and as we were entering the on-ramp to the freeway, as far as you could see there were red taillights.

I arrived about ten minutes late to find the audience just sitting and waiting. As soon as we got there, I came in the back door and rushed up the steps. When I got upstairs, I opened the door leading backstage and saw another open door, and through that door I could see the empty stage. Nobody was out there; it had been empty for probably five or ten minutes because everybody was waiting for me to come out from behind the curtain. Later someone said, "I thought you were testing us." I said, "You thought I was standing behind the curtain just peeking out and seeing how it was going, right?" So when I began the talk I said, "If you plan to go to heaven, don't take the Gulf Freeway." You should have heard the Houstonians applaud. They had fought that freeway since I'd been there, they're still fighting it, and

I'd like to comment about the secret path to heaven.

it looks like they'll fight it a little longer. But we had a good time, and it was a way to bring out the message of ECK, about this secret path to heaven.

Where is heaven? Where can I find it? So often I think back to the biblical reading I did as a student. Very sincerely I looked and struggled, and asked, Where is God? Where is heaven? I won't say my faith was severely shaken, but when I read that St. Paul spoke of a man who was caught up even unto the third heaven, I said, Wait a minute. Nobody told me about anything except one heaven. And I asked about it at the time. What does this third heaven mean? If there's a third heaven, there must be a first and a second. It was very easy for adults and for the people in charge of our religious program to control us: You do good, you go to heaven; you do bad, you go to hell. But if I was going to heaven, I now had a choice.

My faith got shaken once again later when I finally came to understand something that was and still is very precious. It's a state of consciousness that most of us raised in this Christian culture know as the Christ consciousness. Jesus, the man, had this Christ consciousness. It was not a first name and a last name; we wouldn't address him as Mr. Christ. But if you mention this today, people are offended; they think you're making fun of their religion, and you're not.

If you refer to Christ as a state of consciousness, they feel that somehow you're cheating them, that it refers to a man named Jesus Christ. It's used as a name without any understanding of Christ being a state of consciousness; without any understanding that there is always one more heaven, that there is always one more state of consciousness. And so, many of the people have fixed their attention on this

There is always one more heaven, there is always one more state of consciousness.

state of consciousness and stopped there. This is fine for them, but many others can go on.

THE PATH TO SELF-MASTERSHIP

As we do the Spiritual Exercises of ECK, we can go into the inner worlds.

As we do the Spiritual Exercises of ECK, we can go into the inner worlds. We first come to the Astral Plane, and it's so beautiful compared to the Physical that we stop to smell the flowers. But after you've been in the Astral Plane for a while, it gets as commonplace as the Physical, simply because Soul has outrun the physical consciousness, the human consciousness. Soul is ready to go on, and sometimes we and our lower bodies are not. We want to stay there and enjoy it. Then all of a sudden our spiritual experiences stop or they slow down, and we wonder what's wrong. What am I doing wrong?

Nothing. You can smell the flowers forever, but you don't have to do it all on the Astral Plane. You can go on. You can go to the next step, to the Causal Plane.

We were talking about how rituals sometimes become established. There is no worship of the Living ECK Master or any ECK Master. They don't want it. God doesn't want worship, doesn't need it. This is an interesting point. The God that is often looked to is worshipped. And why? Because it is the Kal Niranjan wearing one of many faces. The Kal Niranjan is the most negative force. He has two sides: a smiling face which is out in front, and then the one that reveals what he really is. And this face of the Kal Niranjan needs someone to tell him, Hey, Kal, you're OK. He feels insecure.

A God that was perfect and in all Its fullness would certainly not need praise from the human consciousness. It would not need worship from the human consciousness. The great Sugmad, the one that the ECKist looks to, does not need this. It is not a pitiful God with the characteristics of a spoiled child who expects you to pat him on the head.

STORYTELLERS OF THE CHEYENNE

The Cheyenne Indians came from the area of the Great Lakes. First they lived in wigwams; and then gradually, as they were pushed westward by the white man, they began living in tepees. They did not have TV and radio, of course; and so they needed entertainment. They were people very much like us in many ways. They had their storytellers; and when a good storyteller traveled through, it was considered an event. He was invited in, given some food, and treated really well.

These storytellers had developed their skills over many years. From childhood they were taught the legends of the Indian chiefs, of their heroes, the heroics, the battlefields, everything. They heard these stories over and over, and then the young men would have to repeat them to the elders of the tribe to make sure they got every word right. Some could remember the details better than others, and pretty soon it got to be known who could tell a good story. This man stood in a very exalted position in that culture.

So when a storyteller came through, everybody would come to the lodge. After they had eaten, they would shut the door and sit in perfect silence. They figured some physical ailment would come upon anybody who spoke. The storytellers probably started this myth. Any storyteller worth his salt would make sure that he kept an attentive audience.

It was interesting the way the Indian storyteller would tie one story to another. After talking for a

It was interesting the way the Indian storyteller would tie one story to another.

while he would say, "And this story leads to another." He'd talk awhile longer and then say, "This story ties on to another," and so on. Between stories they would sit around and have a good time—a commercial break.

Paul Twitchell once said that writing a story is very easy: it's like stringing beads—one after another after another. The string goes from here to there. A storyteller would do that too. He would connect one story to another, which would tie in to another, and then there would be another one, like a rest point in eternity, and on and on. The planes are this way, also. There is the Physical, and then there is the Astral. You take a little break, and then you go to the Causal; take a little break, Mental; then to the Etheric, on to the Soul Plane, and from there you go on into the spiritual God Worlds where you find the Sound and Light of ECK at that temple within yourself.

THE SECRET PATH BEYOND SOUL TRAVEL

We have this knowingness inside that our spiritual life is being taken care of.

This is the secret path to heaven. It's found in the ECK discourses. We do the Spiritual Exercises of ECK; we use our creative imagination. We will try a certain technique for a couple of weeks or a couple of months. It may take a while to get there. Even if we don't have a visual experience where we can say, I saw the Blue Light, or I saw the Inner Master, we have this knowingness inside that our spiritual life is being taken care of. There's this knowingness.

Not everyone has to go through this stage where you start at the Physical and then you want to Soul Travel. Soul Travel takes you only through the psychic worlds, through the worlds where there is matter, energy, space, and time. It stands to reason that if you're going to travel, there must be space from here to there, and it's going to have to take a certain amount of time to get from here to there.

When you go into the spiritual God Worlds of ECK, there is no longer space as we think of it here, nor is there time. It collapses, and then there is no need for Soul Travel. Soul Travel will take you so far, up to the Soul Plane, and then you begin to work with the parts of seeing, knowing, and being.

How do you explain this? It works in your everyday life. As we step further along the path to self-mastership, we work with this ECK as It manifests to us and gives us direction. It will be different for everyone. Some will see the Inner Master come and give them hints and directions. Others will feel gentle nudgings. If it's a matter of health, or refilling the wallet and trying to figure out how to get the business going again, the ECK will give nudges. As we do the Spiritual Exercises of ECK, our consciousness opens. We become more aware of the help that is already at hand.

As we do the Spiritual Exercises of ECK, we become more aware of the help that is already at hand.

THE PROTECTION OF THE ECK

The Master says, "I am always with you." There is never any need to panic and say, Why have you forsaken me? The love of the Master is always there, and it takes only our acceptance and our awareness of it.

I might mention that we don't look to the ECK to take care of our daily problems and our daily situations. We do what we can, we put ourselves into it 100 percent, and then the ECK smooths the way wherever needed. Wherever the ditch gets too wide to jump across, It might lead you to a bridge.

A man wrote to report an incident that had

happened to his wife, where she had received the protection of the ECK in her daily life. This took place in another country where there is less freedom and it's easier for the military forces to control people or take them into custody than it is here. This family is not wealthy, and every day the wife would go to the shipyard where she would buy fish, clean and smoke them, and then she would take these fish and resell them. In this way she was able to add a little to the household finances.

This particular day, as usual, she went to buy and sell the fish, when the naval patrol came through and made a lightning raid on the wharf, pulling in a lot of the hawkers and people who were changing foreign currency, which was illegal. Selling fish was not illegal, but the arm of the law in that country isn't very particular until they get you down to the police station to interrogate you and find out who belonged there and who didn't.

When she started to chant HU, this ancient name of God, the Inner Master gave her a nudge.

These people were taken to the naval patrol station where they were interrogated, and some were beaten. The ECKist wasn't beaten, but she was interrogated.

When she started to chant *HU*, this ancient name of God, quietly and inwardly, the Inner Master gave her the nudge to call her husband's name out loud. She wondered, *Why should I be calling my husband's name when I ought to be calling the name of one of the ECK Masters?* But she listened to the nudge, followed it without question, and started chanting her husband's name. All of a sudden one of the naval men walked up to her and said, "Why are you calling my name?"

She said, "I was calling my husband's name. I haven't eaten all day, and I'm getting very dizzy." He then reached into his pocket—and this was interesting—he took some money out, and he said,

"Here, take this money, go to our naval canteen right over there and get yourself something to eat." So she took the money and went across the room to the naval canteen to get herself something to eat.

She was also very bright. She happened to look outside the door just then, and she saw a taxicab sitting there with the door open. Without even a backward glance, she walked outside, got into the cab, shut the door, and the cab took off.

She said the reason they didn't pursue her was because the other naval personnel had seen this naval man talking to her and giving her money, and they just assumed she must be a relative. She felt this very definitely was help from the Inner Master, but she had to use her own common sense too: When you see a taxicab with the door open, get in!

If you are new in ECK, you may want to look at the ECK books. Work with the books, take your time, and don't hurry. When you step onto the path to God and you begin looking for that secret path to heaven, the way will be opened for you; and the way lies through the Spiritual Exercises of ECK. I don't ask you to take my word for it—but try them.

The path of ECK is the path of experience.

The path of ECK is the path of experience. We start out with faith, we start out with belief, but after a time our faith and belief are replaced by actual experience so that we know. We know the reality of God as it is revealed through Divine Spirit, the Voice of God, which can be heard as Sound and seen as Light.

This is the secret path to heaven.

*Eckankar International Youth Conference,
Rosemont, Illinois, Friday, April 9, 1982*

Your secret word may not be working for you, and you wonder, *What should I do?* You can go to the God Worlds chart, find the word that corresponds to your level of initiation, and chant it.

6
THE LAW OF SILENCE

When they put the microphone on me, they're careful not to plug it in until we actually are ready to come on, because you'd hear all kinds of things, such as, "Is the tie straight?" Working with the microphone and not having it plugged in works in very well with my topic tonight, the Law of Silence.

In the works of ECK, we come to that temple within ourselves. We move inwardly, we go to those areas which are unknown to people in most religions. We come to that area where we meet the Inner Master. We hear the Sound, and we see the Light. When we see the Inner Master and when this Master gives us instruction, we begin the discipline of keeping it to ourselves. And this is a hard discipline.

A woman mentioned to me this afternoon that when she was a little girl, before Eckankar had come out in 1965 with the writings of Paul Twitchell, she saw Rebazar Tarzs in her dreams. Rebazar Tarzs gave her experience on the inner planes and gave her a secret word, a charged word of ECK, of Spirit, which could help her open her consciousness. Years before Paul brought Eckankar out, she had met Rebazar Tarzs, one of the great ECK Masters.

Whenever anyone wonders, Is this path of ECK real?—and you see writings that go this way and

In the works of ECK, we go to those areas which are unknown to people in most religions.

that way—there are two things we can do: we can get involved in the controversy, but to do that closes out the temple within ourselves; or we can practice the Law of Silence, with both our inner experiences, and what we see and know, to keep the inner sacred. Because when you go inwardly, you go to that Holy of Holies, the most sacred, ancient part of yourself, the home of Soul. You are Soul.

We practice the Law of Silence to keep the inner sacred.

I was wondering what to say tonight, and in keeping with the topic I wondered if perhaps this would be a night of silence. And yet, there was something that was to be said, to give an insight into how one can prepare himself as he gives service to the ECK. There is also a way that a person can prepare himself to go to the temple within himself and to meet with the Inner Master.

Is ECK Real?

There are those who wonder: Is ECK real? I won't say every last one of you here tonight has consciously had the experience of the Sound and Light of Divine Spirit. Many of you have. Many of the rest of you have the knowingness. Yet there are some of you who have never had this experience and are here out of curiosity.

We are not on an emotional path. It would be very easy for me to stand up here and drum up emotion. For that, all you have to do is turn on your TV and watch the 700 Club; they are masters at it. The ECK Masters are not interested in your worshipping the physical body. You find that most often they are low-key. Oh, we have fun and a good time, but we don't use a club over someone else. We let them have their freedom and their space. We give them the right and the freedom to make their own decision about which path to God they would like to walk, which way they choose to go. We give this freedom. We want the freedom to walk to God in our own way. More importantly, we are willing to give this freedom to others to find God in their own way, in their own time.

The Law of Silence is difficult to follow. Someone this afternoon said, "I finally found something that really works, and I just wanted to go tell everybody about it. But nobody wanted to hear it." You've run into this, and so have I.

When I came across Eckankar, for me it was right. The words rang true. I did the spiritual exercises and was disappointed that I didn't have any experience for two whole months. Then I had an experience. And I wondered why I didn't have one the next night. Was something wrong? I mention this because there are a number of you, like myself, who have found that you may not necessarily be consciously aware of having the Sound and Light of Spirit in your life every moment.

What Is the Sound?

The Sound can be heard as the sound of a flute. It may be heard as the buzzing of bees. At times it may be heard as a whirlpool or a stringed orchestra. These are actual sounds that you hear—pure, uplifting sounds—the action of the atoms as the ECK moves them, which uplifts and purifies the consciousness. It raises us into higher states of awareness so that we are better able to live our lives. When the loneliness and unhappiness come, we are able to look and see why, to get an understanding. We begin to know and recognize the presence of the Inner Master. It may come as a feeling of warmth, a feeling of love. It will just flow in on you.

The presence of the Inner Master may come as a feeling of warmth, a feeling of love.

This afternoon as I went into the children's room, they began to sing "The Sound Is HU, the Light Is HU." It was beautiful. You listen to them and you can tell this song came from pure hearts. You know how children are: they'll be running and tearing around one moment, but when they set their little voices to something like a love song to God, it is something to listen to.

I talked with some young people today who are in high school. We had a panel up here, and they were very interesting. One said, "I was really nervous, and I didn't know what I'd say." Another said, "I was really nervous too." A third said the same thing. Then one said, "Nope, I wasn't nervous at all." I said, "Would you like to go back up there?" He said, "Sure!" And he looked like he was ready to do it. The confidence and strength that develop come from this inner knowing, this inner strength.

When we get the secrets from the Inner Master, we keep it to ourselves.

When we get the secrets from the Inner Master, we keep it to ourselves. If we speak about it, people will try to tear it down. They will try to take away the happiness that one has gained for himself. It makes them angry that anyone would dare to be happy.

How the Law of Silence Works

Once there was an airman in the service whose name had been left off the duty roster. The rest of the sixty men in this flight training school were all listed on it. They all got to help out with cooking, cleaning up the area, and all kinds of little jobs that everyone who's been in the service knows about. But for some reason, they had missed his name. So for the first few days he went to the duty sergeant and said, "Sergeant, I'm here to report for duty." The sergeant looked over the duty roster and said, "I don't see your name here." The airman said, "But it's gotta be there." "Nope, don't have your name."

He did this a few times and then finally said, Hey, wait a minute. I'm being given a good deal here, and I'm trying to get myself in a lot of trouble.

As is the case with anyone who's been in the service and finds he's got a good thing going, he faded into the background. He got really good at this and started to feel proud about it. Each day while everybody else was out there working in the heat down in Mississippi at Keesler Air Force Base, he was having a good time. He'd go for nice, enjoyable walks around the base. Then one day his roommate said, "How come I'm out here working KP and squadron detail and you're not?" He felt really smug and said, "Because they don't have my name on the duty roster."

There's something about the human consciousness: you can't trust it. Great humorists such as Mark Twain never trusted it, and this is what made him great. Well, this airman didn't know any better. Someone was specially sent from the orderly room, and he was told to report. They tried to give him a hard time because he had been off the duty roster for so long without reporting it. They intended to make an issue out of it and were even trying to give him punishment for it, so he was in hot water for a while. In the end, the worst that happened was he had to work a bit before his flight finally shipped out to their permanent stations.

The Law of Silence is good. It's best not to wear our troubles on our shirtsleeve where other people can look at and discuss them. The ECK Masters tell us: Forget gossip; it's something you don't need. It may seem as if they're saying they don't want us to

The ECK Masters tell us: Forget gossip; it's something you don't need.

gossip because somehow it's not upstanding, it's not spiritual—it's just that all those mental concepts don't mean a thing to us.

Karma's Delayed Fuse

There was a time in my unfoldment when I'd come home from work and, as often happened, my wife and I would talk about somebody in the family. Maybe their marriage was going through a rough time, so we'd talk about it, just like the soap operas. The Law of Karma works very quickly, and it works through something like gossip. Two or three days later, for some reason, we were inspired to go at each other. I'd nag and she'd bicker, and we'd just go on and on. We figured at the time that this was just one of those acts of natural law that we were not able to avoid, so we'd have this little tiff in the house. But gradually we came to find out—I was watching—whenever we spoke about someone who was having problems in their marriage, there was a delayed action of about three days, and then it would strike us. But because it would strike so late, we wouldn't notice what had caused it.

ECKists are fortunate because we can work out the karma of this physical life here and now.

ECKists are fortunate because we can work out the karma of this physical life here and now; it comes back to us immediately. By immediately, I mean within this lifetime. Those who have yet to step onto the path of ECK seem to be getting away with this and getting away with that, because they never appear to be held to account.

My daughter went to the store with some friends of hers, all little characters, seven years old or so. She watched as they scooped candy off the shelves and stuffed it into their pockets and shirts. They were very good at it. They urged her to join in: "Come on, do it!" But she's been trained not to steal, and when she came home she wanted to talk about it. "Why do they do it?"

"Because they think they're getting away with it," I explained, "and they're probably going to get away with it for a long time. Nobody will catch them, and then all of a sudden it will all come home to them and they'll wonder why God has forsaken them."

God gets the blame when times get rough. That also applies in matters of health.

THE GREATER DISCIPLINES

The ECK Masters put together the information that ends up in the Shariyat-Ki-Sugmad. They compile it, they gather it through lengthy experience, and it comes from their own hard learning. They didn't just sit on a rock somewhere and say, "Here comes the message from on high—get it down!"

The ECK Masters working at the time of the caveman had to work with the consciousness of the individuals, the Souls that had incarnated as the cavemen. We wouldn't recognize an ECK Master from those days if he came here today. He had to communicate by motions, grunts, or whatever was necessary, because why speak? There was no language in the early days. Man had to be taught how to make a fire.

As human life developed, man raised into the higher spiritual consciousness. With it came the greater disciplines.

As human life developed, man raised into the higher spiritual consciousness. He became capable of going to the temple within himself to meet with inner masters such as Rebazar Tarzs and Peddar Zaskq, like those of you who are meeting Fubbi Quantz and others. They were able to go inward, and as they did, with it came the greater disciplines. One of them was the Law of Silence.

You might have a question about something. Your secret word may not be working for you, and you wonder, *What should I do?* You can write to me. You can also go to the God Worlds of ECK chart in *The Spiritual Notebook*, read it, find the word that corresponds to your level of initiation, and chant it. Try it in many different ways. Try it for a week one way, try it for a week another way. It's an experimental process, it's a creative process, because Soul is creative, infinitely creative.

Soul is creative, infinitely creative.

The imaginative faculty, hitched together with your secret word, is what leads you to the temple within yourself through the different worlds; and this is where you contact the Mahanta, the Inner Master. It takes you into the very heart of God.

There are those who write to tell me they want Self-Realization or God-Realization, and they want it now. Others are willing to take their time, to enjoy the learning, to enjoy it step-by-step; to go to the temple within themselves to see the Light of God. You may see It as a Blue Light; you may see It as a blue globe, a blue star, a six-pointed star. This is the Mahanta. Many ECKists have reported seeing It. This is the first step where you are seeing Divine Spirit—one of Its many manifestations. After this comes the Sound. The Sound and the Light will lift you into the spiritual realms.

In our own life, we will find a word that works for us and we'll do it a certain way for a while, and then all of a sudden it will stop working. Why? Because we have unfolded into another level of expression, another level of awareness. We have to find it; we have to find where this Spirit, this flow, has taken us.

Is ECK Truth?

When we get this ECK working in our lives and we come to the path of Eckankar, there is a period for most of us when we feel very unsure. You wonder: Is this really the way? Is this really the truth? And no one else can answer that for you.

A woman on jury duty went to the jury pool room where all the jurors are kept waiting so that if a trial requires twelve jurors, they are sent out. An ECKist was among them, minding her own business, when this lady came up to her and out of the blue asked: "Do you go to church?" The ECKist simply said, "No," and for some reason this lady really got onto her. She said, "You're going to hell, you aren't saved," and so on. The ECKist, of course, looked to the inner and chanted *HU*. This confrontation took place in front of a number of other people, and there was a time that this woman would have been embarrassed, but now she wasn't. She just looked at that other Soul trying so desperately to prove to Itself that Its own religion was right, because It felt it wasn't.

You'll find that when someone is pressing his faith upon you, it's because he's not very sure of it. This is why, if we have the assurance and the knowing of the Inner Master, we in ECK have no reason to push it upon anyone.

The ECKist didn't know how to get out of this predicament, but she went to the temple within herself and asked for help. She went to that inner silence. Soon another woman joined the group, a Jewish lady, and she engaged the Christian lady in a conversation. The Christian then started to talk to the Jewish lady. Pretty soon their conversation got going, and the ECKist was able to gradually step back. Eventually a call came for the jurors, and the

When someone is pressing his faith upon you, it's because he's not very sure of it.

Christian lady had to leave to go serve on a jury.

The next day they met in the jury room again, and an interesting thing happened: now the Christian lady smothered the ECKist with kindness. She wouldn't even talk to the Jewish woman. It's the nature of the human consciousness. You can't trust the human consciousness.

Before we come into ECK, we are up, we are down. You can't even trust or rely upon yourself from one moment to the next as to what you're going to do. As you come into ECK, you gain strength, you have fewer ups and downs, because you have that firm foundation built upon the two pillars of the Light and Sound of Divine Spirit.

ECK is real. It works. It is the most vital religious teaching on the planet Earth today.

ECK is real. It works. It is the most vital religious teaching on the planet Earth today. There's no way we can prove it to others. There is no way we go out and push it on people; they're going to have to find it out for themselves.

FINDING THE PATH OF ECK

There are many who found the path of ECK and the ECK Masters long before 1965. I have letters attesting to that. It would be easy to put them out for display and say, OK, here's one, here's another. But that would seem as if we were trying to make others believe. There's no reason to do that. If someone is ready, they will hear; and if they're not, they won't. There is nothing that can be done to convince anyone, so save your time, save your energy. Work in your life; listen to that Divine Spirit as It nudges you into a greater expression. If you're in business, It will lead you to a greater expression—and I won't say you'll never have a bankruptcy. There may be some law we haven't understood, and as we followed out these certain laws according to our own imperfect understanding, it led inevitably to failure.

As we follow the ECK, we begin slowly, gradually. It may take years to come to where we begin to succeed a little bit—to come into a happier, fuller life, to shed the loneliness.

BECOMING A CO-WORKER WITH GOD

This afternoon, one of the ECKists who is in the firefighting profession was telling how adventuresome it is and how often he meets people at that point where they translate, or die. Many times he can see Soul leaving the physical body. It is an appropriate time to lightly touch on this because we are in the Easter season.

All Easter was meant to be was a recognition that Soul lives beyond the physical body. Yet this ECKist said just about every time he came to a situation where someone had translated, the relatives on the scene broke down completely. Their faith failed them, and they said, "Why has God done this?" At that point, everything that they had believed, all the faith they had, was completely shattered. As an ECK initiate, he is able to give an understanding that Soul is eternal—It has no beginning and no ending.

People send cards of sympathy which express compassion for the loss of a loved one, but the ECKist is able to tell them something about the spiritual reality of what happens when Soul leaves this body and goes on.

In one case, which has nothing to do with the translation of anyone, there was a fire in the old, junky basement of a very poor household. The ECKist went down there with a fire hose and was finally able

As we follow the ECK, we come into a happier, fuller life.

to put the fire out. He's an interesting ECKist. He's like most of the ECKists—they love life. He's not only a fireman but he also sells furniture.

The ECK may use Its vehicles to take them to the proper house, again and again, as if the laws of chance were bent against odds of about a million to one. Anyway, sometime later, while driving his furniture truck, he gets a call to take furniture to a certain home. It was all brand-new furniture. He gets to this house and recognizes it as the one that had been heavily damaged by the fire which he had put out while he was working as a fireman. He brings the furniture in, and the woman asks if he would take some of it down to the basement. He carries the furniture downstairs, and here he sees this beautiful recreation room.

Well, right after the fire, the woman who owned the house had been completely beside herself. She didn't know what to do. "My possessions, my basement—all gone." She and the ECKist sat on the running board of the fire engine as he talked with her. At the time she had broken down and lost faith in everything she had ever believed in. He had said to her, "We have to learn to give up certain things, because maybe God is trying to bring us something better."

> He said to her, "We have to learn to give up certain things, because maybe God is trying to bring us something better."

Now as the furniture man, he sees the remodeled downstairs area and asks her how all this came about. She looks at him kind of puzzled, and he says, "I'm the fireman who put out the fire." She just looks at him and says something like, "Hmmm."

ECKists, being what they are, have a lot of creativity, and some of them have enough energy to be a fireman and work at a furniture store. This one had enough energy to also work as a deliverer of flowers. These ECKists, especially when they get to the higher initiations, get around here on the physical plane as well as in the inner planes. They *really* get around.

While delivering flowers one day, again he happened to come to this same address, and the door was answered by the same woman as before. She recognized him by now, and she said, "Of all the people I wanted to see now, for some reason, I don't know why, it was you."

One of her relatives had translated, had passed on. Not a very close one, but often when we sorrow at the passing of another, we sorrow for ourselves, for our ignorance and our fear of the life beyond. And he was able to sit and talk with her and bring some of the message of ECK to her. You might think it was coincidence that he would be brought to this place again and again and again in three different guises.

Divine Spirit works in Its own way, in Its own time. It uses the ECKists as vehicles; It uses you.

Divine Spirit works in Its own way, in Its own time.

OUR MISSION IN LIFE

If one would ask, What is my mission in this life? the answer is simply: to become a Co-worker with God.

I once wondered what was so much fun about being a Co-worker. But if you can be a fireman, a furniture mover, and someone who delivers flowers, and you can see people and help them in their daily life and lead them to the Sound and Light of Spirit, this is a small taste of what it means to be a Co-worker with God. It's fulfilling; it's rewarding.

The strength for this initiate came from the temple within himself. He was able to meet the Sound and Light. He had many more stories, but I won't tell you any more of them because you have to find your own stories in your own life. You may not get them every day. It may take a week, or they may be scattered out over months, or you may not have these except once a year.

He practiced the Law of Silence: when he got this from the Inner Master, he held it sacred, he held it dear. And in so doing, he opened himself and will do so even more, as many of you will, as a vehicle for Divine Spirit.

Eckankar International Youth Conference,
Rosemont, Illinois, Saturday, April 10, 1982

Lai Tsi returned from his experience with God to find himself lying on the cave floor with animals gathered around to nourish him and keep him warm.

7

CHILD IN THE WILDERNESS

We're near the beginning of spring and the celebration that is known to the Christian world as Easter. It is the time of rejuvenation of the spiritual body of man, of Soul, and this is all that it has ever meant.

A lot of attention has been put upon the death and the resurrection of Christ, yet there have been instances of different peoples with their own records of men who died and rose again, even before Christianity. In Mithraism this was true, and in the Hindu religion Krishna is said to have gone through the same process as Christ did.

About 700 BC, the ECK Master Vajra Manjushri tried to teach Eckankar to the Persians under King Hakhamanish, but the people of those times were too steeped in the human consciousness. Soul had gone quite far down into that state of consciousness, and Manjushri tried to find ways to bring them up, to raise them into the spiritual worlds. For his trouble he was arrested. Many of you have read this in *The Spiritual Notebook*. He was stretched out on a huge block of wood shaped like the letter *E*, the king's men then fired their arrows, and that was the end of him in the physical body. The next day he appeared to his disciples in a shimmering cloak of light.

Manjushri's body had been placed in a cave. When his disciples came to the cavern, they found that the body was gone—just as in the Christian story. They started to argue, not trusting each other, saying, "You have taken the body." While they were bickering, this great ECK Master appeared and said, "Why are you fighting among yourselves over this piece of clay?"

The temple of clay is nothing more than the home of Soul in the physical body. We are just here visiting.

PAST LIVES

We are as high on the path of spiritual consciousness as we've ever been.

So often we wonder: What can I be? What was I in the past? What about all my past lives? I must have really been great then. We look at ourselves today, and it's a revelation to know that we are as high on the path of spiritual consciousness as we've ever been. Everything that we've been in the past has been put together, as Soul gaining the greater experience. We may have had a greater position in another lifetime, as a king or an emperor, but in this lifetime we have given that up for the opportunity to learn about the Sound and Light of ECK, Divine Spirit.

We have many different values from our past lives as we come through the different religious beliefs. In a radio program about religious matters, the listeners were asked what religion meant to them, and the people called in with their comments. One woman said her religion worked well for her, and when the host asked how, she launched into her reason: "Well, I lost this very expensive diamond setting from my ring; and when I prayed to Saint

Anthony, I got it back." She went on to say, "I lost it the second time, prayed to Saint Anthony again, and I got it back." This happened a third time, and also a fourth.

If we want God to be a lost-and-found person, then we have made God in our own image—a God of materialism, of the human consciousness. The great Sugmad never requires that the ECKist worship It. It is concerned only that Soul return home. It is not concerned with finding lost diamonds. Yet this woman felt that she was getting the spiritual help she needed.

Many of you are struggling to take one more step into the inner worlds with the Spiritual Exercises of ECK. This is the call of Soul, a deep yearning to go back home to the Ocean of Love and Mercy. You find that although you have possessions like diamonds, if they were about to be taken from you or if you had a choice, you'd rather go back to that Ocean of Love and Mercy. And this is the experience of Soul.

This is not meant as a criticism of this woman; there is a religion for every state of consciousness. This is why we never look down on anyone in another belief. We want the freedom to walk the path to Sugmad in our own way. We are willing to let others walk the path to God in their own way, just so their way does not require that we can't follow ours. You know how that goes: We want freedom, we are willing to give freedom, and we expect freedom.

THE CALL OF SOUL

The theme for this seminar is "Building a Spiritual Foundation in ECK," and the title of this talk is "Child in the Wilderness." The child in the wilderness is Soul in the lower worlds, away from Its

This is the call of Soul, a deep yearning to go back home to the Ocean of Love and Mercy.

true home. Soul came out of the heart of God and rested and enjoyed the spiritual planes, but It was not unfolding. In a way, It was an inexperienced Soul that had not learned how to give. Sugmad saw that Soul needed experience, and through the ECK, the lower worlds were created. Soul was sent down into these worlds—into the Etheric, the Mental, the Causal, down into the Astral, and many into the Physical—to begin Its experiences. Soul was unhappy and sorrowful, having left that state of consciousness of bliss.

Soul enters Its first human incarnation, often as a man. We start out with our initial karma, which is given to us to get us going. Soul thereby becomes the child in the wilderness. It begins to experience the troubles of life, balanced by the joys, but never understanding the meaning of it all. It bumbles and stumbles along through the centuries, sometimes meeting the Living ECK Master, taking in a little of the teachings—as much as It can handle at that moment—then steps off the path because It wants to try something else. It wants to try another path.

As the child in the wilderness, Soul once again looks further, ready to go one more step.

A magic show can be very appealing. So the child in the wilderness goes off to the magic show, enjoys himself for another lifetime or two, and then finally, as with all shows, the enjoyment wears off and that hollowness, that emptiness, that spiritual void remains. As the child in the wilderness, Soul once again looks further, ready to go one more step, searching for the Living ECK Master who has been on this planet from the beginning, from the time man first set foot on this earth, so that there would always be a way for every Soul to return to the spiritual planes.

A woman wrote to me and said she had this yearning; she'd had a dream where she remembered saying, "I want to go home. I want to go home."

She woke up very troubled and wondered what it had meant. Later, after she came into ECK, she said, "Oh, now I know. It was Soul; Soul wanting to go home."

THE SOURCE OF OUR PROBLEMS

There are many times the child in the wilderness goes through areas such as anger and has to come to terms with the anger inside. We spoke about it before, about gossip and why it is harmful. It stops us on the spiritual path. It's not for someone else: We think we're hurting another with gossip, but it's really our own self we are hurting. And not in just some intangible spiritual way, but quite often in a definite way right down here.

I'll mention the following story not in the sense that this particular person is the only one who never understood the ways of Spirit correctly, because that's what we're here for. We're learning them. This ECKist was learning too. He felt that another ECKist in the area wasn't doing something quite right and got very upset about it. What he forgot was to go within himself and say: "I've done what I can in the physical, and now I'll let it work out."

I happened to be in his car as we were driving to a meeting, and he told me how upset the ECKists were with the leadership in one area or another. I didn't say anything; I just let it be.

As we were traveling down a freeway that had three lanes, the driver told me how his car had been overheating and that he had taken it into the garage just to make sure that it would be in good condition when we went to this meeting. He was going to be driving me, and he wanted to make absolutely sure everything went right.

There are many times the child in the wilderness goes through areas such as anger, and has to come to terms with the anger inside.

As we drove down the freeway, I noticed that his car was overheating and mentioned it to him. "What?" he said and pulled right through the traffic over to the shoulder. He got out to look, not understanding what had happened. I had brought some bottled water along, so we took the water and poured it into the radiator. It was just to do something for him, because there was actually a broken hose.

He didn't realize that the imbalance he had created by letting anger get the better of him had caused this condition with his car. It happens so often, but there may be a lag period of perhaps two or three days or even weeks before it comes home to us. By then, it's so far removed from the original gossip that we don't remember that we caused the imbalance.

As we do the Spiritual Exercises of ECK, we are raised in consciousness. We gain an understanding of our actions.

As we do the Spiritual Exercises of ECK, as we go to the temple within ourselves, we are raised in consciousness. We gain an understanding of our actions, how they create our life for us, the happiness and the sadness. And as we are raised in consciousness, this understanding widens and we are able to see how *we* overheated the car. Now the reason I could recognize it in him is that I had done this myself. Not just once—it takes a number of times to finally catch on. While learning the laws of ECK, I missed them again and again, until finally I said, "Hey, I'm running out of money for car repairs. What's causing it?"

The ECKist doesn't blame General Motors or Ford or somebody else. He looks to himself as the source of his problems. Knowing this, I began to look through my life and concluded, *If this car is like my body, maybe it's just reflecting something that I have set forth.* I noticed, also, that whenever a negative thought went out instead of goodwill and love, it would affect my health too. Not that I don't catch colds now, but there were some unexplained ones that would come at a certain time. Or the car problems. This doesn't mean every time your car gets a flat tire that you've had a negative thought. The important thing is that we are learning; it makes no difference how.

You take life as it comes. You do the best you can. As you learn your lesson, or as you miss your lesson, you move on. You don't look back; you just move on.

Paul Twitchell had looked for the God Consciousness. He was the child in the wilderness, and most of you have heard the tape where he said he had expected the God Consciousness, prayed for it, did everything for it, and then he finally said: I want it at two o'clock on a certain day. When that day came, he lay down on his bed and waited for it. He probably waited all afternoon, and nothing happened. So he gave up, greatly discouraged. A couple of weeks later, when he wasn't expecting it, it came. It came in its own time, in its own way. He had done what he could to raise himself in consciousness, to open the consciousness through the Spiritual Exercises of ECK, but then it was up to Spirit.

You take life as it comes. You do the best you can. As you learn your lesson, you move on.

THE WAYSHOWERS

One of the ECK Masters who struggled greatly—and they all have—was Lai Tsi, the Chinese ECK Master. He studied in the religious schools of his time and became a doctor of divinity, but he knew from his study that the way to God was not in any book. He came from an influential and wealthy family, but he left it and went up into the hills. After many years all his friends and relatives forgot him, but during this time the ECK Masters came to him, bringing him upliftment; and at one point, he was raised to the God Consciousness.

The ECK Masters will hardly ever attempt to describe the consciousness of Self-Realization or God-Realization. This is a personal relationship with God, between Soul and Sugmad. They will give the methods, they will give the spiritual exercises, and they will show the way. The ECK Masters are the Wayshowers. They will help and assist anyone who is willing to step onto the path of ECK and make his own honest efforts. They won't push you if you're not willing to go.

Lai Tsi returned from his experience with God to find himself lying on a cave floor with animals gathered around to nourish him and keep him warm.

"Should anyone be in distress or need to reach the great Sugmad," he said, "use this contemplation; repeat it slowly and it certainly brings results." And he gave this seed of contemplation which I have found helpful and which is helpful to anyone who wants to reach that source:

Show me Thy ways, O Sugmad;
Teach me Thy path.
Lead me in Thy truth, and teach me;
On Thee do I wait all day.
Remember, O Beloved, Thy guiding light
And Thy loving care.
For it has been ever Thy will,
To lead the least of Thy servants to Thee!

The child in the wilderness reaches into the pure positive God Worlds and becomes a Master in his own right.

The child in the wilderness reaches into the planes of the pure positive God Worlds and becomes a Master in his own right. The way is there for everyone who is willing to undertake the discipline of the Spiritual Exercises of ECK. It's there through the rich and abundant years, and through the lean years; through the weeks where there is something happening and the weeks when you are not aware of anything happening.

Just go forward in full confidence, and trust in the love and the blessings of Divine Spirit.

Eckankar International Youth Conference,
Rosemont, Illinois, Sunday, April 11, 1982

You can be a silent vehicle for ECK anywhere by simply
declaring yourself to be one.

8
SPIRITUAL LIBERATION

When someone asks about the path of ECK and wants to know, What's it all about? the best I can say is that it is for spiritual liberation. You might say, OK, spiritual liberation. What does this involve? Throughout the day you've heard many of the fine speakers tell about the Sound and the Light of ECK. The ECK is the Holy Spirit, the Voice of God. It is the creative force that creates and sustains all life.

The way to this spiritual liberation is first of all through the Living ECK Master. The idea of a living master is relatively new to the Western culture but it is something that the religions of the Far East are well aware of. They realize that in order for a religious teaching to have any life, there must be a living master. The Living ECK Master leads one to the Sound Wave, which is the ECK, and this, then, leads to spiritual liberation.

All I do in the physical is make the books available, meet with you, give a talk, try to show you how to work with the Spiritual Exercises of ECK on your own, as you find them in the ECK books, and suggest that you try them out to see if this really works for you or not. If it does, you may want to look further and go step-by-step, because Spirit takes us one step

The Living ECK Master leads one to the Sound Wave, which is the ECK, and this, then, leads to spiritual liberation.

at a time, always a little bit further. As we get more of the Sound and Light, which are the two manifestations of Divine Spirit, we get more responsibility. And freedom.

THE LIGHT AND SOUND OF GOD

Maybe some of you are familiar with the story of Saul of Tarsus from the Christian Bible. He was on his way to persecute some other people for their religious beliefs; and on the road to Damascus he saw this Light, and he heard this Sound as a voice. This was merely the action of the ECK, Divine Spirit, coming down and striking his consciousness. The men who were with him heard the voice of someone speaking, but they couldn't see anyone.

Most instances reported in Western religious teachings are those where an individual encounters the Light of God. There's Jakob Böhme, the shoemaker, for one. He had this Light of God, and at certain times, everywhere he looked he'd see pink light. We in ECK know that this pink light came from the Astral Plane, which is the next heaven right beyond this Physical Plane of existence. And there were others. Most of them had the Light, this Light of God, but they never had the Sound.

The purpose of the Sound is to neutralize the Light.

Now, the purpose of the Sound is to neutralize the Light. If one opens himself to Spirit without knowing what he's doing, or by accident, this Light could burn one. It could hurt him. I don't say burn in the way that you'd see a campfire burning, but in the sense that It could unbalance one mentally. You might say It could fry his mental apparatus. This ECK Sound neutralizes It. The Light gives the illumination only; It does not give an understanding of what the experience meant to the person who had it. The Sound does. When you have both the Sound and Light within, you come to some understanding of the reality of ECK.

THE PURIFYING OF SOUL

If someone wonders whether ECK is real, there is no one—myself included—who can say, "Yes, ECK is real." Each person has to find it out for himself. No amount of talking is going to let another person realize this truth and find the uplifting and purifying action of Spirit upon Soul.

When this purifying of Soul begins, we may find a couple of things happening in our outer life: Things go a little bit on the fast side, and for a while we really have to step along. Spirit will open up new avenues in our life. And if we go along with them, things will go smoothly. Every so often someone will say to me, "I'm just about ready for an initiation in ECK, and I'm afraid that there are going to be hard times." There don't have to be hard times. Things will straighten out as quickly as we can pick up the new direction that Divine Spirit is giving us.

When this purifying of Soul begins, Spirit will open up new avenues in our life.

It may be in a matter of health.

HEALING AND KARMA

Someone will say, "I want to be a healer," and will try to take upon himself the healing of another person. Generally what happens is that he ends up taking on the karma of that individual without ever knowing how it happened. It's no fault of his own; it's simply Soul learning the laws of Spirit.

If someone is in distress of any kind, there is a safe way to handle it. Besides getting professional help when it's needed, the safest and easiest way is just to mention to the person: "You know, there is a Living ECK Master, and you may want to write to him. All you have to do is write what you want in a letter and mail it. It will be in the hands of Spirit to act upon as It chooses, in Its own time. The Living ECK Master may not even have time to answer you, and he probably won't answer you with a letter, but that has nothing to do with it." Then, of course, it's up to the individual.

When someone wants to be a healer and then takes on another's illness, this karma from the other person was earned. It is often because the individual did not know the laws of Spirit, or perhaps was under the control of one of the five passions of the mind: greed, anger, lust, attachment, and vanity. This is what causes our karma.

The five passions of the mind—greed, anger, lust, attachment, and vanity—this is what causes our karma.

What Is Illusion?

Once when I was employed at a print shop, for a while I was working a double shift. This job got to be a very heavy load. Sometimes I didn't know if I'd be able to get enough sleep to come back the next day and do more work. So one time I drew this little picture of a stick figure of a man working in a field. There was a cloud overhead, it was raining on him, his back was bent, and he was hoeing away. I included this caption with my little drawing: "A man harboring an illusion or working under an illusion." Other people looked at it and said, "Oh, harboring an illusion . . ." and they just kind of wondered what it meant.

In a way, all of life is like this: it is an illusion, but not in the sense that this life is not real. There are some religious teachings that say there is no such thing as sickness or illness. If you've ever had a cold or if you've ever had treatment of an acute nature, you know it's a little difficult to believe that. I'm not saying anything about the people who feel this way, but when I speak of illusion I'm not speaking of this physical plane not being real—I'm saying it's how we perceive it. We are under the hand of illusion, and we do not see it as it really is.

As we do the Spiritual Exercises of ECK, our consciousness is raised bit by bit so we do not go too fast. We keep our balance so that we can function from day to day, so that we can hold our job, support our family, and handle the responsibilities that we have taken upon ourselves.

As we do the Spiritual Exercises of ECK, our consciousness is raised bit by bit so we do not go too fast.

The ECK Masters are generally family men. Paul Twitchell once said about his wife, Gail: "Whenever I get too far out there, there's always my wife." A family helps me to keep my feet on the ground too. When you have spiritual work to do, sometimes you may think, "I'd really like to go off in the hills somewhere." It's like a writer who says, "Someday I'm going to sit down and write that novel, but I'm too busy right now." He says, "I have to go to work in the morning, and when I come home I'm tired and there's just enough energy left to watch a little TV; but someday I'm going to retire or take a month off from work. I'm going to earn my money now, then I'll go off to a cabin in the hills somewhere, and I'm going to write that novel." I feel like that sometimes, too, but it never works.

My dad, who never had any use for lazy men, used to say, "If you ever have any work to do, give it to a lazy man, because he'll get it done." He didn't mean it in the sense that it was really something great—he had nothing but scorn for the lazy man— but that the guy was really using his time right. Whatever had to get done, he'd get done quickly so that he could go and have a little more time in the shade. And sometimes I'd like to do this too—not answer the phone at home or not call the office. But on the other hand, I am grateful and appreciative to work with those of you who are also interested in bringing out the message of ECK.

HOW TO BE A VEHICLE FOR ECK

There are all kinds of predictions in the ECK-Vidya, the ancient science of prophecy, about things that can happen in this universe several hundred thousand years down the line, as the earth runs its natural course toward the destruction of the lower worlds. You and I aren't concerned about it, because that's many thousands of years away; it's not tomorrow.

If anyone wonders, How can I be a vehicle for ECK? you can do the spiritual exercises.

If anyone wonders, How can I be a vehicle for ECK? you can do the spiritual exercises. You can be a silent vehicle. You can go into the grocery store and simply declare yourself a vehicle for ECK. You can say something very simple early in the morning, just one time a day: "I declare myself a vehicle for the Sugmad (which means God), the ECK (Spirit), and the Mahanta (which is the highest state of consciousness)." Then just forget it and go about your day, knowing that everything you do is for the good of the whole, for upliftment, that it's being done in the name of the Mahanta and is a karmaless act. You go ahead, get your lessons that day, and never think twice about it. And you certainly never feel guilt.

One of the most dreadful things I believe that a religion could ever put upon an individual is guilt. It makes one afraid to step out into life. He's afraid to try something new. All he has enough energy for is to come home and sit in front of the TV set, because actually he wonders if there is anything more to living. Through the creative Spiritual Exercises of ECK, we tap into this inner self and we begin to find things to help us grow and ways to do it.

RECOGNIZING SPIRITUAL EXPERIENCES

My first year in Eckankar, I wanted to know if this Eckankar was real. I wanted experiences on the inner planes. I'd had a couple of experiences in the Sound and Light, but it's interesting how fast they fade and how quickly you forget. It's like a ball player who had a good year last year, but this year if he's hitting .201 and his fielding errors get way up there, the coach puts him on the bench. It's the old story of, What have you done for me lately? And in the same way, you forget past spiritual experiences.

So one night I asked Paul Twitchell about this on the inner planes. He was sitting in an easy chair just watching me as I paced the floor in front of him, deep in thought, with my hands crossed behind my back in the classic thinker position. I was walking back and forth for show. I said, "When am I ever going to have experiences on the inner planes, with you or with the Sound and the Light of ECK?" Of course, I didn't realize it was happening. This was in the dream state, and I thought I was wide awake.

He just looked at me for a while, and then he turned his head toward a picture of a lady who had been on the earth plane about 199 years. She had gone the entire route, from childhood to adulthood, and she'd had experiences at every level. Paul looked at me again and pointed to the picture. It was as if he said, "I don't know how to break this to you. You are a young man, but even when you get to be that age, it doesn't look good."

Through the creative Spiritual Exercises of ECK, we begin to find things to help us grow.

I knew it was all over then. "Yeah," I said, "the spiritual path is too hard. I've been on it a year, and I remember a couple of experiences, but they don't happen often enough. It doesn't look as though I'm ever going to make any progress on this path to God." Paul just sat there with his arms folded, watching me. I walked away very upset and immediately woke up in my bed wondering, *When am I ever going to have an inner experience with the Sound and Light?* The experience had come about so naturally that it took me almost half a day to figure it out. The ECK Masters work in subtle ways.

The three attributes that come from the practice of the Spiritual Exercises of ECK are charity, wisdom, and freedom.

The three attributes that come from the practice of the Spiritual Exercises of ECK are charity, wisdom, and freedom. Wisdom is something beyond what we're usually taught in the lower worlds—and here I'm referring to the Physical, Astral, Causal, Mental, and Etheric planes—where we gather only information of the shallowest kind. As soon as you come into the spiritual worlds above the Fifth Plane, you begin to get some of the spiritual knowledge for the first time. And it's different.

After you've been in the spiritual planes for a while, at the Ninth Plane and beyond, then you begin to come into the wisdom of ECK. Much of what is passed off as wisdom in books and elsewhere really isn't wisdom at all. It's a form of information, and it's only information about some man's opinion. There is nothing wrong with this since it may lead some person to the next step where he can look to that inner temple and find the way to step onto this path himself. It can help one to find a path that will enhance his own efforts toward self-recognition of Truth, and finally the God-knowledge or God-Realization.

Overcoming the Fear of Death

Some stories, though not of the cheeriest nature, do help to bring across a point. What ECK can do for one is to give more insight into life and take away the fear of death. There is often a dramatic difference between the viewpoints of one who has experience in the other worlds, such as an ECKist, and someone leaving this plane in translation, or death, who has never heard about Eckankar. The ECKist is filled with confidence because he knows that the Inner Master is going to meet him in the inner planes. Very often those who do not have this confidence in the existence of the spiritual travelers, who are there to help and assist, will have fear. They cling to the body because they are afraid. Even when it's very seriously damaged, sometimes they will not let go.

What ECK can do for one is to give more insight into life and take away the fear of death.

One ECKist told of an experience he had while in contemplation. He was doing the Spiritual Exercises of ECK when a young man came to him and said, "I wish you would tell my brother about Eckankar."

"Does he want to know about Eckankar?" the ECKist asked.

"He won't pay attention to me because I'm only his younger brother."

"Well," said the ECKist, "I'm not able to go tell anyone about ECK unless he first asks."

The young man became very upset. "But you have to tell my brother," he said. "Come with me."

The ECKist wouldn't do it. He turned and walked away from the young man. Then he came out of contemplation.

Several weeks later, in his capacity as a firefighter, the ECKist was working on the rescue squad when a call came in about a motorbike accident down the road. As soon as they got to the scene, he could see that one of the individuals was so badly injured that it was just a matter of time before he would leave the physical body. They very carefully put him in the ambulance, and as they were pulling away, someone yelled, "Hey, there's somebody else here behind the hedge!" He went back there and found that it was the individual he had met during contemplation. This individual had translated already, but it had gone very smoothly for him because he knew about ECK.

The ECKist got another surprise when he returned to the station. In reviewing the report of the accident, he discovered that the other person, the one who had been so seriously injured, was the brother of the individual who had translated. Then he understood: The young man had been so insistent on the inner planes about wanting his brother to know about Eckankar because he knew he was getting ready to leave the physical plane. He knew this in the Soul body, not in the physical consciousness. The one who did not know about ECK struggled and tried to hold on to the physical body for several more days, causing himself a whole lot of pain that simply wasn't necessary, before he finally let go.

The ECKist learns through direct experience on the inner planes that there is no reason for fear.

The ECKist learns through direct experience on the inner planes that there is no reason for fear. In a gentle and easy way, in most cases, you are gradually introduced to the other planes so that you can become acquainted with living there while you are still in the physical body.

Lessons in Charity

The ECK Masters walk among us at all times. A university student wrote to tell me that on his way home from school one evening, a man approached him as he was waiting for the tram. Though the man was dressed like a beggar, his eyes were remarkably clear and glittering. He shook the student's hand, and they started talking. The man told him that his ship, which had been scheduled to leave that evening, had been delayed until the next morning, so he had to stay in town overnight. He said he needed just enough money to tide him over until he could ship out.

All of a sudden the tram pulled up, and the student said, "Excuse me, I gotta go." As he hurried off, the beggar said in a sad tone of voice, "Yes, Eric, go on. Catch your tram."

After the student got on the tram, the words haunted him—they had not been spoken in an ordinary way—and only later did it dawn on him that he had met an ECK Master in disguise, just as Paul Twitchell described in *The Flute of God.*

Only later did it dawn on him that he had met an ECK Master in disguise.

Most of you know the story: Paul was experiencing the hard side of life at the time, back when a quarter meant a little more than it does today. A beggar came up to him and asked for money to buy a cup of coffee. "Times have been hard for me too," Paul said. He reached into his pocket and gave the man one of his two quarters, which was all the money he had at the time, and directed him to a coffee shop around the corner. It wasn't much, but it was half of everything Paul had, and he was willing to give it up. Within a few days, he said, his affairs took a turn for the better.

Frequently I get letters from those who are still looking for a materialistic God. They'll know better soon; when you do the spiritual exercises, your values change. Someone will say, "I'm asking Spirit for help—I've entered the *Reader's Digest* Sweepstakes, and if I win I'm going to take a little money right off the top for ECK." Somebody else recently wrote: "I want to be a yachtsman. I'd like to have a yacht, and I want to travel all around the world."

Many of the letters I receive, however, are to request a spiritual healing, and it's turned over to Spirit. If there is a way to give spiritual help, to assist someone to take a more direct step toward his goal of spiritual unfoldment, I'm more than happy to help, as the Inner Master.

How the Master Gives Love

When Paul first brought the message of ECK out, the path was new to many people and they started out with certain types of astral experiences. Some of those first experiences in the dream state are very vivid and phenomenal; they're often necessary to allow the individual to experience the reality of the inner worlds. The Master does not continue to give a whole string of inner experiences of the same kind, however, because he wants to lift Soul out of the lower worlds of phenomena and take us beyond that.

After two or three years of spiritual experience, one can actually begin to work in direct consciousness in the other worlds.

As we are raised out of this, we have less of the splashy stuff and more of the Sound and the Light of ECK. You may see It as the Blue Light, or you may hear a sound. You may hear the buzzing of bees. Some people hear birds twittering. You might hear It as a chorus, or anything else. This is just the representative Sound of ECK on the different planes, the atoms in motion on a particular plane producing a certain sound. This is Divine Spirit.

After two or three years of spiritual experience, one has been led beyond many of the phenomenal experiences. At some point he can actually begin to work in direct consciousness in the other worlds, having an experience of Sound and Light every so often. Sometimes at this stage one might wonder why he no longer has the same vivid experiences as before. He completely overlooks the fact that he has unfolded beyond them, and he may try to blame this on a new Master.

It goes something like this: The parents have raised three or four children, and then down the line they have another child. The older children say of the younger one, "You're treating him better than you ever treated us when we were that age." And this isn't necessarily true. The first child usually has it a little rough, because somebody has to break ground for the others.

When you're two and three and four years old, you need a lot more hugging. As you get a little older, especially if you're a boy, you say, "Eehhh! Don't do that to me when my buddies are around!" You know how it is—the mother will kiss the boy when she drops him off at school, and he'll look around to make sure that all his buddies saw him wipe it off. But then when the older ones see the kind of warmth that the parent is giving to a child who's several years younger, they'll say, "You're treating him special." It's just that the older child is now getting love in a different way, while the youngest child is getting love in a way that he needs.

So when someone just steps onto the path, the Master gives love in the way that individual needs at that time. Then after a few years, that person is now an older child in a sense, no longer needing the same coddling as the youngster. But not realizing this, he may say, "Something's wrong. This Master isn't as good as the last one." What's the Master supposed to do—put you back in the crib? Could the mother hen squeeze the chick back into the shell? It's not possible. There's absolutely no way we can

When someone just steps onto the path, the Master gives love in the way that individual needs at that time.

go backward, and yet often when we say, "I'm not having the experiences I did before," we're actually asking to be squeezed back into the shell.

INTERPRETING DREAMS

One woman
had a
dream that
demonstrates
how the Inner
Master often
works with us
and how the
ECK comes into
one's life.

One woman, newly on the path of ECK, had a dream that demonstrates how the Inner Master often works with us and how the ECK comes into one's life. It happened through the dream state so that it would come to her gently. Instead of having an experience of the Sound and Light pouring in directly, which might have shocked her consciousness, the Inner Master saw that it was necessary to take it a little bit slow for the sake of her well-being and stability.

The dream was this: She was watching TV on the inner planes when a news flash announced an earthquake. Running outside, she saw that all the big buildings, including a university up the street, had started to crumble and shatter. She noticed that although the university had fallen into a heap, it didn't bother her. A little farther down the street was a skyscraper bank building, and because of the earthquake it started to tilt. It remained standing but ended up leaning against the capitol building. Then she saw a huge block building, peculiarly shaped with rounded edges, shake loose from its foundation and come sliding down a hill right past her.

She asked someone what the dream meant and was given this interpretation: "Well, looks like there are going to be changes in your life and in your finances." And that was OK as far as it went.

What happened was that Spirit had come into her consciousness when she began the Spiritual Exercises of ECK, and she saw this on the inner plane as the earthquake. It shook her foundations. When Spirit comes in, It has to kind of shake us awake.

The earthquake was the ECK coming into her consciousness, and the university represented the mental structure, the mental thought process which is generally very strong in some of us as we step onto the path. It stands in the way of Spirit working freely in our life. This mental process is the one that works by logic and reason. It says, If I go to that party tonight, I know this or that will happen; so I'm not going. Pretty soon we can become withdrawn and inward, and we start missing out on life.

When she saw this university building fall in the earthquake, it meant that the ECK was coming in and working to break down that rigid, unbending Mental body to make it the servant of Soul, instead of trying to make Soul be the servant of mind. She said she hadn't felt badly about it.

Then the bank building shifted over. A lot of times we think our security depends on how much is in our bank account or wallet. When this building started to lean, the security in money wasn't quite as strong and upright as before. It had lost a bit of its character, and the reliance on money wasn't as strong.

But Spirit had come in. There's more reliance on Spirit when you come to know that as you work in your daily life, the ECK will let you take the first step, then It will take the second, and so on.

The big blocks from that building with the rounded edges that slid by her were some of the huge blocks of karma that can pass off in the dream state. This helps to get rid of karma from our past so that we can be free, so that we can be open to let Divine Spirit begin working through us. It brings an upliftment

As you work in your daily life, the ECK will let you take the first step, then It will take the second, and so on.

of consciousness and begins paving our way and making it better.

CLIMBING THE MOUNTAIN TO GOD

I won't say that the path of ECK is going to be a path of roses, because it won't; but there will be times when you'll get to rest. Picture it as climbing a mountain to God: Although there will be times you'll have to climb up the side of the mountain, you may come to a cliff and want to rest for a while, and there might even be some roses there for you to enjoy. But once you have rested, you have a choice: you can go up or you can go down. Why did you climb the mountain? It's the same call of Soul that's within each of us.

And why do we search? Why do we look? We're looking for this Voice of God.

And why do we search? Why do we look? What are we looking for? We're looking for this Voice of God which comes down through all the different worlds. We want to hook up with the Sound Current, to catch It as Soul and ride It back into the heart of God, to the God center.

There is a spiritual exercise I'd like to mention briefly called the Easy Way technique. There are some individuals wanting to step onto the path of ECK who first need to drop the drug habit. They are finding that it's holding them back, it's destroying their life. In a case like this, of course you get professional help and work with the medical people. But inwardly you can work with this Easy Way technique, which can be found in *In My Soul I Am Free*[1] by Brad Steiger.

The path of ECK is merely to enhance your own efforts for spiritual unfoldment. It's to enhance them and to enrich your life to where you become the person in charge of your destiny.

---

1. See footnote on page 26.

We can give help, but I'm not going to push you if you don't want to go. A man would be foolish to push a mule—they kick. And you can't pull it either. If a mule wants to stand there, he's going to stand there; and if the rider is smart, he'll let the mule do just exactly what he wants to do. If the rider is really intent on taking a ride, he'll wait until the mule decides to move and then jump on and go as far as the mule will go, to guide him. This is not to say that we're like mules—we're not. We are learning every moment.

We are learning every moment.

ECK may not be the path for you. You may be perfectly happy as a Christian—a Pentecostal, a Baptist, or a Catholic. Or you may want to step onto the path of ECK, but your family is of another religion and you aren't sure what to do. In either case, I'd say you are better off to stay with your religion until this can be worked out so that you can make a smooth step to the path of ECK sometime later. In other words, stay with what you have now if you're happy.

The path of ECK is for those who are between paths, or for those who are looking for true and actual experience of a kind that is hard to find in any of the orthodox religious teachings that I have ever studied.

But that is not for me to tell you. You have to decide that for yourself.

Denver Regional Seminar, Denver, Colorado, May 8, 1982

"Oh, do you belong to that ECK club too?"

9

THE
LIBERATION OF SOUL

The path of ECK is an individual matter. If someone would ask, What's it all about? the best I could say is that it's a path to God. It's your own path to God. Really, what more can be said about it?

The path of ECK is an individual matter. It's your own path to God.

Some of our initiates were in Denver for a regional seminar a couple of weeks ago and took part in a radio interview. The questions the interviewer asked about Eckankar were quite interesting.

"What are some of the things that you do and know that other people don't?" he asked. "For instance, what about death?"

One of the Higher Initiates said, "Well, we have the knowledge and the ability to survive death; and there are even times we have the experience where we leave the physical state of consciousness and go beyond into the higher worlds."

The man quite rightfully asked, "How do you know it was like death?"

The ECKist replied, "Because this is a parallel occurrence."

The interviewer said, "But have you ever died?"

And, of course, the initiates got quiet because it's

a difficult thing to answer. They stumbled through, but the best thing to do if someone comes up with a question like that is to give them a book, because this path is a personal experience.

Those of you who have had awareness in a state of consciousness beyond the physical plane know. You know the difference between a dream and being in a higher state of consciousness. The man asked a number of questions, as though it seemed difficult to believe that there might be some key which would give purpose to our existence.

A KEY TO LIFE

I noticed that cliff behind us. Looking at it, you wonder what ravages the earth went through to form this very pretty area. In a real sense, most of you were here as Soul in another form, at another time, to witness the ravages that occurred. You lived through the experiences that went with those days, and this is a memory which lies within. You might say, well, why would I care? And that's a good question. Maybe there is no reason, except to point out that the human consciousness is limited to this physical body, but Soul transcends one life or the memory of another life farther back.

At one time I wondered why I bothered to get up in the morning. Why did I bother to go to work, because after all, someday I would leave this earth— so what was the purpose? In the same way as many of you did, I looked. I asked questions, but never really found many answers before Eckankar; and many of you have found that too. The path you're on, whatever it is, is a bridge; and if you are in a religion and find that it suits you—that you are happy, that you have purpose for getting up in the morning—

The human consciousness is limited to this physical body, but Soul transcends one life or the memory of another life farther back.

by all means, stay with it. You've got more than a lot of people do.

One of the computer programmers at the Eckankar International Office recently told me of a man she had met in a delicatessen. He looked at her T-shirt, which had something on it about Eckankar, and said, "Oh, do you belong to that ECK club too?" She just said, "Yes, I belong to that ECK club." That's how it sounded to him, so she went along with it. "What's it all about?" he asked. And she simply said, "It's learning how to live my life better."

"Yeah, I can understand that," he said. "About a week or two ago I was talking with another fellow who belongs to your ECK club, and I didn't understand one word he said." It's not easy to talk about.

The saints and others who have had experiences of God found it difficult to relate them to their fellowman. The experience of God comes as Sound and Light, which are manifestations of the atoms moving at a certain rate. When we have this experience, there is no way to tell someone else, "I am changed in consciousness." And many times it's difficult to carry on in your everyday life, because now you have gained an insight into human nature and beyond. It's as if you can see through the motives and purposes of the people around you. You can read them like a book. I used to do this at school, before I came onto the path of ECK.

In college I had a friend who liked to spin a good tale, hoping I'd buy it. As he talked, I'd sit there and just look at him. It was as if I could see completely through him and knew he was trying to put one over on me, generally with a story about why he needed to borrow some money. When he'd finish his tale I'd say, "Well, I don't have the money to lend you today," because maybe he didn't pay

When we have this experience, there is no way to tell someone else, "I am changed in consciousness."

me back last time. I have a long memory for things like that!

This reminds me of Arnold, an old farmer back home who had a reputation for being very tight with money. As a young man during the Depression, when a lot of the farm youth left home to earn a little money in the big city, Arnold went off to Milwaukee to find work. He was walking downtown one day, when a pickpocket came along—times had been hard for him too, I imagine—and reached into the farmer's back pocket. He didn't quite get a good enough hold on the wallet, and Arnold felt him back there. He spun around, grabbed the pickpocket's hand, and gave him a crushing handshake. The man must have been quite impressed, because he just returned the handshake and left. Quickly.

When people tried to use a tall tale to get some money from me, I'd look right through them. One time a friend said, "You know, Harold, I don't know how to tell you this, but there are times you have an absolutely unnerving ability to look right through people, and it makes them nervous." So I had to stop doing that because, in a way, I was getting in their space. I still did it, though, when someone wanted to borrow money and I needed to check out their story.

Sometimes I wonder what can be said about the message of ECK that can give you a key and take you one step further. The whole key, of course, is the Spiritual Exercises of ECK, and these are found in the ECK books.

The whole key is the Spiritual Exercises of ECK, and these are found in the ECK books.

How to Figure It Out

Generally, before we come to the path of ECK, we are interested in theory. We have a whole lot of ideas about what life is about even without having had any experience. With theory come the questions, and we look to philosophers, psychologists, psychiatrists, and anybody else who has hung out a shingle and claims to have any answers. What's it all about? we ask, and everybody will give us a little answer here and there.

The mistake is when we override our own judgment and listen to someone else who gives us information or advice which is not for our own good. How do you figure this out? All you have to do is stick around a little while and see how good that person's advice has been for you. This holds true whether it's someone claiming to know exactly what you need for your health, or exactly what you need as far as understanding your dreams. The best thing is to learn how to do these things for ourselves.

Health is an individual matter. Those of you who have been in Eckankar for any length of time find that the ECK, or Divine Spirit, begins bringing different diets to your attention in a very gentle way. You learn how to improve the health of your body, because a healthy body aids one as he reaches for God-Realization. Someone may tell you that a certain diet worked for him, and he figures it's got to work for you too. It may, or it may not. I've listened to others and tried a lot of diets, and I know many of you have, too. In most cases I've found that somebody else's just doesn't work for me.

It's the same with dreams. When something in your dream comes through in a symbolic meaning and you don't understand it, it's easy to go and ask someone else for an opinion and get their idea of what that dream meant. That's OK, but it is you who has to be the final judge and jury of your own inner life. *You* have to decide: What does that dream mean to me? How does it tie in to a lesson that I need to know about right now? Many times the dream

You learn how to improve the health of your body, because a healthy body aids one as he reaches for God-Realization.

symbols are so garbled that they don't make any sense at all. The mind gives you symbols simply because you're not able to handle the truth directly.

I get letters from individuals who say they don't remember anything about their inner experiences at all: "I don't remember dreams," or "I don't remember any of the experiences during the contemplative exercises." Many times it's a guard and a protection to prevent the emotional body from getting an overload as Spirit tries to come through to give you clear insight on your diet, where you stand spiritually, or some of the laws that you may have inadvertently broken. Maybe you suspect this already, but you aren't quite ready to have it come through clearly. In many cases, we're still carrying the old factor of guilt that has been instilled from some of our previous training.

SHEDDING GUILT

If there is a way to stifle spiritual unfoldment, it's to carry the burden of guilt.

If there is a way to stifle spiritual unfoldment, it's to carry the burden of guilt. Guilt has been put forward by many teachings, even those before our present time, simply as a means of controlling the people. In the old days, when God spoke to men directly, there was no need for an intermediary, a middleman, the guy who takes all the profit. But as time went on, we lost the ability to go within ourselves and get our own answers. That didn't make any difference until trouble cropped up in our life: We lost a loved one, a tornado or a hailstorm came through and ripped up the crops, or something of this nature.

In the face of disaster man feels helpless. He doesn't know where to turn. And it was very easy, during vulnerable times, for someone who may have correctly predicted an eclipse of the moon to come forward and say, "I know why this happened. I know why you're having these hard times. You have angered the gods, and there is only one way to make things right. Fortunately for you, I know how to do it." In the old days, it usually involved an animal sacrifice of some kind which, of course, would be given to the priest. This was a matter of control.

In Eckankar we look for self-responsibility. If we do an action, we know definitely that someday we're going to have to pay for it, that it will come due. And this holds true whether it's positive karma or the negative kind.

In Eckankar we look for self-responsibility. If we do an action, we know someday we're going to pay for it.

CAUSE AND EFFECT

I wanted to explain the Law of Karma, the Law of Cause and Effect, to my daughter. In the New Testament Paul referred to it when he said, "Whatsoever a man soweth, that shall he also reap." My daughter had just turned four, and sometimes the best way to teach children is to tell them stories, the old standby stories that have been passed down for centuries. One of them was the story of the Little Red Hen.

Here's the story: Once upon a time there was a hen, a cat, and a dog who lived together in a house. One day the Little Red Hen found some grain and said, "Well, if we plant the grain, we can bake us a cake." The others looked at it and said, "Yeah, that sounds like a good idea." So she said, "Who's going to plant the grain?" And the cat and the dog, of course, said, "Not I. Not I." Being a good little hen, she put the wheat in the ground, and after a while it started to come up. "All right," she said, "Who's going to water the wheat? If we're going to have the cake, we have to water the wheat." And the cat and the dog said, "Not I. Not I," because it meant work.

The wheat grew higher and higher and eventually the day came for harvest. The Little Red Hen said, "All right, who's going to harvest it? If we're going to have the cake, somebody's going to have to harvest the wheat." And the cat said, "Not I," and the dog said, "Not I," because they were having a good time in the living room, resting and lounging on the sofa. They weren't about to go out in the heat of the day and thresh this wheat. So she threshed it and put it in a little bag. Then she said, "All right, now somebody's going to have to carry this into town to have it ground. Who's going to do it?" You know the answer. The cat and the dog were too comfortable to move.

So the hen got the wheat ground into flour and then came home and said, "Who's going to bake the cake?" And they said, "Not I. Not I." She said, "All right. I'll bake the cake," and the good Little Red Hen baked the cake.

Then came the moment of truth.

Then came the moment of truth. She had baked the cake, put on the frosting, and set it on the table. Of course, the cat and the dog were right there. They pulled up their chairs and sat there licking their chops, and the hen said, "All right, now who's going to eat the cake?" The dog said, "I'll eat the cake," and the cat said, "I'll eat the cake."

While I was telling the story, my little daughter just sat there and listened to everything. I had planned to use this story as an illustration to show her how the people who do the work get to eat the cake. So at this point I said, "The Little Red Hen made the cake, then at the end she asked the others, 'Who's going to eat the cake?' Now, can you tell me who gets to eat the cake?"

My daughter said, "The cat and the dog." I said, "The cat and the dog? But the Little Red Hen did all the work. Why would the cat and dog get to eat the cake?" And she said, "Because they asked first."

I hate to say it, but too often our attitude toward God is similar. We're willing to do whatever we want in life, but when it comes to the eleventh hour and times get hard, we say, "Please God, remove this from me." It's a nice dream, but we have to face our own life.

I get letters about some of the karmic conditions that are working off for the individuals who step onto the path; there is a heavy load, and they wonder what's the purpose. They want help, and I can give them help in some ways. When I say "I" can give them help, I don't mean myself but as a vehicle for Spirit. I turn it over to Spirit, and whatever It does, It does; I have no say in the matter. Sometimes, though, there is a little help that can be given: some people have a burden lifted—you might call it a quick healing— others are led to a doctor, others to a dentist.

I turn it over to Spirit, and whatever It does, It does; I have no say in the matter.

In the days before I knew about the damage that sugar could cause to the body, I ate quite a lot of it. Even if I suspected it, I did it anyway, because you can eat sugar all year long but you go to the dentist only once a year—so it's easy to forget.

When my teeth started aching, I went to the dentist and he said, "Well, looks like we're going to have to pull some of those." Anyone who has been in a dentist's chair knows it's not a lot of fun. I had been in Eckankar for just a little while then, and I said, "I'd sure like to get out of this one." So I looked to the Inner Master during the spiritual exercises one night and asked if I could have a spiritual healing so that I wouldn't have to go through this tooth extraction. I was really hoping that the infection at the root of the teeth would be cured miraculously.

Insight on Healing

A couple of nights later, while in full conscious-ness in one of the other worlds, I found myself sitting in a dentist's chair. The dentist and an assistant were using a rather crude set of tools—it wasn't the finest place to be. I just sat there and thought, *Uh-oh, here we go.* The dentist went at it and started digging around, pulling and tugging and just having a grand old time. As far as I was concerned, there had to be a neater way to go about it; they were a little messy.

By the time I woke up, I had been through the whole experience. I must have worked it out on the inner planes, I thought, because I'd heard stories of people having car accidents, for instance, on an inner plane so they wouldn't have to go through it out here. I thought this was such a case. But my teeth still ached. When the appointment time came and I went to the dentist, I had to sit through the whole thing again, from start to finish.

I had asked for a spiritual healing and, though I'd hoped it would come in the dream state, what I actually got was a long-term healing. If the infection had been taken away and I had gone back to eating sugar the same as before, I would have been back in the dentist's chair a year later, and he would have probably been there with his little pliers, pulling and having an even better time than before.

Sometimes the spiritual healing is a deeper healing.

Sometimes the spiritual healing is a deeper heal-ing. If I remember the pain caused by the sugar, I ought to be cured for a lifetime. I know any of you who've had the same experience begin to think very carefully about how much sugar your body can handle. We all have different capacities. Some people can handle it very well, others not so well.

Paul Twitchell said that when he took over the responsibility as the Living ECK Master, some of the load that he helped lift from you and me affected his health. Sometimes it is a little bit hard to keep the physical body operating well. Some of the things that an individual goes through in this position—and I speak with a little bit of experience now—are unbelievable. And anyone who takes on the position knows this before they accept it. You know what lies ahead. Those of you who have passed the Second Initiation know that at this point you will no longer have to return to the physical world.

For myself, I was very grateful to be given the opportunity to go to the temple within myself to find the Sound and Light of Spirit, which is the actual Voice of God. This Sound can be heard in different ways during the spiritual contemplation: as running water, the buzzing of bees, the flute. When you hear this sound, it is Divine Spirit working directly in your life, uplifting your state of consciousness, pulling you out of the state of human consciousness which, without the insight of the higher worlds, is a life of misery, not knowing the purpose, not knowing why we're here.

Living in Spirit, we have happiness come into our life; and it also brings a life of action.

As the spiritual man, living in Spirit, we have happiness come into our life; and it also brings a life of action.

Beavers Bend Campout, Broken Bow, Oklahoma, Friday, May 21, 1982

The door was closed when he walked into the kitchen, but he saw it open and heard a voice say, "The door is open whenever you are ready. May the blessings be."

10

THE DIVINE KNOWLEDGE

*I*n the sixteenth century, Martin Luther, the Protestant reformer, was taught that the way to become holy was to step back from life. His superiors said, "To keep a pure heart, you must keep apart," and they supported this precept by quoting one of the saints of the church at that time who asked, "How can the angels visit if I defile myself and consort with men?" This idea was introduced to Europe—medieval Germany— from India around the first or second century AD, and it is an idea that we in Eckankar, of course, do not subscribe to.

WHAT TRUE DETACHMENT MEANS

We are in this world but not of this world. We are detached from this world, but this does not mean that we say good-bye to our emotions and our mind or anything else. We have the Spiritual Exercises of ECK, and these are exercises for the spiritual body.

The Mental body needs exercise too, so if we want a job promotion or if the mind needs something for self-satisfaction or growth, it's all right to take

We are in this world but not of this world.

a course at a college. Or it can be anything that you enjoy, such as literature or even some of the crafts. The emotional body also needs exercise. Sometimes if the ECK love is flowing through so strongly that you want a good cry, it's OK. Go off and have yourself a good cry, because it exercises the emotional body; and there's nothing wrong with this.

The physical body needs exercise too. I don't really like to do it because before I got this job, I had plenty. To get to work every morning, I'd have to run quite a few blocks to catch the bus. I'd usually get up in just enough time to run like crazy down the street, because if I missed the bus, then I'd have to catch the train, which was more expensive. The bus would drop me off several blocks from the Eckankar office, and I would have to run a bit more. A lot of exercise.

In my earlier days on the path of ECK, for a while everything was Eckankar. I gave up all my other interests, but it's not necessary. We don't have to be the way the medieval monks were told to be, or go live in the sanctuary of the monastery. We can live life; we can go out in the mainstream of life and enjoy the fellowship of other ECKists and people who are not in Eckankar.

We don't have to go live in the sanctuary of the monastery. We can go out in the mainstream of life and enjoy the fellowship of other people.

BEING INVOLVED IN LIFE

Maybe you want to get involved in some cause. A lady told me today that it really upset her, from a personal point of view, that in the future her child was possibly going to be exposed to prayer in school. She didn't have any use for it, and she said, "What should I do?" I said, "Well, what do you want to do? Make up your own mind. If you feel this threatens the individuality of your child, you as a parent have a right to say whatever you want to say. Go ahead, let your voice be heard. Let the school board know who you are. Sometimes letters to the editor are effective. Do what you think is best."

CONTACT WITH DIVINE SPIRIT

Some of us have experiences on the path of ECK, and sometimes I put letters describing these in the *Mystic World* and incorporate them into my writings. I do this to let those of you who haven't yet had the experiences know that there are others who do see the Blue Light, who do have some experience with Divine Spirit, which can be heard as Sound and seen as Light.

Others write to say, "I'm not having any experiences, and I'd like to have them." But if they come too strongly before you're ready, you might not know what you're asking for. It's better to turn the pacing of your experiences over to the Inner Master and just let them come at their natural pace, whenever you're ready. Let the Inner Master decide.

It's better to turn the pacing of your experiences over to the Inner Master and just let them come at their natural pace.

This afternoon someone told me about a time when he'd had strong reservations, to put it mildly, about Eckankar. When his wife became a member, he felt it was his mission to save her. So he spent a lot of time at it. But once he made up his mind and got going in ECK, he had quite a reaction to Spirit coming into his life. He'd look at the situation and say: Here are the teachings, here are the writings in *The Shariyat-Ki-Sugmad* and in the ECK discourses—why am I having such a reaction? But he did.

There were times he'd get into a dispute with the Arahata, the teacher of the ECK class, and he'd just jump up and leave. He said one time he went home, secluded himself in the closet, and just stared at the wall for a long time. He knew he was in a crisis, and he didn't know how to get through it.

Gradually it came to him that his reaction was just a balancing out of his initial resistance to Spirit; and eventually things changed. He's a Higher Initiate now.

It's not always easy to step onto the path of ECK. There had been times in this life when I wished that all I had to do was work hard Monday through Friday, get drunk Friday and Saturday nights, sleep it off in church on Sunday morning, and rest up a little bit Sunday afternoon so I could start all over again on Monday. And it's kind of a comforting existence in a way, but it's a thoughtless, mindless existence to those of you who have some experience in the works of ECK.

THE PATH OF DIRECT EXPERIENCE

You realize you can no longer form your spiritual path based on what someone else tells you.

You realize you can no longer form your spiritual path based on what someone else tells you. It must now be direct experience. Sometimes the experience comes directly through the contemplative exercises, where you actually see the Blue Light or hear the Sound. You might get it in the dream state, or you may see the ECK working in your everyday life. Frankly, I would recommend seeing the ECK work in your everyday life, because when times get hard, it's amazing how fast those inner experiences fade away, as though you never had them.

For myself, I found the monthly initiate reports to be exceedingly helpful to recall the inner experiences that I'd had during the month. This holds true whether a person mails them or not. If you have a good linkup with the Inner Master, it's not necessary to mail the monthly initiate reports; but you may find it helpful to write them for your own use so that you can look back and see what has happened, if anything, whether on the inner or the outer.

I have a letter from a lady about her husband's difficulty in accepting the fact that she was an ECK student. She wrote, "My husband has been looking into Eckankar for about a year and a half, and he has been having some mental struggles with some of the writings. Just before the Eckankar International Youth Conference in Chicago, we were socializing with an ECKist couple, and after a discussion about spiritual awareness we came home." Then her husband encountered one of the ECK Masters.

The husband said the door was closed when he walked into the kitchen, but he saw it open and heard a voice say, "The door is open whenever you are ready. May the blessings be."

She went on to say: "A few nights later we were lying in bed talking, and he saw a blue star floating above us and a dark shape eclipsing the blue star the way a cloud covers the moon. He told me later what had happened. The voice said, 'You are the dark cloud blocking the Light. You have really tied yourself to the earth this time.'" You have to understand, he was already having a hard time accepting the writings and works of ECK.

She continues, "The voice was loving and warm, almost on the verge of laughing; and my husband said inwardly, 'I know.' The voice said, 'Let's see about untangling this, shall we?' And he said, in that moment, he accepted the Master and he felt the Blue Light enter into his Third Eye, the Tisra Til. At this moment, I saw blue lights illuminate his face like a halo. I told him what I saw, not knowing what was going on with him at that point. He then told me that

He heard a voice say, "The door is open whenever you are ready. May the blessings be."

the Master had said, 'I am always with you. May the blessings be.' "

Frankly, I wish I'd get stacks of letters like this, and I know you wish you were sending stacks of them. But the fact is that you may see one of these aspects of Spirit only occasionally. It may come once a week; some of you have it more often. You may hear the Sound, and It goes with you. Others of you don't, but you wake up with the knowingness. You wake up in the morning, and you know that something has happened. You're not exactly sure what, but there's a feeling of spaciousness and goodwill that goes with you.

When we are walking in Spirit, we have awareness and happiness. We have a life of action. This is the way of ECK.

A LIFE OF ACTION

When we are walking in Spirit, we have awareness and happiness. We have a life of action. This is the way of ECK.

Someone mentioned to me that he was staying in an A-frame cabin. He was a little bit apologetic about it, saying he didn't have much money. But I knew—and he really knew, too—there was no reason to be apologetic about the money you have or don't have. If you're on the path of ECK, somewhere along the line you've scrambled, wondering, Where am I going to get the money to make it until tomorrow? And it comes. There's no reason to be apologetic about it, because the Inner Master, whether before you stepped on the path of ECK or after, has put you through the paces to toughen you and bring you a little bit further, step-by-step, to the point where you could handle it.

At each point, when you were given a test, you had a choice: Do I wish to go on, or do I want to step off?

We were talking quite a bit this afternoon with

some of the Higher Initiates. One lady said, "When I went to the first ECK lecture, I really couldn't understand what was being said. There were so many new terms. I couldn't help wondering what I was doing there." She got up to leave, and at the door were some Higher Initiates. She looked at their faces, and she could see a sense of serenity and peace. She talked with them for a while and as she left, she just knew within herself that she had found the answer, not in the words that were spoken but in the presence of the two people who had spoken with her.

The mind likes to question. This is one of its functions. It likes to put everything into a nice, neat mental framework where it can form questions: What is Soul? What is life? The physical body's only interest is in trying to find happiness through the senses or through pleasure, and this is what has tied Soul to the lower worlds for all these centuries.

I receive many letters from people requesting an ECK-Vidya reading. We're not interested in the past. It's an empty dream; it's gone. Whether we like it or not, the highest expression that we have achieved as Soul sits here tonight. And sometimes I would look at myself and say, "Is this the best I've been throughout all those centuries?" But maybe we take a beating in our physical lives and by the time Soul gets to the end of the road, It's ready to leave.

Whether we like it or not, the highest expression that we have achieved as Soul sits here tonight.

We don't look to the future very much, either, for another reason. We make our plans, but yet, as it says in the Bible, "Take therefore no thought for the morrow," spiritually. We do have to plan for the rent and car payments and insurance, because even though we are in this world and not of it, we have responsibilities.

FACING RESPONSIBILITIES

Stepping back from society and going off somewhere might appeal to us at times, and it hits strongest when we've grown up, gone through struggles, tried to attain the goals of our youth, and perhaps realized we are not going to reach them. Not too many of us can face failure well, so we sometimes decide to change our direction to a spiritual goal of some sort.

We sometimes decide to change our direction to a spiritual goal of some sort.

Every so often a lady from another country writes to me about her husband, a doctor, who had decided to give up everything, leave the family, leave the children, and serve God. He was going off to a retreat somewhere, and she was heartbroken. But there isn't much I can say when it involves the personal matters of a family. It has to be turned over to Spirit. In many cases I won't even answer a letter like that, simply because it would be interfering between the husband and wife, and I won't do that.

The husband felt this was the only way he could serve God—at least this was the excuse he gave himself for his failure. He had not been able to hold a successful medical practice. Each time he tried something, he would defeat himself every few years by one of his decisions. He got to the point where he saw he wasn't going to be a success in the physical life, so he said, OK, I'm going to serve God. And this was his solution. Of course, he took no responsibility for his wife or children and felt everything was taken care of. And this is wrong.

There were times, as I was going along this path, when I thought I'd be better off to stay single. First I wanted to get married, but the ECK just never brought anyone along. Then I met my future wife, but by that time I'd gotten pretty obstinate and wasn't sure I wanted to get married anymore. Finally I said, "OK, if this is the next step, I'll get married." Then when the decision was made to have a child, I thought for a while that this would stop me from the path.

If someone asks, "Do you recommend marriage?" or "Do you recommend having children?" I generally say, "No, I wouldn't recommend that anyone get married, and I certainly wouldn't recommend planning to have children, because if you have to ask, you aren't ready." And then if you go ahead and decide on your own responsibility to start a family, sometimes you barely have enough steam to pull it off. Yet the opportunity for growth is there, where we learn how to give.

Sometimes when people write or talk with me, they'll say, "I'm having problems in my life. I simply am not able to meet my financial obligations. I'm having health problems; I'm having this and that. I'm in ECK, and I thought the path would become easier somewhere along the line." Well, some of it is karma working off from before, though some of it works off in the dream state. Yet much of this is unnecessary.

The opportunity for growth is there, where we learn how to give.

INFLOW AND OUTFLOW

When we first come onto the path of ECK and we begin the spiritual exercises, it's like turning on a water faucet. The ECK starts flowing through, and It just flows through like an impartial energy field, like magnetism or electricity. It just comes through, and It has Its own laws. We're like a big bottle. After about one year It has filled us up about halfway; after about two years, It's up to the top.

When I did my first two years, as I imagine most of you did despite everything that was said about spiritual gluttony, I was taking as many discourses as I was allowed, reading outside books, stuffing myself. At the same time I held membership in two other organizations that had their own sets of initiations. It was a mess. I had a really tough time.

Back in 1967 when I got onto the path, the Shariyat-Ki-Sugmad had not been translated. Paul Twitchell had not yet brought it out. So I didn't realize what I was doing. I ignorantly kept stuffing myself. And everything went wrong. I didn't have any money to speak of, I was working really hard and getting nowhere, and I thought I was trapped for the rest of my stay on earth. Then gradually it began to fall away as I started to give—to give in little ways.

This began the outflow for the first time.

This began the outflow for the first time. Many will let the ECK flow in and flow in and flow in, and all of a sudden It goes over the top and It actually begins to burn a person. When I see this happen, generally I'll recommend that the individual get physical exercise, or in some cases get counseling. This may come as a surprise, but sometimes that's the best and most direct way.

If we get a spiritual healing for emotional problems or for physical or mental conditions or anything else, often the cure is too easy. We haven't taken the first step toward mastership. This can all be done for us, but we haven't learned anything, especially how to stand on our own two feet.

NO WORSHIP IN ECK

I was in the library the other day reading a book on quaint customs, and one of them was kissing the pope's toe. This struck me as funny, though I don't mean it as a lack of respect. This custom has a history behind it: It was said to have started with the

Assyrians several hundred years BC, and then it was passed over to the ancient Egyptians, whose foot-kissing ceremony was for the slave to the ruler. From the Egyptians it was passed to the ancient Greeks, then it came to the Romans. Some time after that, about AD 329, was the first recorded instance of an individual kissing the toe of the pope.

First the ritual involved actually kissing the toe, then later they refined it by putting a covering of some sort on the toe. I found this highly interesting. Even today, in Istanbul and other places, it is said that the ruler gets his toe kissed, a privilege reserved for only the highest-ranked people in government; those who are of lesser rank only get to kiss the coat. Those who have no rank at all are allowed only to bow low from a distance.

If there is one thing that the ECK Masters are working for us to realize and understand, it is that there is no worship in Eckankar—not of the Higher Initiates, of the Living ECK Master, or even of the Sugmad. We're wasting our time if we do this. Individuals who come from countries in the East where this is part of their customs will occasionally come up to me at an ECK seminar and kiss my coat. It's done with love, it's a sign of spiritual respect, and I'm not making fun of it in that regard, but still I'm very uncomfortable about it. After all, how would you feel if you were in the grocery store and someone came up and kissed your coat?

We each have a line within ourselves. A person who is of a high ethical character, his ethics being a reflection of his high spiritual unfoldment, will never cross that line. In other words, we never resort to that level of sarcasm which crosses this line and can cut a person to the bone. I used to be very good at it; I had a really sharp tongue when I was in my

There is no worship in Eckankar—not of the Higher Initiates, of the Living ECK Master, or even of the Sugmad.

early years. It's a sign of anger, and I had as much as anyone. If someone crossed me, I would know how to use words to whittle him down to size. And he wouldn't forget it. I took great pride in it which, of course, was ego and vanity. I worked with the whole line of these passions of the mind. I used them all, enjoyed them, gloried in them. But there comes a time when we have to give them up.

THE KEY TO LIBERATION

The liberation of Soul comes in meeting the Living ECK Master, who then leads us to the spiritual exercises which lead to the Sound and Light.

The liberation of Soul comes in meeting the Living ECK Master, who then leads us to the spiritual exercises which lead to the Sound and Light. And then comes the liberation. This liberation is being freed from the endless cycle of birth and rebirth, from the pain and the sorrow and the unhappiness which come from being under the hand of fate, or destiny.

When we step on this path, we have the privilege of having direct experience of the greater awareness which is unknown to any orthodox religion. I won't prove it to you; and you, as members of Eckankar, are not expected to prove it to anyone else. Make the message available through the books; let the person come to his own understanding.

There is a spiritual exercise given by Paul Twitchell in *In My Soul I Am Free*[1] called the Easy Way technique. There is also a series given in *ECKANKAR—The Key to Secret Worlds*. For those of you who are new to ECK and would like to look further, I would suggest you read the books and take your time. And when you feel uncomfortable inside, I'd say to put aside the books, let it be, and do some-

―――――

1. See footnote on page 26.

thing else. When you're strong enough and you feel comfortable again to take another step, then take a little bit more. But don't push and don't hurry.

Don't rush. We've been at this a long time, and in this lifetime we have the opportunity to finally gain this liberty of Soul.

*Beavers Bend Campout, Broken Bow, Oklahoma,
Saturday, May 22, 1982*

They did not know that what had made Greece and its civilization great was the presence of the ECK Masters. Some of them worked on the beautiful temples, such as the Parthenon.

11
THE ENIGMA OF ECK

*T*he EK symbol is one that has appeared many places in centuries past, from Greece to the Himalayas. Perhaps in the years to come more will be revealed about its role. The EK symbol is merely a symbol of Spirit, the Voice of God. There is no special connotation connected to it; it's not worshipped or revered except in the sense that it points to that source—the Light and Sound of God—which we all carry within us.

And if you wonder about the importance of the ECK or this Divine Spirit in our life—you may want to call It the Ocean of Love and Mercy—it is simply that we learn the way back home to God again.

The function of the Living ECK Master is to link one up with this Holy Spirit, or Divine Spirit. When this happens, our lives are not miraculously made easy where we become millionaires or have no health problems. This doesn't happen. Our life continues as before, but with one difference: We are being opened to the source of life itself, which brings a solution at the temple within ourselves for everything that comes up in our lives.

Many times this ECK, this Spirit, will nudge us gently, as It nudged us before we came onto this path, but then we didn't listen. We couldn't hear. When the linkup is made with Spirit, the

The function of the Living ECK Master is to link one up with Divine Spirit.

inner hearing is opened. It's like putting on a spiritual hearing aid, except it's more natural. We can see the Light clearly in our inner vision, and this guides us through the pitfalls of life so that we can make our way more direct.

A Nudge from Spirit

This evening I got a little nudge from Spirit, and it happened in a funny way. You know how it is: just when you get in the shower, the phone rings. You wonder if you can get to the phone before the person hangs up, and whether it's worth the trouble to get the whole floor wet. Finally you either go or you don't, but no matter what you do, you don't feel right about it.

The ECK works very subtly in our lives, in little ways.

What happened to me tonight was just a little thing, but the ECK works very subtly in our lives, in little ways. If I had gotten this same nudge fifteen years ago, I would have reacted differently.

This is what happened: I have a walkie-talkie in my room. I use it to keep in communication with the ECK staff; if someone wants to get in touch, all they have to do is call me. I didn't get one call on that walkie-talkie all day. But I took it into the bathroom, finished shaving, and when I was ready to get in the shower I made sure the little switch was turned on.

It's interesting that as you go further in your spiritual unfoldment, you find that you have to be cleaner than you were before. You find that order comes into your life, that you want to be clean, and you want to know where to find something. This happens a little bit at a time, more and more. So when you see individuals who claim to be holy men and you visit their temple and find it's filthy, you might suspect that their claims are not true. But if you're still not convinced, you may follow them for a while and find out—if you can stand the smell and the dirt.

As I got ready to go into the shower, I turned up the volume on the walkie-talkie. Of course the noise from the shower drowned it out; I couldn't hear what was going on. Then, for some reason, the water stopped. It didn't just trickle to a stop—you know how it does sometimes when it's teasing you. It just stopped. Fifteen years ago, or before I got into ECK, I would have probably pounded on the faucet, pounded on the wall, and made tracks to the phone to get the hotel manager. But just then, when the shower stopped, I could hear somebody calling me on the walkie-talkie, wanting to ask something of great importance.

So I was able to get out of the shower easily and walk over to the walkie-talkie and take the call. Then I got back into the shower and turned it on, and it worked just fine.

It's one of the little ways that the ECK will come in and begin working with us. If I were to tell you a secret about this path, it would be that the ECK is working and doing this every moment in your life. This may come as a surprise. You were expecting that when you got past a certain initiation in ECK, after a year or two, that a bright light would flash, a great big secret would be revealed, and you'd be knocked flat on your back.

We were joking about that in Denver recently. A couple of years ago we had a meeting there, and one of the Higher Initiates drove in from Wyoming. He had to stop along the way to make a phone call. He tried at several places and just couldn't get through. Finally he got to this little grocery store just as a thunderstorm came up. There was a particularly vicious series of thunderstorms going on at that particular time, just as we were all trying to

If I were to tell you a secret about this path, it would be that the ECK is working and doing this every moment in your life.

get to Denver. This was just the ECK force, the pure positive force, coming into conflict with the negative. Not that we ourselves did anything, but the ECK was flowing through us as vehicles. It's very much like the weatherman says: When a cold front comes into an area, you end up with thunderstorms and tornadoes.

So the Higher Initiate got out of his car and went into the grocery store, but the clerk refused to let him use the phone inside the store. So the ECKist had to use the one in the phone booth outside. He picked up the phone just about the time the lightning struck—and it knocked him flat. I believe he said that the lightning came off the tip of his nose. But he picked himself up, shook his head, got himself together, and made it to the meeting. It was quite an experience, but he got through it. These things do occur.

THE ECK MASTERS' ROLE IN HISTORY

As the ECK culture comes out, we can look back through history and see the renaissances which have occurred. During the Middle Ages, the fourteenth, fifteenth, and sixteenth centuries, there was a revival of sorts, a renaissance coming out of the Dark Ages, where the humanists of the era were looking back to classical Greece. They looked to the beauty, the aesthetics, and the ethics of that great culture, and they wanted to duplicate it.

What made Greece and its civilization great was the presence of the ECK Masters.

But they did not know that what had made Greece and its civilization great was the presence of the ECK Masters. Some of them worked on the beautiful temples, such as the Parthenon. It was an expression of truth that the individuals at that time were looking for in their everyday life. As they reached for this, they put forth the greatest they were capable of, whether it was in music, art, or writing. This is how their search for truth came out—as an expression.

Whenever the spiritual forces stir and the ECK Masters step forth to light the spiritual fire which has grown dim, you can see changes of one sort or another in the society of the times. This certainly happened during the Renaissance. There was Michelangelo and many of the other great painters; there were the musicians. They were looking back to the classical Greeks and wondering what made these people produce such great works of art. At the same time, during the Middle Ages, when the church of the time had failed the people, Martin Luther became one of the leaders of the Reformation, and new thought was brought in.

The ECK Masters worked quietly in the background with many individuals in history; we realize much later that they made a significant contribution to the spiritual unfoldment of man. Such ECK Masters were Fubbi Quantz, during the time of Buddha, and Rebazar Tarzs. This is always happening. You find when the social structure is in an upheaval, men like Copernicus come along and dislodge the earth as the center of man's universe. Copernicus came out with the discovery that the sun was the center of the universe, but he had to be careful about making this claim known during his time because of the persecution which he would have faced.

The ECK Masters worked quietly in the background with many individuals in history.

About the same time, Christopher Columbus was moving his ships across the Atlantic to America, and Magellan was out there in his little boats. They served to broaden the viewpoint of mankind. In effect, their discoveries made smaller man's opinion of his own importance and that of Europe and the Mediterranean area, which had been the great seat of civilization as it is known in our current history.

The Culture of ECK

The music that I've heard tonight is far superior to what I listened to in 1969 at my first ECK seminar. I remember distinctly that it sounded like hymns. I have nothing against hymns. But I don't sing very well, and as I was growing up, the people in our little country church were very straightforward if you sat behind them and sang off-key with gusto, the way I did. I can remember one lady turning around in the church to see who was making that awful racket. She wasn't doing so great herself, but I didn't care. When you're in a small church like that, you pretty well know who can sing well and who can just sing loud. I was one of those who, the more I sang, the quieter I got and the further to the back of the church I went. I finally ended up in the balcony. It was a kindness to my fellow creatures.

I do like to sing, but I keep it to myself. I think even my whistling is beautiful. My daughter, who's eight years old, says it's great—but that's about the extent of my fan club.

The ECK culture is formed on the Sound and Light of God, which the EK symbol represents.

The ECK culture is not formed on a historical basis but on something more sure and more solid, the Sound and Light of God, the ECK, which the EK symbol represents. The ancient EK symbol, with its distinctive design, strikes a chord within people. Often without knowing it, they are remembering a time in Greece, Egypt, or more ancient times when this symbol stood for Spirit. In the Golden Age long before our current history, when man looked to the temple within himself, he did not have to look to outer churches or graven images. This is why we never look to a symbol as a graven image to replace something that is alive within ourselves. But the question is: How do we tap into this, how do we reach this temple within ourselves?

The Spiritual Laws

The ECK Masters want us to develop the self-reliance to step forth into our own worlds, to go forth with increasing confidence, to know that for everything we encounter in this life and the life beyond, we are able to handle whatever comes our way.

I don't mean that your life necessarily will be easy. So often when people write in and ask for a spiritual healing after they've tried all the medical cures, they'll say, "I'd like some help because the doctors I've approached are not able to do anything for me." There are some individuals who get the spiritual healing; it depends upon whether or not that person has learned the spiritual laws.

When we break a spiritual law, whether willfully or in ignorance, it sets up a series of events that affect our health. It may affect our finances, it may affect our mental and emotional well-being. This happens time and time again, so that we add up what's called karma—children of the five passions of the mind: anger, greed, lust, attachment, and vanity. These passions of the mind are the claws that hold Soul in the materialistic worlds. My role as the Living ECK Master is to reach every individual who has gotten enough experience in the classroom of the world to realize that there must be something more to life.

When we break a spiritual law, whether willfully or in ignorance, it sets up a series of events.

My wife is attending college to finish up and to take some of the courses that she never did before. In observing the young people today, she noticed a striking difference from what she remembers when she was that age. In those days the students were happy and light, and they'd joke and goof around. Even though the weight of nuclear weapons was hanging over them, they found something to be light and happy about.

Yet she notices, at least at the school she attends, that there is a deadly seriousness about the students.

They'll get good grades if they can, but that's not their
main consideration. All they want to do is get through
school and get out there in life. They're almost like
people who are fifty or sixty years old, who have had
maybe thirty years more living under their belts; it's
like they're older people in young bodies. They feel
there must be something more to life, but they've
become disillusioned and wonder if the next path they
run into will be just another dead end. They ask, Is
someone there just to take my money? What'll I get
for the price I've paid?

I can't speak for anyone else, and I won't try to
convince you what is right or wrong for you. Only you
can make that decision for yourself.

As one of the ECK staff members was traveling
to this seminar, she flew into Chicago and missed the
connecting flight here to Cleveland. It was very late
before she got in. She took a cab from the airport and
met a cabbie who was learning his lessons too. Before
you get on the path of ECK, you think you can get
away with something. You have this idea that as long
as you can talk a little sweeter or a little faster than
your fellow man, if you've researched a little bit better
than he has, you can pull a fast one on him in real
estate or banking or you name it.

*The Law of Karma for the average individual has
a delayed reaction time.*

The Law of Karma for the average individual has
a delayed reaction time—it could take anywhere from
ten years to fifty lifetimes. By the time you've gone
through one lifetime and you start all over in the
next, your memory is wiped clear. Mankind really
hasn't advanced very far or very fast in the spiritual
sense. We have made strides in science and many
other areas, but the spiritual part of man is ready
for a leap.

So when she got in the cab, the cabdriver said
it would be about twenty dollars to get from the

airport to the hotel. Most of you know that in every town there are cabbies who have their own little tricks for extending the ride. If you're a stranger in town, he'll take the freeway that loops the town, and with a big smile he'll overcharge you by about five or ten dollars and expect a 15 percent tip on top of that. Well, when the meter hit the thirteen-dollar mark, the cabbie reached over, threw down the flag, and clicked it off. The ECKist thought they were going to get seven dollars off the fare.

Of course, the cabbie thought he was being really clever. Why? First of all, he didn't know about the Law of Karma, that at some time he would have to pay for that seven dollars—plus the tip—in the true coin. It might have taken longer, but after he put the flag down, another car hit the taxi causing a fender bender. He was lucky, except for one thing: He didn't have the ECK lighting up his understanding to see what had happened.

The ECK staff member just rolled her eyes up toward heaven and said, "What else is going to stand between me and getting to that ECK seminar?" It had been just one series of delays.

And when they arrived at the hotel, the cabbie got out and said, "That will be twenty dollars." And he expected a tip too.

He was lucky, except for one thing: He didn't have the ECK lighting up his understanding to see what had happened.

STEPPING-STONES

Those of you who attend ECK seminars know that sometimes it takes every bit of creativity just to get there. You're perhaps understanding a little bit of what the ECK Masters go through to get the simplest thing done. It seems the more you open yourself to the ECK, the greater the reaction when you write a letter or whatever, and so you learn very quickly to work with the laws of harmony. You learn to work in the spirit of goodwill and harmony with those around you, even when you find that coming to a seminar is sometimes like running an obstacle course, like somebody has thrown a bunch of suitcases in your path and you're trying to figure out how to get around them.

These things come up, and you wonder about them. You say, OK, why are all these things happening? I thought when I got on the path of ECK, I'd have fewer problems and life would get smoother. Now it looks like I'm not able to take another step.

This is where you become like the duck when the rain falls on it—the rain beads and just rolls off its back. You will see these things coming through life, and you will see that what you've called problems or situations are no longer obstacles holding you back from your own goals in life. You will come to see them as stepping-stones. And furthermore, you will see that there is help given when you've done absolutely everything you can to make it work and you've met with little success. That is when Divine Spirit, or ECK, steps in and helps you out.

What you've called problems or situations are no longer obstacles holding you back from your own goals in life. You will come to see them as stepping-stones.

THE REALITY OF ECK

This afternoon I had the good fortune to speak with a lady who told me about the reality of ECK in her life and how she had learned to work with this creative flow. She had belonged to an orthodox church for a long time, for forty years, and had attended every Sunday. She was a faithful churchgoer, and yet, she never received that fulfillment inside herself where she could say, "I have an answer for something that is crying inside." She did not know the words to describe the feeling. This is the call of Soul, and Soul, of course, wants to go back to Its home, to God.

She had a son and raised him, and during all those years he, too, had gone to church regularly. As he got older, she noticed he didn't go to church as often as he used to. I know some of you have run into this. Your parents will say, "Why aren't you going to church anymore?"—and they'll do it to change your mind and try to get you back. But this lady was very sincere and open when she questioned her son, and he told her, "Well, actually, I'm following another religious teaching." She said, "What is it?" and he just said, "Eckankar." He figured she was just asking because she was concerned that he was going to hell.

I find this an interesting thing: The people who are so concerned about someone else's fate after this life, who will go out and try to save them from hell, are usually those with the least confidence in their own destination when they leave this life. It's one reason that the ECKists, although we give out information, never feel the need to proselytize, to collar someone and say, "I've got just the teaching for you! It worked for me, and if it's good enough for me, it's good enough for you and the whole world."

Many religious wars were begun because of man's intolerance of man and his mistaken belief that God wanted him to kill and slaughter in His name. It's not true. Some people claim to have visions—Ah, that was God talking to me, or it was an angel, or it was Jesus—that inspire them to go out and do the most negative things. It never crosses their mind that if it is a God of love to whom they look, such a God would never countenance an action of that sort. This happens to people who are so unbalanced in their own emotions and mind that they are outcasts even within their own religion and just walk on the fringes.

The people who are so concerned about someone else's fate after this life are usually those with the least confidence in their own destination.

This lady said that shortly after talking with her son, she became interested in the teachings of ECK but she didn't know very much about them yet. She was facing surgery and had to go to the hospital. The night before the operation she was very uncomfortable and nervous. You can't help wondering what will happen, and, of course, for her it was natural to worry. It was during the middle of the night that she had her first encounter with the Blue Star of ECK.

She was lying in her bed, and suddenly she saw this little pinpoint of blue light, and it grew larger and larger. As it grew, it developed a core, and within that core was bright, blinding white light, and in it she saw one of the peace symbols of the sixties. After the operation, when her son came to visit, she mentioned to him what she had seen, and he said, "Oh, yeah! That's the Blue Star of the Mahanta." She said she was so new to the works of ECK—she hadn't read anything yet—that she didn't know about the Blue Star.

He said, "That's the Blue Star of the Mahanta."

This is the Blue Star of the highest state of consciousness that we can look to in order to open up this Sound and Light of Divine Spirit within our own lives.

Sometime after this, she got her Second Initiation in ECK. In Eckankar we wait two years. Many of the other groups will immediately initiate or baptize you as soon as you join the church or religious group, and the newcomer has absolutely no understanding of what he's getting into. Does the path fit him or not? He doesn't know, and he's into it too quickly, before he's ready. In ECK we wait two years. We suggest that an individual who is new to ECK read the books and practice the Spiritual Exercises of ECK described in the books. These are the key for the linkup with that Divine Spirit which very few individuals have access to while they walk the earth in this body.

When this ECKist got her Second Initiation after two years, she became aware of a sweet smell, sort of a musk, and she wondered what it was. She thought it must be something in the house and started looking around for the source. It stayed with her throughout the entire Second Initiation, which for her was several years. When she got her Third Initiation, when she had earned that state of spiritual awareness where she could move on, all of a sudden it went away—and she's missed it. She wanted to know where it went and what it was.

When the ECK Masters come in the Soul body and give the protection and love as you are getting your own feet under you to become masters in your own right, sometimes they'll give you a little signal of their presence. Some see the Inner Master as the Blue Star, others will catch one of these fragrances, perhaps of sandalwood.

At one time when I was going through a big change in my own life, I went to the bank to draw out my savings because I was moving to another town. It was early in the morning, and I was one of the first customers. It was a very cold bank; I believe this was after the days when they gave away a toaster to get your savings account. While the bank teller was doing the paperwork to close out my savings and checking accounts, I said to her, "Boy, somebody's got some nice-smelling roses in here."

I was about to make a change in my life, and I wondered if I was making a mistake or if this was the way Spirit was nudging me. For several months I hadn't gotten any nudge on the inner—no Sound, no Light. I had no assurance. When I mentioned the fragrance of roses, she said, "We don't have any

When the ECK Masters come in the Soul body, sometimes they'll give you a little signal of their presence.

flowers in here." I said, "Well, anyway, the perfume smells good," and she said, "I don't smell anything." The way she said it made me decide I'd better not pursue the subject. So I took my money and ran. But the ECK will come in, and It will bring this upliftment.

Self-Mastery

Since this is the Creative Arts Festival, perhaps later I can bring out how the creative force can work in our lives. Perhaps you are the way I am and you don't sing. You might wonder, What is this creative force? I don't write, I'm not able to play a harmonica, and I can't even tap dance. There is a way to bring this creative force into our life, to help us in making our business decisions, to help us when we make decisions about how to resolve a rough edge in our marriage. How can you smooth this out? How can you tap into this temple within yourself, this eternal fountain, and get your answers without having to write to someone such as myself and say, "I would like an ECK-Vidya reading (the ancient science of prophecy); I would like someone else to tell me what's happening."

As the Inner Master, I am able to work with the individual through various states of consciousness.

As the Inner Master, I am able to work with the individual through various states of consciousness. Many times it is done during the dream state at first. As you begin to move into those inner worlds, toward the heavens, moving toward the pure positive God Worlds in this lifetime without having to wait for the translation or death of the physical body, you begin to gain a little bit more strength. One of the ECK Masters will come to you—Wah Z, Peddar Zaskq, Rebazar Tarzs, or any one of the other Masters—and the Inner Master will begin working with you in the dream state. This is to work out the karma that's standing between you and the self-recognition which comes on the Fifth Plane, the Soul Plane, or that which stands between you and God-Realization.

We come to the awakened state of consciousness, and then we go to this Self-Realization—the self-recognition, the self-consciousness of Soul—and then to the recognition of the highest state. When an individual has achieved the ability to meet life on his terms and to go with the flow of ECK, to roll with the punches, then he becomes a master in his own right.

I have mentioned before that when one comes to the point of being an ECK Master, he really becomes one who is the servant of Spirit.

The ECK Master knows the laws of Spirit. He will not break them under any circumstances. Knowing the will of Spirit, he acts in full harmony. He works with each individual to show him how to work with these laws of Spirit which are unknown to the average man.

Every trouble and hardship that comes into our life is of our own making, and it's there only for the purpose of the upliftment of Soul. There is a healing that goes on inside as this Spirit, this Sound and Light of God, comes into expression through the music, through the vehicle, through yourselves.

When an individual has achieved the ability to meet life on his terms and to go with the flow of ECK, then he becomes a master in his own right.

Eckankar International Creative Arts Festival, Cleveland, Ohio, Friday, June 11, 1982

We can love our children, but the greatest service we can give them is discipline. We can show them how to grow up as ECK children who are acquainted with the Sound and Light of Divine Spirit.

12
THE KNACK OF SELF-RELIANCE

*T*he ECK Masters who came centuries ago worked on a one-to-one basis, with one individual at a time; and there were advantages to that. Nowadays, you put on the microphone, and this is just part of the way the ECK message is presented today.

This is the Creative Arts Festival, and there's a lot of creativity that goes on. We asked for an extra piano this weekend. Some of the things that happen are quite humorous. When the piano arrived at the rehearsal room, somebody said, "The piano's here." I was listening on the walkie-talkie and heard the message that came back: "But it doesn't have any keys."

Throughout the day I did some work, sometimes up in the room and sometimes with consultations, meeting with various individuals, and then I'd listen to the next episode on the walkie-talkie. When they finally got a piano tuner to the piano, there still were no keys. He said, "Where are the keys?"

Well, apparently somebody else had the keys for one reason or another. Another voice came on a little later and said, "Why don't we have the keys?" and the reply was, "Because we didn't *ask* for the keys!"

The ECK Masters who came centuries ago worked with one individual at a time.

But there has been a lot of creativity from all of you. Many of you helped in one way or another, and everyone had to do just a little bit more to get this message and this program presented.

CHILDREN'S DAY

This is also the weekend of Children's Day, a tradition that came over from Europe about 1856. You can almost mark a civilization's greatness by the way they treat their children. We also have an annual Eckankar Youth Conference. I'm not saying that you should treat children like little gods and goddesses, especially when they knock over the flower vase, or they forget to clean their feet when they walk across a light-colored rug, or when the little boy next door jumps up and down on the front wheel of your daughter's new bike as it's lying on the ground and breaks off the reflector.

There is a respect that we must give to each other as Soul, recognizing the uniqueness of the other as a spark of God.

Children need discipline, but there is a respect that we must give to each other as Soul, recognizing the uniqueness of the other as a spark of God. Once we see this within ourselves and others, how can we treat each other in any way except with harmony and love?

The country of Turkey has an interesting custom which was still being observed in the mid-1950s. They set up a special day for children. It was a symbol and an image for them to build on for the future. They established this day to look toward the youth, toward the future, toward that which changes. In this way they hoped to make more rapid steps into the twentieth century. History will prove whether it has had a great deal of success or not, but on this particular day, it really is the children's day. The merchants give them ice cream, free rides on the buses, and do all these nice things for them. If children had more than one day of this, they'd get such big heads that you couldn't live with them.

CHILDREN AND DISCIPLINE

If any of you who are parents have ever sent your child off to the grandparents for a week, then you know what it's like when children have it all their own way, without any discipline. Some grandparents don't listen when you tell them, "Bedtime's at nine o'clock." You find out later, when the child comes home, that bedtime was eleven or twelve o'clock or whenever the child would fall asleep from sheer exhaustion.

We can love our children, but the greatest service we can give them is discipline. We can show them how to grow up in this society as ECK children who are acquainted with the Sound and Light of Divine Spirit. We can do the Spiritual Exercises of ECK with them so that they can establish for themselves a foundation built on something other than the human love of their parents or, later in life, their loved ones.

As we grow older there comes a time we find that there are those close to us who leave. They go across the borders of life. Man, in his ignorance, has feared this transition, this translation.

Sometimes you just wonder, What are we as a civilization doing? The other evening I went downstairs in the hotel and saw all these video games. I was curious about Pac-Man. Games like this are like anything else: It's not the game but what we do with it. Unfortunately, it has become almost an addiction for some children. They don't have anything to replace it that they consider to be better.

Whenever we get too much of any one thing and it rules our life so that we lose control, then we have

We can love our children, but the greatest service we can give them is discipline.

to consider very carefully: Is this for our best interest? This is when our lives are out of balance, with excesses of any kind—the passions of the mind.

It's an interesting thing: People are looking for adventure, and when we are not able to go inwardly and find this adventure, we look outwardly. We look to our videocassette recorders. There's nothing wrong with videocassette recorders; this is not a criticism of them. But we owe ourselves a greater awareness than accepting the consciousness of another individual feeding us his ideas in a steady stream through the television set, through stories, and even through games like Pac-Man.

I didn't do so well in the game, really. You get caught up in it, and it's a real adventure. It's like the old days when a knight would be in battle, he'd actually be doing something. Or the saints, as we know of them, would be the adventurers and go out into the spiritual worlds and seek this Sound and Light of God.

Pac-Man won't be around forever, but it's an interesting game. There's this little Pac-Man who runs around, up these hallways and corridors, running like crazy. You're controlling his movements with a little stick, and you try to coordinate yourself, moving left and right. As he runs, four little creatures come after him, and they always know where he is! You've got him up in the northeast corner of the field, running around up there and doing really great, gobbling up those dots. All of a sudden they know: He's up in the northeast square—go get him! And they come from all corners and zoom in after him. You're almost trapped, and you go off into a side corner and you wait; but they know you're there. Then you're trapped. But it's OK: you've got a few more turns.

Our lives are out of balance, with excesses of any kind—the passions of the mind.

I'd have to say that people like you and I are on the path of ECK because we love life. So what we do is to look for ways we can grow.

Yet I looked at the whole idea of Pac-Man, and its whole purpose is to destroy. The little man gobbles up dots, and after he gobbles up a certain amount of dots he becomes empowered. That means he can turn around and go chasing the little monsters who were chasing him, but only until they revitalize their forces and come back chasing him. The game teaches our children something we have to consider very carefully.

An ECK parent can say, "My son, my child, please don't do that," or better yet, find other activities for him to do. In other words, what most people in this world do to cure a negative trait, whether it's drinking or whatever, is to try to get rid of it. They'll say, "I will go on a fast," or, "I will stop drinking at a certain time." There's a better technique, and that's to replace it with something that will help you more than this negative trait has hurt you. Replace it with something better.

People like you and I are on the path of ECK because we love life. So what we do is to look for ways we can grow.

IMMOBILITY TRAPS

I noticed the creativity of Soul working through the human consciousness during the gas shortages in 1974, when you'd drive up to a gas station and end up in a long line. The negative powers that control the lower worlds, which are around us at all times, do not want Soul to be free or to have mobility or communication. This shows up here on the physical plane.

The first thing I found was that the mobility of the American people had been stopped. They were not able to drive around as freely. There wasn't enough gas to go on summer vacation. This physical immobility carried over to the mind. Thought processes slowed down and became more constrictive, as the distance between points became more of a barrier. Communication between people suffered. Then, in their creativity, people started to find new ways to break through the immobility and establish a communication that was not restricted by distance.

They found it in the home computers. Now, of course, these get monitored and checked too. And it goes on and on like this. Soul must constantly transcend barriers to new levels of freedom.

THE PLUS FACTOR

There is no civilization that ever reaches a golden age unless it's imbued with the Sound and Light of ECK. It must have this as its foundation. This goes all the way back to the classical Greek civilization. It's not the refined manners or the superior mentality that forms a great civilization; it is actually the wisdom, power, and freedom of Divine Spirit.

These three attributes, or essences, of Divine Spirit are the law of the spiritual world. We go beyond the physical plane and through those worlds which include the various heavens with which orthodox religions have become acquainted. We go beyond this into the pure spiritual worlds, and we find there is no karma; we work under the one law of wisdom, power, and freedom.

When you have this within a civilization, and there are those people who are acquainted with the Spiritual Exercises of ECK and practice them for themselves, this brings an upliftment to the individual. This does not mean directing this Divine Spirit toward someone else or in any other way, but to chant the HU, which is the secret name of God. Then you, as the individual, go out in your community as you look for the greater expression of Truth.

There is no civilization that ever reaches a golden age unless it's imbued with the Sound and Light of ECK.

You look for it even in your job and your profession.

It's what is called the plus factor. You put a little bit more into your job than the contract requires. This is what sets the creative person apart from the masses. He will put a little extra in, no matter what he does. He'll give added quality in every case.

Sometimes when talking about creativity, I wonder what would be the most important point to bring up next. You can see creativity working in many different ways.

An ECKist mentioned that she went to a college campus because she wanted to put up ECK posters and leave some ECK books. She went first to the campus officials and was told, "No, you can't do that. We don't allow that here." She was very upset by this, and she wondered, *What am I going to do?* She felt this nudging from Spirit inwardly that there was some way to be of service because of the Light and Sound flowing into her. She found that to keep in balance and keep the state of well-being and harmony, of joy and feeling good, she had to give some service. So she tried to give it on this college campus, and she ran right smack into a stone wall.

Finally she said, "OK, I'll just turn it over to the Divine ECK"; and as she started to leave, she walked past the campus newspaper office. It hit her: Why don't I go in there? She walked in and talked to some of the people, and after a while they said, "Sure, we'll do an article on Eckankar." And it worked out. She was using this creativity; she was going one step further.

> It's what is called the plus factor. You put a little bit more into your job than the contract requires.

AWAKENING YOUR SELF-RELIANCE

The ECK Masters wish to awaken self-reliance in an individual so you learn that the key or the solution lies within yourself. You learn through the Spiritual Exercises of ECK to go forth into the inner worlds and draw on that source of knowledge which will guide you gently in one way or another through your everyday life. Once the Master has worked with the chela in this way, and that individual has gained this self-reliance and has become confident in meeting life on his terms, then the Master will let that individual go. He will go on and find someone else who needs that opportunity or has earned it or wants it. When I say "his terms," I mean in the sense that the individual recognizes the direction of Spirit and where It wants him to go.

It's interesting how very few people truly want to take one more step. Wherever you have groups of people, you will find that there are more who want to be the follower than the leader—unless you find a leader who has some success.

A lady was telling me this story: She said that when she was in school no one wanted to be the school newspaper editor or the yearbook editor. I mention this because we're now coming to the end of the school year and some of you have had that particular job. So this woman said she would take it on. She went at it vigorously, got a staff together, helped on this and that, and she did such a good job that it turned out really well. Some of the students were envious—those who hadn't had the courage to take the job before— and the next year they said, "Well, heck, if she can do it, we can do it." She was disarmingly deceptive in that it didn't show how well organized she was. By the next year, everybody wanted to be the leader.

You learn through the Spiritual Exercises of ECK to go forth into the inner worlds and draw on that source of knowledge which will guide you gently in one way or another through your everyday life.

How to Talk about ECK

I was talking with some of the children yesterday, and I asked one who was eight years old, "What do you do when someone at school asks you what your religion is?" The children use a great deal of discretion; they know how to be discreet, how to answer their friends. If they find it safe to do so, they'll say, "Oh, I belong to Eckankar." Other children will ask, "Do you believe in God?" and they'll say, "Yes, I believe in God," because they do. Children have their own way of speaking with each other, but they won't go around carrying a banner the way many adults do.

After we've left a particular religious path and we come to Eckankar, many times we are still carrying banners. And it's really not part of the path of ECK to carry a banner in the sense of going out, grabbing someone by the arm, and saying, "Hey, you know, this great teaching works for me and it's gotta work for you too!" It doesn't work that way. We give out the information, we present it—we may go on the radio or on television or leave books around our community—in ways that make it possible for someone to find the message of ECK through the public forum. We don't have to pound on doors and say, "I have something great for you!" It's not necessary.

After we've left a particular religious path and we come to Eckankar, many times we are still carrying banners.

KEEPING A GOOD THING GOING

At times I do a lot of research, looking here and there for one thing or another. I was reading some books the other day about the post–Civil War times and about the men in the cavalry on the Western frontier. Life was very hard in the posts out West, and the fort had only so many homes for the officers, but they had to have living quarters. When someone of a higher rank arrived, he could go and look over the living quarters of everybody else beneath him in rank. There wasn't very much room for creativity in selecting what you wanted, but there was a lot of creativity in figuring out how to keep a place that you liked. This may seem like a long time ago—a hundred years or more—but to me it seems like yesterday, and it might be that way for those of you who have experiences that you remember, perhaps in the dream state.

In this one particular case, the news came that a new officer had arrived on the post. The new officer went around and looked at all the different housing units that he could choose from, and he found this one really good house. It had several more rooms than a second lieutenant was entitled to, yet there was a second lieutenant living in it, even though he's right at the bottom of the officer ranks. He should have had a little hut or a tent out in the field somewhere, but here he had this nice house with three rooms and a basement.

"That looks like a good place," the newly arrived officer said. "Who's staying in there now?" The officer escorting the newcomer said, "Well, it's only a second lieutenant." Because this man had a right to go over there and kick him out, he said, "Well, let's go look at that place."

Everybody was always curious at first and said, "How does a second lieutenant rate that?" They found out. As soon as a new officer made an inspection, it became very obvious: The whole basement was flooded with water bubbling up from an underground spring. This happened every time a new officer came on base.

Only after the second lieutenant left did they find out what had happened. When he had arrived at the post, being at the bottom of the ladder, there was nothing available for him except a tent. But he looked around a little bit more until he saw this house with three rooms and a basement, and it was vacant. He

There was a lot of creativity in figuring out how to keep a place that you liked.

asked, "Why isn't anybody living here?" and the man escorting him took him downstairs and showed him. "Look, the whole basement is flooded." The second lieutenant said, "Well, I'll take it, anyway."

This man was very clever and used his creativity. He got himself some plumbing supplies, and the first thing he did was to make a cap for the spring. He put a cap on it just like a regular plumber would, and that shut it off. Next, he put in a drain with a removable plug, just like in a bathtub. He would pull the plug and drain out all the water. The basement would dry out in a day or two, and he was in good shape.

Whenever news came that a new officer had arrived on the post, the second lieutenant went to the basement and took the cap off the spring. In just a few short hours, the basement was bubbling with water. It took the newcomer a little while to sign in, and by the time he would come in to look around, the basement was flooded. No one ever found out about this until the second lieutenant left the post after a couple of years. He never told anyone. So this is often what the ECK Masters tell you: "If you've got a good thing going, keep it going."

A FIRM FOUNDATION

With the principles of ECK, we look to see how we can make ECK work in our everyday life; how we can go to the temple within us and find that source for ourselves. There are those who step onto the path of ECK and get a good mental knowledge of the teachings, but they have not caught the spirit. When the first little ripple comes along from the psychic waves or the negative waves, it's just like a bowling ball going down the alley. The ball will knock over perhaps one, two, or three pins, but it won't knock

We look to see how we can make ECK work in our everyday life.

down every pin. When this negative wave comes through, there are some who leave the path of ECK; but interestingly, there are more who stay.

You ask, Why is this? It's simply because some have taken more time to build a firm foundation in ECK through the spiritual exercises and the contemplative practices day by day. They set a time and they'll do it for the twenty or thirty minutes recommended, and they'll do this every day.

Some have taken more time to build a firm foundation in ECK through the spiritual exercises and the contemplative practices day by day.

MIXED BLESSING

A point about the expression, "God bless you" or "God bless it." In Ireland saying this was a peculiar custom.

There was great superstition, and superstition, of course, is just fear of the unknown. The Irish were very frightened of this thing called the evil eye, which is a very negative and very psychic belief. In their ignorance of the laws of life, it was very easy to quickly look at someone and say, "You have the evil eye."

The only way a person could avoid this label and avoid being persecuted by his neighbors was to look at a person or an animal or a thing as he walked around and say, "God bless you, God bless you, God bless you." Today, many times we feel that sayings such as "God bless you" are positive, and yet often they are born of fear. It's something deeply instilled.

In Eckankar, rather than directing this blessing at someone in such a way, we say, "Baraka Bashad," or "May the blessings be."

Eckankar International Creative Arts Festival, Cleveland, Ohio, Saturday, June 12, 1982

I read them a story about this little person who goes through his own dream state, and it illustrates how Soul goes along and creates whatever It needs.

13
THE NATURE OF SOUL

*T*he nature of Soul is something that has been on my mind, and probably yours too, for a number of lifetimes.

At the Creative Arts Festival a few weeks ago in Cleveland, Ohio, I went down to the children's room. Children are their own little people. I decided to read a story to them, a little book that came out a number of years ago called *Harold and the Purple Crayon.* Someone thought it was fitting and had sent it to me.

CREATING YOUR OWN WORLD AS SOUL

The children were seated on the floor. I sat down with them and began to read this story. It was about a boy who went into the dream state and actually created his own dream using a purple crayon. He decided to go for a walk, but first he had to have something to walk on; so he took his purple crayon and drew a road. But it was such a long road and not very interesting, so he decided to leave the road and take a shortcut through the forest. For this he drew a single tree; he didn't want to make the forest so big that he'd get lost.

Soul goes along and creates whatever It needs.

It's a wonderful story about this little person who goes through his own dream state, and it illustrates how Soul goes along and creates whatever It needs.

173

The little boy always kept his eye on the moon; he took his little crayon and drew the moon up in the sky, and it stayed with him throughout his whole adventure. I explained to the children that this was like the Blue Star of ECK—it's always with them. Finally he was ready to go back home, and how did he do it? He said, "I know the moon is always right outside my bedroom window," so he drew a window around the moon, and then he knew he was home.

While I was reading this story, every once in a while I'd hold up the book so the children could see the pictures. They couldn't really see it unless they were close, so the kids would crawl all over each other and hang on me to get a better look—except this one little girl about six years old. She simply sat in the back and said, "I can't see." I wondered why she didn't act like the others and jump up to get a closer look. I'd read another page, hold up the book, and she would just sit back there and call out, "I can't see." Each time, I would lean over and hold the book so that she could take a good look at it, and then she was satisfied. I realized she was actually acting very much like a grown-up. We get that way.

Children in ECK

At home one time when my daughter was about four years old, out of the corner of my eye I saw a very smart-looking little man dressed in green clothes, about so tall. My daughter was standing nearby and I said, "Did you see something?" She said, "Yep." I said, "Well, what did you see?" and she told me what she saw. I said, "Yep, same thing I saw." But I couldn't help wondering, so I asked her: "Do you see this stuff a lot?"

I explained to the children that this was like the Blue Star of ECK— it's always with them.

This vision goes away from the children; it left us as we grew older. We went to elementary school, and the education and everything else began to close in on us. By the time you're eight or nine years old, you no longer see many of these things, and even less so by the time you reach thirteen or fourteen. When we are young, we have this openness, an open communion with the other worlds; but then we go to school, the education closes in on us, and we lose it. We no longer see "the little people."

The staff planned to film some clips from the children's room and perhaps use it in a documentary sometime in the future. Of course, they had an idea of what they wanted the children to say, but children don't always cooperate. And I can't make them say what someone wants them to say, either.

So in our conversation, I tried opening up questions along certain lines. I asked them whether they'd had any dreams lately, and sometimes they'd just say, "Yes." You try to get away from questions where they can answer with yes or no and ask the kind where they have to actually say something.

I realized I hadn't phrased the question properly, so I said, "What kind of dreams have you had lately?"

"Um, a good one."

Well, if you're going to try to do something like this, you ought to actually look for a little one who's a live wire; somebody who isn't going to be tired by the time you get to the children's room at the end of the day when it's about time for them to go home. There happened to be such a little girl there. But she had her own thing she wanted to talk about, and every time I'd steer her toward something that the film crew might like, she'd yawn. You know how you work with children: "Oh, are you tired?" I said, and right away that was a threat. Her eyes opened wide,

When we are young, we have this openness, an open communion with the other worlds.

and she perked up. Then when she got to talking about what *she* wanted to talk about, she was wide awake and everything went fine. Of course, then the film crew went to sleep.

The room was set up in an interesting way. It was a large room with a partition in the center. This was where I read to the children. On the other side they had a camera set up where I was supposed to be talking with one of the children. We wanted to see if we could come up with something which would illuminate the ages—no matter what the child thought about it. When we were just about done talking, I said to this little girl and all the rest of the children, "Well, I guess I'm going to have to go now." She said, "Where to?" I said, "Only to the other side of the room." She said, "Why don't you stay here?" I said, "Well, that's how things are in life. You do something here for a little while and enjoy it, and then you go on to something else over there and enjoy that too."

All of a sudden she jumped up—the little ones can move fast—and she ran away. I got up, carefully stepped around the toys and little fingers, with some of the children hanging on to my legs, and started to go over to the other side of the room. Just then the little girl came back. She said she'd gone over next door to see what it was like—as a scout—because if I was going to go over there, she wanted to make sure it was OK. "Harold, you don't want to go over there," she said. I said, "Oh? Why not?" "Because nobody's over there," she said. "The people are all over here."

"Harold, you don't want to go over there," she said. I said, "Oh? Why not?"

I said, "Well, let's go over there and see what happens." We walked over there and, of course, everybody came with us. She and I sat down and prepared to have a nice conversation. They had the camera right in front of us, set very low. If you're going to sit down on the floor and talk to a child, you put the camera at eye level.

Just about the time they're ready to start filming, this other dear little child comes walking in and sits down in front of me, right in front of the camera. All she wants to do is sit there and look. When someone from the film crew came over and tried to move her, the little girl who was supposed to be talking with me said, "That's my friend." How do you tell the little girl's friend to leave because she's blocking the camera view? So she continues to sit there, the camera crew's back there wondering what to do, and the little girl I'm talking to won't say anything the crew wants to hear.

A little eight-year-old boy came over then and started talking about the things he ran into at school among his classmates, none of whom knew about Eckankar. I said, "What do you have to do so your friends won't make fun of you?"

"Well," he said, "I usually don't talk too much about Eckankar to them. I just keep it to myself." They had prayer in his school, and he was forced to pray, even though he didn't want to. He said he just gently put his attention on his Spiritual Eye and he'd chant *HU*. The children have their own ways of getting by in this world. It's not always wise, but they often use a great deal of discretion. They know when it's a good idea to talk about the ECK and when it's not. They know who's ready to hear about ECK and who isn't, and they use a great deal of common sense. They may not say one word of ECK to anyone for weeks at a time; then when the time comes, they'll mention it to a friend.

He just gently put his attention on his Spiritual Eye and he'd chant HU. The children have their own ways of getting by in this world.

The Spiritual Consciousness of the Child

Just a few minutes ago I was speaking with one of the parents, and he said, "What do you do about discipline?" My daughter is eight years old now. I know this doesn't affect all of you; others of you who are grandparents have put your time in. It's a lot of fun now to spoil the grandchildren and let the parents take care of the rest. You've paid your dues. When my daughter was small, I was much more strict with discipline than I am today. At the earliest age children have an incredible ability, an uncanny knack of knowing how to drive a wedge between their parents. They know just how to do it. I'm speaking about babies who are six months or a year old. They're much happier—delighted at times, in fact—if they can drive their parents apart. If the parents disagree with each other about the discipline of the child, this is just great. The child knows this instinctively.

There are the two natures in the child as well as in the adult—the positive and the negative—and they come into balance.

In a sense, we speak about the spiritual consciousness of the child, but there is also the other part. There are the two natures in the child as well as in the adult—the positive and the negative—and they come into balance. The role of the parents is to show the children how to come to the temple within themselves, even when they're young; to show them how to work with the sacred names of God and come to this Sound and Light of Divine Spirit. And it will take every bit of creativity that you have to learn how to work with children.

Someone told me about a child who could see colors around people. She was learning for herself how to look at people and interpret the purity of colors, and what a certain color and the shade of that color meant. The adult understood this, and he said to the child, "Now, you realize that others don't see colors around people, and you have to be a little careful when you talk about this." He just treated it in a very natural manner. Children have this ability, and the parents can begin to work with it. Even those of you who are grandparents today can develop the child with these ECK principles. The ECK principles are the life of ECK; we are in It from moment to moment.

The benefit of the path of Eckankar is simply that we open our awareness to what is around us anyway. Very often when I'm about to come out for a talk, part of the talk will be developed because someone backstage all of a sudden wants to talk about one thing or another. It's at a moment like this that we are the most open, and we hear; Spirit is telling us something that is important for us to know. Most of the rest of the time in our life, though the ECK is present everywhere at all times, our awareness is closed. We gradually learn to expand the consciousness, to open it up and pull it back a little bit more, so that we can hear the sweet whisperings of Divine Spirit as It is giving us answers in our everyday life.

The benefit of the path of Eckankar is simply that we open our awareness to what is around us.

THE FOUNDATION OF THE LIGHT AND SOUND

I was speaking last night about the shadow of truth, and this refers only to those teachings which do not incorporate the Sound and Light as the foundation. We have this foundation in Eckankar.

Recently someone came up to me and said, "I've been in Eckankar for years, and I haven't had any experiences." So we got to talking a little, and the person said, "Well, yes, I've had the Sound; I had the Sound even before I came into Eckankar, but it's changed." The Sound, of course, is direct communication with God. This is why we emphasize It in

Eckankar. This is what gives it vitality. We talked for a while, and as she spoke, she realized that she had been having experiences. She hadn't seen the Blue Light, and she wanted that experience; but she had the Sound which, in a sense, is greater.

The Sound performs an unusual function: It neutralizes the effects of the Light. We have the stories of the saints who, in their search for God, came to the first step and saw the Light. Many of them were thrown out of balance because the Light burned them. Not outwardly—there were no charcoaled humans walking around—but inwardly. It affected their minds: many of them went off the deep end and were no longer of any use to anyone else.

The Sound performs an unusual function: It neutralizes the effects of the Light.

PROOF OF THE EXISTENCE OF SOUL?

A great emphasis was placed upon Soul at the beginning of the 1950s. There was a prospector who had gone into the Superstition Mountains in Arizona looking for the treasure of the Lost Dutchman mine. Many prospectors had gone into that wasteland before him, but none had ever come back with the treasure.

Prospectors don't usually talk too much about how things are going, whether they had any luck or if they got close, but this man went out there time and time again. He lived in a room that rented for four dollars a week and didn't even have a car. Every so often one of his prospecting friends would drive him out to the desert and drop him off, and then for a while no one would see him. One time he left for the desert, and he never came back. The desert had claimed its toll, they figured, and nobody was too concerned.

It was discovered later that he had a safe-deposit box in the bank that contained a will, some cash, and all kinds of stocks, bonds, and securities. It turned out that this penniless prospector, who had lived in poverty, had left more than a quarter of a million dollars.

There was a peculiar provision in his will: His money would go to anyone who could give scientific proof of the existence of Soul.

With a quarter of a million dollars at stake, there was a lot of interest from many organizations. There were the universities—they sent their best professors to give discourses on Plato recording the talks of Socrates on the nature of the Soul as It left the body. That was their approach. Add to that the medical men who saw the drama of life and death in the hospital every day, the occult people with their various ideas, the religious people with their angle, the scientists—everybody came in, all wanting a chunk of that money.

This went on for eighteen years, and I believe it was finally resolved in 1967. By then, the judge had listened to over 134 claims for the money. He now had to come to a decision on something he didn't really have any personal knowledge about, and before doing so, he decided that he should ask for divine help.

It's curious, I suppose, that the works of Eckankar had just come out—Paul Twitchell brought them out in 1965, and this was 1967. The proof the judge was looking for was something like a photograph of Soul leaving the body. But the judge never found any organization that had a camera capable of recording that. So he decided to do what he considered the next best thing: He gave the money to a neurological society to gather information from the medical, the psychiatric, and the psychological fields. He figured this organization had the best chance of any to discover the nature of Soul.

His money would go to anyone who could give scientific proof of the existence of Soul.

Some of you may have been acquainted with this case. At the time the newspapers called it, "The Ghost Trial of the Century," and there was even a book about it entitled *The Great Soul Trial*. A great deal of attention was focused on the nature of Soul at that time, and yet we find that the answer, the key, is at the temple within you.

MOTIVATION

I could probably speak for an hour or two on the Temples of Golden Wisdom. These are all described in the ECK works. But actually, in its simplicity, you yourself must go to the temple within you. You will be met there by the Inner Master, by the Light Giver. He has the ability to combine, or bring together, the physical and the spiritual; he is able to lead you through the outer planes to the books, the ECK discourses, and the Spiritual Exercises of ECK. As you do these with love in your heart, and with interest and motivation, you will be led to that temple within yourself. This is the source of life, the source and fountain where you can find the solution to every problem that comes up.

We were talking about motivation the other day. Letters come in that say, "I haven't been able to have this expansion of consciousness; I don't know how to get it. What can I do?" There has to be a lot of motivation, and if you don't have it naturally, you've got to create it.

I had the motivation when I joined the military service and was sent to another country: I was homesick. I didn't want to be there; I'd rather have been home. About this time I came into contact with the works of ECK. Paul said, "I can show you this ability to move through the spiritual planes and also

As you do the Spiritual Exercises of ECK with love in your heart, and with interest and motivation, you will be led to that temple within yourself.

to move from here to there in the physical plane." I thought: I'm going to try it! If you leave the military base physically and take a flight home without permission, that's called AWOL. You have all kinds of people coming to look for you, so you have to decide on some other way. So I had the motivation.

I mentioned at the Creative Arts Festival that there are so many things that vie for our attention, such as the TV and other media. We can watch TV, and we can go to the movies. I enjoy all of these, when I have the time. But we stay in control of ourselves. We decide how much to allow a certain TV program or anything else to come into our life. We decide to what measure we will be the recipient of someone else's state of consciousness.

Touched by the ECK

A man who hadn't yet come across Eckankar and this ability to move in other states of awareness learned that the ECK will get in touch with you when the time is right. He was in the library preparing a research paper. While digging through the books on a lower shelf, all of a sudden a book fell on top of his head from the shelf above—for no reason. It was *The Spiritual Notebook* by Paul Twitchell. He picked it up and was just going to stick it back on the shelf, but first he opened it. "Oh, yeah!" he said. "This is what I've been looking for." A few of the creative techniques are given in this book, and it's available here for those of you who would like to try some of them.

Read some of the books, look Eckankar over, and if there is any interest, decide: Is this something that you are looking for? What we're looking for in learning the way of ECK is a greater ability to meet our

We decide how much to allow a certain TV program or anything else to come into our life. We decide to what measure we will be the recipient of someone else's state of consciousness.

life. When anything comes up, instead of being plowed under by the forces of life, flattened by the steamrollers of the negative forces, we say, "I have the temple within myself," and we figure out what to do. It will give an idea, a nudge to take the next step, to figuring a way out of the predicament.

It will give an idea, a nudge to take the next step, to figuring a way out of the predicament.

A secretary told about the time she had just moved to another town. She was short of cash and had no rent money and only enough food money to allow her to eat for about a week. She took that money and a little hibachi, went to a store, and bought herself a supply of spareribs and cold drinks. This isn't exactly the way the licensing departments of the state work, but she went out alongside the road and set up a little stand with a sign that announced, "Spareribs and Cold Drinks." Charging enough money to recover her costs and make a profit, she was astounded by the number of people who pulled over to buy the food. This venture enabled her to sustain herself until she found a job and the first paycheck came in.

She touched into this creative stream. She tried something which she would never have done otherwise—going out to the side of the highway and selling food. I'm sure she also kept an eye out for the highway patrol, trying to figure out when they slowed down if they were hungry or if they were planning to give her a ticket.

I like to prepare my daughter for the rebellious teenage years when the individual is looking for that self-identity, the way we all did. You won't walk on the same side of the street as your parents because you're ashamed of them. I try to inform her, to open up her mind, give her information. I say, "Yeah, when you get to be about thirteen or fourteen, you're going to be ashamed of me and you won't want to walk with me." Of course, she's at that age now where she'll say, "Oh, Daddy, I'll always love you." I say, "Well, you know I'm just laying a good trip on you, don't you?" She'll insist, "I don't care, I'll always love you!" "That's great," I'll tell her. "I'll always love you too!"

It's a lot of fun with children, but sometimes it can be hard; I won't say it's always a pure delight. The best we can do is prepare them for the time when they're able to stand on their own, with the Spiritual Exercises of ECK, so they know how to get in touch with the Inner Temple.

The best we can do is prepare them, so they know how to get in touch with the Inner Temple.

Many of you have come here from miles and miles away. Enjoy it, and put yourself into the weekend 100 percent. It'll give you food for Soul for weeks to come.

Victoria Regional Seminar, Victoria, B.C., Canada, June 27, 1982

The old man said to Alexander, "That water left me too old to live, too old to die."

14

ECKANKAR, THE CROSSROADS OF LIFE

*O*nce, during a good time in my life, even though I didn't have a job and didn't know where I was going, I was free to get on the road and just drive and drive. It was a wonderful feeling, and I didn't want to stop. Finally I realized it was a matter of responsibility to myself to step out into life again, get a job, and get some money together so I could keep paying my own way.

A newspaper article I recently read contained a variety of different answers to an interviewer's question: Why don't you believe in God? A number of people responded to it. I found their comments interesting. It wasn't that they didn't believe in God, but they had a concept that they hadn't been able to put into words yet.

The man-on-the-street interviewer asked, "Why don't you believe in God?" A female law student said, "I am basically an existentialist," and then explained a little about what that meant. She felt that people are responsible for their own actions. In organized religions, an omnipotent being is used too often as a crutch.

An electronics installer said, "I am agnostic. I

It wasn't that they didn't believe in God, but they had a concept that they hadn't been able to put into words yet.

believe in a supreme being but it's not something I pray to. I just figure all this organized mess on earth couldn't be an accident. Somebody planned it."

A nurse responded, "Well, I believe there is a supreme power that has a lot to do with controlling what goes on, but I don't pray. I don't feel that's necessary because it won't make any difference." And here I suppose you'd have to say that it depends on what you're praying for.

The Right Way to Pray

Prayer is fine when it's used in its rightful way to pray for our own spiritual unfoldment.

There is a controversy today about whether or not to have prayer in schools. Prayer is fine when it's used in its rightful way to pray for our own spiritual unfoldment. Too often it is used in another way: to control another person.

An individual may feel that if you don't follow his religion, you are going to hell or perdition. He will pray to change the mind of the person who doesn't fit his philosophy. This is wrong. This is a violation of the use of prayer; it's black magic.

If many of the people today understood the true purpose of prayer, they would be very shocked to find that under the spiritual law, they are coming under the label of black magicians. They would be astounded.

One More Step

In ECK we have the opportunity to bring the message of ECK to the individuals who are looking for another path to God, who are ready to take one more step. I found this on my recent trip to Wisconsin after the Creative Arts Festival. I wanted to go into the area just to look around, put up some posters, meet the ECK leaders, and see what could be done to bring the message of ECK to everyone who was interested in it.

I'd driven all day, and by 9:30 that evening I came to this town way up north, near Lake Superior. Seeing a launderette, I decided to stop and put up a poster; but after jiggling on the door handle, I noticed a sign that said it closed at eight o'clock. It had been closed for a while. Through the window I could see two men: one of them was lying on a folding table, just relaxing. The other was a big formidable-looking individual with a beard. *OK*, I thought. *I wonder what's going to happen now. I've done my best.*

As I started back to the car, one of the men came out the side door and asked, "What do you want?" I said, "I just wanted to put up a poster." He asked, "What about?" and I said, "About Eckankar."

"What's Eckankar?" he asked. "Well," I said, "it's a teaching about how you can find the temple within yourself." He said, "Let me see it." I showed it to him, and he said OK.

When we went inside, I saw a bulletin board filled with posters and little business cards. He said, "There isn't any room up there, but I'll tell you what. You can put your poster up right here on the wall by the door where people come in." All I had with me were thumbtacks, and I didn't want to stick those in his wall. I said, "I have some tape in the car; we'll use that, and it won't hurt your wall." He said, "Sounds good," and he put up the poster.

This was a town in northern Wisconsin where the TV reception isn't so good and they had nothing to do at night except lie around on the folding tables. They would just pass time until it got too late to do anything else, and then go home and just fall asleep. That was it. So he wanted to talk.

"What's Eckankar?" he asked. "Well," I said, "it's a teaching about how you can find the temple within yourself."

We talked for a while. He said he was concerned about the unions up there and what they were doing to the creative part of man, to Soul. He felt this was killing creativity. I just listened. He went on to talk about the town for five or ten minutes. He didn't ask one question about Eckankar, and I didn't mention one word about it. He was feeling me out. He wanted to see what kind of a person I was. Well, I was hungry. I hadn't eaten all afternoon except for a snack. So he gave me some directions to a restaurant, and I left. He let it be at that, and so did I.

I was willing to give the ECK message, and just by giving of himself, he had opened himself in a little way to Spirit. He didn't have to let me in there, but he did. It's a step for one at the crossroads of life.

The Living ECK Master has roamed the earth for centuries. He gives the opportunity again and again to individual Souls who have come to that point where they are just about ready to step on the path of ECK. Many times we, ourselves, have met one of these agents of God, whose only message is that there is a way to learn of the Sound and Light of Spirit. You can work with these ECK Masters for the upliftment of spiritual consciousness, to help you get through your own life.

You can work with these ECK Masters for the upliftment of spiritual consciousness, to help you get through your own life.

There Is Always an Answer

I can talk about all the adventures you will have in the heavens and beyond. But it's of little use if you're wondering, How am I going to get a job? or How will I get through these times of recession? We can learn to know that in the spiritual consciousness there is always an answer for every situation that comes up in our lives; there is always a way. What holds us back is one of our attitudes.

As an example, we can look at some of the wealthy men in this country who have amassed fortunes. Some of them inherited it; there are others who were able to take the steps to attain this wealth. You look at two people with similar educational backgrounds—one is a success financially or spiritually, and the other is not—and you wonder what made the difference. The difference is in their attitudes.

To bring news of Spirit, this Holy Spirit, of how to begin working with Its aspects of Sound and Light that come into our life, and to begin getting the insight into how to make our life better—this is the purpose of ECK.

SOUL AT THE CROSSROADS

We'll reach the crossroads again and again in our search. Many times we will meet an ECK Master, and we may or may not recognize him. He might be a businessman hurrying through an airport, or he may look like a beggar standing on the street who comes up to you and asks for a handout, as is recorded in *The Flute of God* by Paul Twitchell. These beings come in any number of different ways to bring a blessing of God and to raise and expand the consciousness of anyone who opens himself.

Eckankar won't take away all your problems. The most I can guarantee you is that once you've learned to overcome one situation in your life, you'll probably get another one twice as big. If you think I'm out here beating the drums for ECK membership, you're probably wondering, *Why is he saying that?*

The path of ECK is designed to give every individual his own mastership. But it won't happen

The path of ECK is designed to give every individual his own mastership.

overnight. If you're studying in any profession, whether it's to be a schoolteacher or a medical assistant, you are not going to be at the top of your profession after one year of college. Most of the professionals in the field you've chosen get a chuckle out of this and say, "Yeah, well, three more years, and then maybe he'll get out in the job market, and then after he puts in about four or five years, he may be worth something." This is the reason employers think twice about whether they want to hire someone without any experience. It takes a little bit of time to grow into the field of our interest, whether it's in the physical in business, or whether it's in the spiritual.

The Voice of God

Letters come very often from people who say, "I'm not having any success in my spiritual life, and I wish you could give me some help. I've seen the Blue Light now for two years—but that's all I see." Or they'll say, "I've heard the Sound; It has changed in pitch from what It used to be, but that's about it. Could you give me any help to unfold spiritually?"

This Sound and Light, the two manifestations of Spirit, are actually the Voice of God.

They don't recognize that this Sound and Light, the two manifestations of Spirit, are actually the Voice of God. They are in direct communication with God. It does not necessarily come as a big voice booming from the sky, like a 747 streaking through the cumulus clouds. It comes in a way that many of the orthodox religions have never understood.

There is some mention of the Sound and Light in the Christian Bible at Pentecost. They saw flames that looked like tongues of fire, they heard the sound of the rushing wind; these are two manifestations of this Divine Spirit. This is what comes through. In Eckankar we learn how to tap into this.

STUDYING THE ECK-VIDYA

One of the aspects of Eckankar is the ECK-Vidya; this is the ancient science of prophecy. I haven't put too much attention on it as a general thing. I won't read it for someone else, but for those who would like to develop it for themselves, we have classes on the ECK-Vidya. This is one of the more interesting aspects that attracts us when we first step onto the path of ECK. We say, I would like to know my future and my past. There is a feeling that if we knew the future and the past, we could somehow make our present life better. There is some truth in this, but I would rather that someone who has an interest in this particular aspect of Eckankar read and study the book by Paul Twitchell, *The ECK-Vidya, Ancient Science of Prophecy.*

There are classes on the ECK-Vidya: you can contact the local ECK leaders and simply say you would like to study this. We don't teach how to do the ECK-Vidya readings in this class. But you study the book and, through your spiritual exercises, begin to develop your own techniques for getting a little insight, opening this up just a little bit.

An individual had a question about the role of the ancient oracles in the spiritual life of man in the time of the Oracle of Delphi. To learn and open up, he decided to study the ECK-Vidya. First he went into a contemplative state and asked, "What is this all about?" He then visualized himself in ancient Greece, sitting on the side of a mountain. After a while, an ECK Master came along and asked him what he wanted. He said he wanted an understanding about the role of oracles in the spiritual life.

He then visualized himself in ancient Greece, sitting on the side of a mountain.

He came to understand that the oracles were used in those times because the consciousness of man was so low. They were not able to go to the temple within themselves directly, through the Spiritual Exercises of ECK, and meet the Inner Master to get information on whatever they were looking for. So the ECK Masters at the time would work through oracles. What has come down to us in history is a poor shadow of the original message that was given; it's merely a rehashing of the psychic and occult techniques which have lost their original meaning.

As he sat there on the mountainside and got insight into his question, the ECK Master showed him some incidents from his past lives, revealing something that was of importance to him in this lifetime, something which had a direct bearing on his spiritual unfoldment. Little objects that looked like electromagnetic cards were pulled out of a file. You may either read them directly, or they may display pictures that give the complete scope of the individual and of those lives which were of importance. The ECK Master pulled these out for him and gave him a look. He considered this an added bonus, but it happened through his own efforts. He worked with his creativity to figure out how he could go about getting a deeper, more penetrating insight into his own life, and this is how he did it.

The ECK Master showed him some incidents from his past lives, revealing something that was of importance to him in this lifetime.

THE WATERS OF IMMORTALITY

A while ago on late-night TV there was a series on Alexander the Great—maybe some of you saw it. Alexander conquered all the then-known lands, but some of the history about him that does not appear in man's records is revealed in the ECK works. For instance, Paul Twitchell made reference to the time Alexander marched over the Hindu Kush mountains and came through the Khyber Pass and through all the lands still to be conquered. He set up camp down in the plains and called his soothsayers together. "I've heard about this place where there's a spring of the waters of immortality," he said. "Find me the fountain of youth and bring back some of the water."

The ECK Masters know the location of something like this, but it's the spiritual that they are concerned with. This spring of water is for those who have a mission here: to bring out the news of Divine Spirit and how the Soul that is looking for unfoldment can contact It, reach the Sound and Light, and start incorporating these into his own life to gain greater understanding.

While Alexander waited back in camp, his men followed the Jhelum River up to one of the springs far back in the mountains. They studied all the sacred signs and concluded that this was the real thing. Scooping some of it into the water bag, they rode back to the camp and presented it to Alexander. "Here it is," they said. "We brought you some water from the fountain of youth." He was just about to take a drink when a wrinkled little old man came running up, carrying on and making a big scene. "Don't drink it, Alexander!" he shouted.

Alexander stopped. The old man went on, "Look at me. Centuries ago I drank that water, and look what it did to me." Alexander, a strong young man in his prime, said, "What do you mean?" The man said, "That water left me too old to live, too old to die." Alexander stared at the old man for a moment longer, then dumped the water.

Many times, at the crossroads of his life, Alexander the Great was approached by the ECK Masters and given the opportunity to take a step, to go on either the spiritual path or the path of materialism. Each

Many times, at the crossroads of his life, Alexander the Great was approached by the ECK Masters and given the opportunity to take a step.

time, when this blessing came to him, he decided to go on the path of conquest instead of the path of self-surrender to the Divine Being. And because of this, one of the ECK Masters disguised himself as an old man and came to stop him because he would have used this water for the wrong purposes.

There are a few individuals who do drink from this water of immortality; they learn to work with the enzymes and to reverse the aging process because they have a mission. They are not concerned about staying in the body or not. They just do their work. The person who qualifies is one who learns to work in the state of vairag, or detachment. This does not mean giving up all interest in the family, throwing away all emotions and walking through life like a zombie, a computer-controlled robot, and then saying, I am now in the detached state. No. One who does that is actually in the sleep state.

EMBRACE LIFE WITH RESPONSIBILITY

The ECK Masters, whether men or women, have loved life and have embraced it, but with responsibility. We do not have the concept of sin in Eckankar, because with that concept goes guilt. Guilt ties people up in fear and dread. With every move they wonder, Is this act going to take me to heaven or hell?

In ECK we take full responsibility for each of our actions.

In ECK we take full responsibility for each of our actions, knowing the principle that is spoken of in the Christian Bible by Paul: Whatsoever a man soweth, that shall he also reap. If you live this principle, you are living the Golden Rule: Do unto others as you would have others do unto you. Certainly there are very few people, except in the most negative states of consciousness, who want anything but good for themselves.

I often mention that children are close to this Divine Spirit within. It doesn't mean I'm blind to the fact that as they are growing up, if you don't keep your eyes on them, any minute you could be in for surprises. But in the spiritual consciousness they are very open to this divine essence, to the God-center. Gradually it closes off as they reach about six years old and begin going to school.

I received a letter from a lady who was a grandmother. Her son was dating a woman with a five-year-old child. That child's mother was very much like the people interviewed in the article I spoke of earlier—she didn't believe in a God, and she had never given her child any religious instruction.

One day when this grandmother's son and his woman friend went out, the five-year-old stayed with Grandma. She and the little boy settled down to talk about all the good things that children like to discuss—candy and their dreams of being a spaceman. Then the little fellow looked on the wall, saw a picture of one of the ECK Masters, and out of the blue he said, "Grandma, how can I get to heaven?" He tied that picture in with his spiritual unfoldment because he just knew. Many children meet the ECK Masters in the dream state.

Once we gain reassurance of ourselves as Soul, we gain confidence in life.

I and the other ECK Masters use the dream state because it's a good way for many people who are a little afraid of taking a step into the other worlds and getting the reassurance that Soul lives forever, that It has no beginning and no end. Once we gain reassurance of ourselves as Soul, we gain confidence in life. No longer are our actions tempered by fear— What will happen if I do this or that? Our life becomes tempered by common sense. There is a great difference.

Those of you who are new might want to look

through the ECK books for yourself. Take your time, study, and look them over. Weigh it all in the privacy of your own home. Ask yourself: Is this a path I'm looking for? Has Eckankar something to give me that I haven't ever had before? Is there hope? Is there a chance to really make some spiritual progress in this life?

Quite frankly, we don't make much progress, even from lifetime to lifetime, because as soon as we get the lessons learned, it's time to translate, or die, and we come back with a clean slate. The lessons have been learned, but since they're not at our fingertips, we start all over again.

HOW COME YOU ARE ALWAYS CALM?

Look within for the answer whenever something comes up: What am I learning here? How can I get on top of this situation?

My wife went out with some friends this afternoon, and one of the ladies works with disadvantaged children who have had some problems with school in the past. Since she was the new teacher at this particular school, she inherited the rowdy class, the ones with the discipline problems. But she's a Higher Initiate in ECK, and she works from the temple within herself. She has learned to look within for the answer whenever something comes up: What am I learning here? How can I get on top of this situation?

The children tried to get under her skin, to needle and bug her, and see if they could get her furious the way they had done with all their other teachers. She didn't get flustered; instead, she helped them. Using the regular educational system, she was able to give them insights into how they could begin developing values in their own life.

They began to learn to have respect for themselves so that when they grew up, they could go out into life and have at least somewhat of a positive experience as Soul in the present physical form.

One of the students came up to her one day and said, "How come you are always calm?" He wondered why they had not been able to get to her. She said, "Because I go to the temple within myself." He said, "What's that?" She explained, "That's the place where one can go for his own answers to get through life. It's the source of all wisdom, knowledge, and understanding." It was a new concept to him, and since he had never heard of it before, he couldn't begin working with it yet.

She didn't say, Only in my religion can you find this temple within you, but instead she said, "The temple within you is there. Become aware of it, and through your own awareness you will come to a greater understanding of your true being." And the boy understood.

MEETINGS WITH THE VAIRAGI MASTERS

There is just one more thing I'd like to mention. As we are at the crossroads of life again and again, through past lifetimes and in this lifetime, there will be these beings, the ECK Masters of the Order of the Vairagi, who come to meet us. Many times we don't recognize them because no one has ever told us that such beings really walk the earth.

During the summer, our daughter had the opportunity to spend some time in the country. This was a new experience for her, a chance to go out and learn something. We live in town now. I grew up on a farm and have known the deep resources that were opened by just having that background, and I wished many times that she could have that experience too.

This meant that, at eight years old, she would have to get on a plane and fly off to another state. We didn't know if she would enjoy it or not, or whether she would be homesick. She had her own doubts too.

As we are at the cross-roads of life again and again, there will be these beings, the ECK Masters of the Order of the Vairagi, who come to meet us.

At the airport, we had to fill out all kinds of forms to authorize the flight attendant to take her from her parents, put her on the plane, and then turn her over to the people who were going to meet her when she deplaned in the other state. While these arrangements were being handled, we couldn't help wondering how she was going to get along out there.

Our little daughter stood there dressed up in her old cowboy hat, a cowboy shirt, and her blue jeans. When the flight attendant came over to take her to the plane, she couldn't quite make out if this child was a boy or a girl. She wanted to be discreet about it, and yet she didn't know how to approach it. Finally she said, "Is this my Master Klemp?" I said, "It sure is!" I think she missed the point. She was a little flustered because she hadn't expected such an enthusiastic response. She was at the crossroads too; she had made good progress. Whenever she decides that she wants to take the next step in her spiritual unfoldment, maybe someday she'll recognize that she had the opportunity that many of us have had in the past.

THE POINT OF SELF-MASTERY

I'd like nothing more than just to sit down in a room with each of you and find out what you've learned in ECK, the experiences you've had, the successes you've had, the apparent failures when you say ECK is not working, or when ECK is working. But it's not necessary. You are learning how to come into contact with the temple within yourself, with the Inner Master, and to get your own answers so you can go through life with self-mastery.

You are learning how to get your own answers so you can go through life with self-mastery.

In that sense, you come to the point where you no longer have to ask someone in authority: Give me my answers. Tell me, am I going to have a successful life? or any of these things.

When you come to the point of self-mastery, as you are working toward it, you learn that you can shape your own future. You are making your own present through self-responsibility and the attention on the Sound and Light of ECK at the temple within yourself.

Atlanta Regional Seminar, Atlanta, Georgia,
July 16, 1982

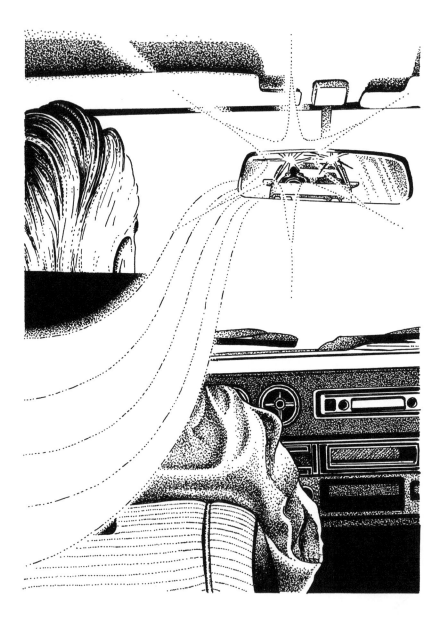

He'd started out late from home and was making pretty good time, when all of a sudden he saw this blue light in his mirror. And, of course, he also heard the sound that comes with it.

15

ECKANKAR, THE GREAT ADVENTURE

I understand you've been having a pretty good time. We have a lot of company in town this weekend: the Jehovah's Witnesses, the Roman Catholics, and six thousand members of the American Legion.

It's interesting how it goes with preparing talks. Sometimes it's easy, and the talks just come together. Other times it's a struggle as some of these outer things affect us. Somebody mentioned just a little while ago that it's quite probable that one of these groups is sitting there praying for us. This has to be neutralized. As we, the ECKists, come into an area, we are determined to be vehicles for the ECK no matter what's going on around us.

EFFECT OF THE SOUND ON THE LIGHT

In Eckankar, we know about the Light and we know about the Sound. The Sound is that which neutralizes the effects of the Light. An interesting point about the Light and Sound is that here in America, few of the religions know about even the

We know about the Light and we know about the Sound.

203

Light. In the East, some of the religions get only the Light. They have the great inner experience, but it can burn the individual. This was the case with Saul of Tarsus and with Jakob Böhme, the inspired cobbler who went around seeing a pink light. They were burned by this Light; they had too much of It. It can unbalance one to the point where he doesn't know how to get along.

We get both the Light and Sound—the balance—and we have this protection.

We get both the Light and Sound—the balance—and we have this protection. The Light is important, but Soul cannot do without the Sound. It must have the Sound in one way or another.

Communicating with God

I met with an ECKist who was deaf, and through an interpreter the ECKist asked, "What is this Sound? What is the Word?" Because he's deaf, he wondered, *Is Soul deaf?* I had to reassure him that Soul is not deaf.

"On the inner planes, do you see any of the ECK Masters?" I asked. The ECKist said, "Oh, yes, I see them." He went on to describe all kinds of inner communication with them—he'd seen a whole row of them. I said, "If in the dream state or during your contemplation you see one of the ECK Masters, you are seeing the Light and hearing the Sound."

He indicated that he wasn't able to hear the ECK Master speak, and I asked, "Then how does he communicate with you?" He said, "He writes."

"That," I said, "is the Word. You are getting it directly." He didn't realize that there were many ECKists who would do just about anything to have his degree of contact with this inner reality at that inner temple.

I've mentioned this before, and I'll probably mention it again and again. In letters or conversations, someone will say, "I haven't had any experiences with the Light and Sound. Please help me; I'm having a real spiritual problem." If I'm speaking with the person and I can tell that he is having this experience, the conversation might go like this:

I'll ask, "Do you ever see one of the basic things such as the Blue Light?"

"Oh, yeah. I see the Blue Light."

"Well," I'll say, "what's the problem then?"

He'll say something like, "Actually, all I've seen for the last two years is the Blue Light."

"That doesn't seem to be too great of a spiritual problem. Do you hear the Sound?"

"Yeah," he'll say, "but it's mostly the same Sound. It's changed a little bit in tone, but it's mostly the same old Sound."

I'll try to explain it to him very carefully: "Do you realize when you have the Sound and Light in your life, you are having actual communication with God?"

"Really?"

"Really."

All too often we have been led to believe that communication with God is a big voice in the sky—coming from somewhere in the cumulus clouds at thirty thousand feet. Who told us this? People who didn't know. We have the legends that have come down to us, such as Moses on the mountain hearing God speak to him. They didn't know how God spoke. It comes sometimes as the still small voice, or it may come as the booming voice from the mountaintop. Some of you know.

Sometimes the ECK may work in a gentle way. It may give you just a nudge, a feeling of how to act, what to do.

Sometimes the ECK may work in a gentle way. It may give you just a nudge, a feeling of how to act, what to do, which dentist to go see. Something down to earth.

Three Basics in ECK

There are three basics in ECK. The first, of course, is Sugmad, or God; next comes Spirit, the creative principle; and then Soul. Sugmad, of course, is the center of all. God is the center of all, and the Ocean of Love and Mercy is the home of Soul, where God creates Soul. Spirit, then, is the substance out of which Soul is made, and Soul is the spark of God that is sent into the lower worlds.

Every religion has as its thesis how to get freedom for Soul. How can we get Soul back to heaven? Every religion establishes its own heaven—here, there, some higher, some lower, some better, some worse—and this is how they work.

In Eckankar we look to the inner temple. How do we get there? Through the Spiritual Exercises of ECK. This is how we become freed from the bondage to the lower self, to the causes that have held us here.

Through the Spiritual Exercises of ECK we become freed from the bondage to the lower self.

If He's Real, You'd Know

This morning when I visited the children's room, there were just a few children there, and they were looking through an older copy of the little book *Alphabet for Young ECKists*. Under "W" was the Wheel of the Eighty-Four. The Arahata asked the children, "Do you know what this wheel is?" They were really puzzled. We don't put much emphasis on the Wheel of the Eighty-Four; it's that cycle of cause and effect, of reincarnation, that keeps us here. I asked them, "Do you suppose this Wheel of the Eighty-Four is a bicycle wheel?" And, of course, they were offended that I would talk down to them.

Children are very straightforward. They have their own reality and their own worlds. One little girl had her teddy bear, and I said, "Is he alive?" My daughter tells me hers is, but grown-ups don't believe her. The little girl looked at me, and she wasn't quite sure if this was just the usual adult question. Do you tell your secrets to an adult who will laugh? She finally gave me a pointed look with this little secret smile that said, "If he's real, you'd know."

In the other worlds, the children meet with the ECK Masters, especially Gopal Das, at one of the inner temples. The ECK Masters will often work with the children using cartoon characters, which is a good method because it gives them a happy way to learn.

The children, and perhaps we adults, would like nothing more than to be outside at a seminar like this, walking around on the grass—if we could find someplace like that. Yet we of the twentieth century require something that is more convenient: a hotel room with a good rate, a good restaurant, a place to have meetings, and so on. The children would like to be outside, but sometimes it isn't possible. We are trying to make it easier for them, as well as for ourselves, to have a more direct way to learn about ECK.

In the other worlds, the children meet with the ECK Masters, especially Gopal Das.

AN OPENNESS OF HEART

We had a meeting yesterday with one of the ECKists from Africa. There is an element in that culture which is different from ours. Here we are weighted down with the mind—this is something I carry within myself too. In this ECKist's culture, they walk around with an openness of heart; they'll take a chance on a person.

Here, with the social pressures, as we get more advanced and sophisticated, the laws get more restrictive. We think we are becoming quite a civilization, yet our laws restrict us more and more. They don't have that over there in the same way. Of course, these are the lower worlds, and it's not heaven no matter where you are.

When this African chela was ready to step onto the path of ECK, he already had a connection with the inner. He was already beginning to help himself through the inner direction when something would come up. In preparation for the path of ECK, he went to a man he trusted for advice. The man said, "You are going to have to purify yourself."

"How do I do it?" he asked.

The man said, "In the morning, when the dew runs off the roof and down the drain, have a bucket under there to catch the water. This will be pure water which you can use for purification." This was supposed to go on for a certain number of days.

The first night, the person who was about to become an ECKist went to sleep, and when he awoke the next morning, he bathed himself in the dew water. It worked the same way the second night. Everything was going fine.

He lived upstairs where he could look out his window and watch the little bucket as the dew ran into it. Down on the first floor there lived a quiet little man who never said anything and seemed to be a good neighbor in every way.

On the third night, the African awoke and found himself standing outside. His body was upstairs on the bed sleeping.

On the third night, the African awoke and found himself standing outside. His body was upstairs on the bed sleeping, but in the Soul awareness he was standing by this bucket where the dew was trickling in. To his amazement, he saw his neighbor pick up the bucket, dump out the dew water, replace it with ordinary water, and set it back down under the drain.

The next morning the African awoke, jumped out of bed, and went storming to the door. His wife knew how much this sacred water meant to him, and when he ran outside and began to dump it out, she was mystified. She said, "What are you doing?" He said, "This water is no good!" Then he knocked on the neighbor's door and demanded to know why he had dumped his water. The neighbor, of course, was shocked—he thought no one had seen him in the middle of the night.

In our culture, everything is constructed along a mental framework. Actions have a certain logic behind them. Before the police can act on anything, there has to be a motive. This guy on the first floor had no logical motive that the Western mind could understand. He just seemed to act out of sheer orneriness—he'd go outside, dump the pure water, and replace it with polluted water. Why did he do it?

SPEAKING SOUL TO SOUL

Many of us may speak English, but it's the inner communication that is important to us. Each one of us is working in the spirit of love and harmony, which is the way the ECK will work through us. Though we are communicating through this outer language, we often speak Soul to Soul.

Each one of us is working in the spirit of love and harmony, which is the way the ECK will work through us.

When a person says something that sounds strange and you don't know what he's talking about, take a little time to understand him. We can show a little patience and take the time to ask, What do you mean? or Do you really mean this or do you mean that? Find out what the other person is trying to say. This will build harmony and goodwill which are so important and necessary for our spiritual unfoldment.

ECK FOO YUNG

Sometimes the question comes up about what the Masters eat. Actually, when you're on the road, you eat anything you can. Some days I don't eat very much, but then there are other days when I catch up. Then I pay the price. I'll go home and fast because the next seminar is maybe a week or two down the road and I have to squeeze so much work in.

You can think about the ECK so much that It gets into your everyday conversation and you don't even know It's there.

My daughter was about to go on a summer trip, and I wanted to spend a little time with her before she left. As you who are parents know, sometimes you don't have as much time as you'd like to spend with your children. Time passes, and all of a sudden they're eighteen. You wonder where their childhood went and why you let it go by without appreciating the child and just having a good time.

My daughter's eight years old, not too far from the age of six when children are cute in their own way. By the time they're going on nine, they have developed this little sophistication which always amazes parents, when they remember the two- or three-year-old child. I said, "Would you like to go to this health-food restaurant?" She said, "No." I asked, "Why not?" and she said, "Because the selection isn't very good." My own feeling usually is that you look at the menu, and you eat what's there or you don't. But I said, "OK, where would you like to go?" She said, "Well, let's look around."

We ended up in a Chinese restaurant. We sat down and started to look through the menu. There's often a lot of monosodium glutamate in Chinese food. I get a heavy throbbing in my head when I eat something with monosodium glutamate, but sometimes I'll go ahead and have it anyway.

When you eat at a Chinese restaurant, it's fun to order family style—everybody orders what he wants, you put it in the center of the table, each person helps himself, and you just have a good time trying this and that. I started making out a list. One of the items I put down was egg foo yung, but I spelled it differently. The waitress came over while I was in the middle of making this list; I was pricing the food to make sure the meal would fit the budget. She looked down at the slip of paper and started to laugh. I asked her what was so funny. She pointed at the list and read aloud, "ECK foo yung." I was really surprised and explained that it had to do with my work. It also gave me an opportunity to leave a book with her.

A LITTLE MESSAGE

A lot of times I'll leave a copy of *The Wind of Change*, *The Tiger's Fang*, or *The Spiritual Notebook* with a little message written inside the cover. I try to find ways to personalize it so it won't seem like a book that someone discarded because it wasn't good enough to read.

Up in the right-hand corner I'll put the date, the name of the town I'm in, and include a little note. I'll change it each time to let it be creative, but it will usually say something like: Dear Reader, I've enjoyed this book. It has meant a lot to me. If it fits your thinking, you're welcome to it. Happy reading. Then I'll sign my name.

In a way it's like putting a note in a bottle and tossing it into the ocean. In the comic strip *B.C.* by Johnny Hart, the guy will throw his bottle with a note into the ocean and then sit there, waiting for about four or five frames. Finally the bottle comes back, he opens it up expecting this great piece of information, and it's usually something he didn't want. I become awfully curious about where the ECK

A lot of times I'll leave a copy of The Wind of Change, The Tiger's Fang, or The Spiritual Notebook with a little message written inside the cover.

books really go. We have put out well over half a
million books—they're out there somewhere. I've
thought about writing, Is anybody really reading this
book? If so . . . or If you read this book, pass it on.
But before you do, please write and let me know
where this book is going. I'm just curious. I'd like to
get some feedback, and I just may do this someday.

FITTING IN THE SPIRITUAL EXERCISES

The other night we were in Atlanta, and we went
into a restaurant. It was very late; we had just
finished a bunch of meetings, and sometimes it helps
to wind down if you go out and get something to eat.
The waitress was a student. She was working the
night shift, and she said it was really difficult. She
was studying math and physics and, in the meantime,
trying to make her way in life. So we got to talking
about this.

One of the fellows at our table began to tell us
about how he used to work on rotating shifts—a week
on the evening shift, the next week on the midnight
shift, and the following week he'd work the day shift.
Then it would start all over again with the evening
shift. This does horrible things to your body clock.
You never know if it is morning or midnight, and as
an ECKist, you wonder how you are going to work
your spiritual exercises in.

*You wonder
how you are
going to work
your spiritual
exercises in.*

This person was just stepping onto the path of
ECK at the time. He had come across *The Flute of
God* by Paul Twitchell, and he was very anxious to
start it. It meant so much to him to be able to read
it, but he had to work those strange hours and he
was always tired. In his job at a plastics factory, he
worked on the conveyer line. He had to take everything off the belt as it came through, then put it away

or box it. One day he figured out that if he worked really fast for five minutes, he could clear away all the boxes that had accumulated in the previous ten minutes. So he'd work very fast for five minutes and then take a ten-minute break during which he would read *The Flute of God.*

We make every effort because when we find the works of ECK, they are golden. They are the golden writings that strike the chords of Soul. We often say, I've heard this somewhere before. The memory is dim to the outer ears, but Soul remembers and is trying to get through the mind, trying to get through the emotions.

As we raise ourselves in the spiritual consciousness, as we go higher, we are better able to solve the problems of life. We are happier. We are more at home in every environment. So often when we first step onto the path of ECK, the problems of life have crushed us and it looks as if there's no way out. We think the rest of our life is going to be a burden, and sometimes we wonder: Is it worth the trouble?

As we raise ourselves in the spiritual consciousness, as we go higher, we are better able to solve the problems of life.

WHAT IS THE PURPOSE OF SOUL?

What is the purpose of Soul? To have the experience of life on this earth, to go through every experience, to one day become a Co-worker with God, and to have our talents used in a way we enjoy.

Recently I mentioned that someone came up to me and said, "Before I got married, I seemed to have a lot of freedom to go out and just put the ECK message out in any way I wanted to. Now my wife and children are holding me back." He really felt this way, and he was speaking honestly. I could understand his position because I had felt that way too, in the past.

But we are exactly where we belong in the

present moment, in the Soul awareness.

I told him, "At one time it bothered me too." So what I would do was to ask my daughter if she would like to help me make a poster or two. She was delighted, of course. The poster wasn't folded too straight, but we went out and hung it up anyway. You help them a little if it's too rough, because it also has to be acceptable to the people who see it, but it was a real work of art from the heart.

We would also arrange family trips to little towns nearby. We'd save our money, make plans to stay at a Motel 6, and just take a trip in the car and put up some posters while we were there. Besides putting up the posters, we would explore the town or go swimming or pick fruit off the trees—whatever we wanted to do. It's fun for everyone.

We incorporate the ECK teachings into our everyday life.

We incorporate the ECK teachings into our everyday life, but we don't make the mistake of giving up the things we've enjoyed doing before we came onto the path of ECK. We don't need to feel that somehow we are closer to God because we are now just reading ECK books.

Life is too short and too precious. Its purpose is for us to live, to enjoy our families, and to find a way to answer the nudge of Spirit that comes through and says, You're learning how to be a Co-worker; you must give out my message. There is a way we can learn to do this so that one can grow while at the same time enjoy himself and his family.

THE BLUE LIGHT SPECIAL

I'd like to tell you a story I call the Blue Light Special. We're taught about the Blue Light, and this means the Mahanta on the inner planes at the inner temple. Those of you who have been able to see this are seeing the Light of God. Over the weekend someone was telling us a story about this Light.

He was rushing to get to the ECK Center to teach an ECK Satsang class, and he arrived there late. The ECK leaders know that you arrive on time and you start on time. He felt he should explain to the people in the class why he was late, so he said, "Well, on the way down here, I was delayed because I saw the blue light and heard the sound."

He'd started out late from home, and it was so hot outside that he shut the car windows and turned on the air conditioning. He was moving down the highway, thinking about the upcoming Satsang class, and not watching the speedometer. He was making pretty good time, when all of a sudden he saw this blue light in his mirror. And, of course, he also heard the sound that comes with it.

He pulled over to the side of the road and just sat there waiting for the highway patrol officer. When the officer approached the car, the ECKist rolled down his window, and the two of them just looked at each other. The officer waited for him to say he was guilty or to explain or make excuses. Finally he said, "You were speeding." The ECKist simply said, "I know." The officer began writing, and the ECKist just knew the ticket was coming; but when he reached for it, he saw that it was only a warning.

If you plan to be somewhere, start out on time and don't rush; if you start out late, follow the natural cycle of things, and finish out that cycle.

He did have the protection, but there was also a lesson: If you plan to be somewhere, start out on time and don't rush; if you start out late, follow the natural cycle of things, and finish out that cycle. Take the things that come if there isn't a good way to get out of it. But be prepared so that you are always at peace inside yourself. Feel that you are prepared and know that the answer, or the solution, for every moment in your life is at hand as long as you are patient and look to the Sound and Light. This may come as a gentle nudge; it may come as a feeling. Listen to it.

I would like to thank you for coming. I've gotten to meet some of you here and the rest of you in the dream state or in contemplation. Sometimes you'll meet Peddar Zaskq or one of the other ECK Masters. Whenever there's a question about what or who you see in the inner, my answer is always: Go to the temple within. Go within and what do you see? Go within and what do you feel? What do you realize? The ECK is the ECK, and It will come to you in the form that is right for you.

If you see one of the ECK Masters, accept it and know that you have the highest assistance always with you.

If you see one of the ECK Masters, accept it and know that you have the highest assistance always with you. It is always there.

San Antonio Regional Seminar, San Antonio, Texas, July 18, 1982

"You want to know what I'm taking out of here?" the worker said. "I'm taking wheelbarrows."

16

THE SECRETS OF ECK

*I*n this life we are looking to learn the secret of the power of ECK, to bring It into our life. Many of us have searched for centuries, following one path or another, and looking—without success—for the source of the call of Soul.

Someone asked me, "Can you give us an answer that will appease this spiritual hunger?" The only thing that can ever take away the thirst, or hunger, for God is the Word of God, Itself, which we know as the Holy Spirit, the ECK, Divine Spirit, the cosmic Sound Current, and the Audible Life Stream. We want to bring this ECK into our life in order to live in greater harmony with ourselves.

To bring this ECK into our life is to release the God power within us.

We went on a trip to Australia, New Zealand, and the Far East a little less than a year ago, just after I got this position. After the 1981 World Wide in California, we left almost immediately. There were three of us traveling together. When we got to New Zealand, some of the ECKists asked if we would like some cheese and crackers. We said yes, thank you, and ate the cheese and crackers. By the time we got to the next stop in the southern part of New Zealand, in Dunedin, we all had colds. We weren't used to that much cheese and crackers.

The only thing that can ever take away the thirst, or hunger, for God is the Word of God, the ECK.

THE ECK PROVIDES

As we come into ECK, as this ECK power comes through us, we look to make our lives a little more creative, a little more interesting. So when we travel, to give a little bit of variety to life, we'd order ahead a different airline meal—sometimes without sugar or salt—just to see what the airline people would actually come up with.

On one particular flight, my traveling companion and I had put in our special orders. He wanted fruit and vegetables. Ours were the only special meals on that flight, and the flight attendants still got them mixed up. My companion sat at the front of the plane and I was sitting near the middle, well behind him. The meal came, and it wasn't what I ordered. But I take life as I find it; food is food, and I was hungry—so I ate it. Up in front I could see my companion having a conversation with the flight attendant. Well, it turns out it was not the food he had ordered either, but he decided not to eat his.

The stewardesses were wondering where they could find this man some apples or oranges, but there weren't any on the plane. He sent the food back and sat there hungry. If I had known he was going to send it back, I would have taken it. My whole life, whether it's been spiritual food or any other kind of food, I've always had my plate out.

It was a very short flight, and we were just going to be on the ground long enough to open the doors, bring on some mail and one or two people. No passengers were going to get off, and they were going to shut the doors and take right off again. As we were coming in for a landing, I heard something rolling down the aisle behind me from the back of the plane. I looked back, and right down the middle of the aisle, past all the passengers, came this big red apple.

As the plane landed, the apple rolled against the door to the pilot compartment and stopped. The flight attendants opened the door of the plane, and although I didn't notice what happened to the apple, I knew they did not bring any more food on board. We were on the ground just long enough to open and shut the door, then the plane taxied out to the runway and we took off.

All of a sudden, a flight attendant came out of the galley carrying a tray with nothing on it but one big red apple. She took it over to my traveling companion. He didn't know where it had come from, but he ate it and was very grateful. I wanted to jump up and say, "Do you know where that apple came from?" but I didn't want to spoil his lunch. I waited until he finished. When we landed, I said, "How did you like your apple?" He said it was just fine. And then I told him where it had come from—and he had mixed feelings. I said, "Well, I'm sure they washed it."

The point of all this is that once we learn how to tap this ECK force, It provides everything in our life. This is how the ECK works.

Once we learn how to tap this ECK force, It provides everything in our life.

HOW SPIRIT COMES INTO OUR LIFE

When I first began giving ECK talks, I struggled to give the doctrines of ECK straight out. I would go to sleep on myself with this approach, and my audience would go to sleep too. Since I wasn't the Living ECK Master then, if it got too complicated, they would say, "Oh, what was that you said?" They weren't sure if I was talking straight ECK or not. So I decided to talk about the things I knew—how ECK has worked in my life. Maybe someone else would hear one of these stories and say, "I would like to read a little bit more about this Eckankar and learn about the Sound and Light of God," to bring a little more happiness into his or her life.

The first step to bring this ECK power into our lives is to harmonize ourselves inwardly and outwardly. The way to do this is through the Tisra Til, the Spiritual Eye, which is described in *ECKANKAR—The Key to Secret Worlds*. To use this spiritual faculty, the ECKist practices the Spiritual Exercises of ECK. This spiritual faculty, the Spiritual Eye, needs exercise; it needs daily exercise. For the ECK, or Holy Spirit, to come into your life, this is one of the main secrets of ECK: to practice—faithfully and daily—these contemplative, creative exercises.

The first step to bring this ECK power into our lives is to harmonize ourselves inwardly and outwardly.

The ECK will come into our life through the back door, when we're not looking for It. We'll look for the Voice of God, this Audible Life Current, without recognizing that It is here, every moment. Then what can we do? We must open ourselves to hear the music of God. Many of you have heard It as the flute, as thunder, as the buzzing of bees, or you may hear other, different sounds of God. This ECK comes in such a subtle way that many times we do not recognize Its presence.

When I was a youngster, we used to get the Sunday paper with the comics at home, and in the paper was a magazine. I read a little humorous story in it that has stuck with me for years. It was about a factory worker in Poland. This story is an illustration of how the ECK is right here, but we're looking for It everywhere else but within.

Every day this worker would leave the factory pushing a wheelbarrow with some kind of goods on it—sometimes boxes, sometimes straw, sometimes burlap bags. The guards work with an inner faculty, and they can *feel* if someone is doing something illegal.

This particular guard knew the worker was taking something out of the factory, so every day he searched each load that this man wheeled out.

One day he said to the worker, "I know you're taking something out of this factory. I don't know what it is, but since this is my last day here, would you please tell me? I have searched every load; I have looked through all the burlap sacks and all the little boxes. Even though I haven't found anything, I know you're taking something out. I can't figure out what it is."

"You want to know what I'm taking out of here?" the worker said. "I'm taking wheelbarrows." And the guard was satisfied—this mystery which had been gnawing at him for months was finally solved.

WHAT IS THE KEY?

When I first came into ECK, I wanted to know, Where is this key to Eckankar? One of the first writings that Paul Twitchell put out was something called *The Key to ECKANKAR*. I picked up the book and wondered, *What is the key that will open me to the Sound and Light of God?*

The spiritual hunger was so great. I was looking for this secret of ECK.

After that, another book came out called *ECKANKAR—The Key to Secret Worlds*. I read through it, and again I said, What is the key? By this time, I had learned the ECK works at a mental level. I had the ability to know and remember the different spiritual concepts and precepts scattered throughout these ECK works. But I didn't know them in my heart: I had not had the realization of Soul. I thought I knew the meaning of ECK, and yet Soul said, Keep searching for that key. It's at the temple within you.

I thought I knew the meaning of ECK, and yet Soul said, Keep searching for that key.

THE HEART OF THE TEACHINGS

I had a meeting with two ladies. And when there is a consultation, generally a donation is given. To get from Spirit, we must first give. These ladies seemed to be wealthy and well-traveled; they figured if they were very smart in a businesslike way, both of them could come see me for the price of one. One of them said, "Since the donation you request for the time is so much, we would like to use half for myself and half for her. How about that?" I said it would be all right.

To get from Spirit, we must first give.

They came in, and I could tell they really wanted to check me out: Does this guy really have the key to Spirit? They chattered and seemed very open socially, and yet they kept looking at me very carefully. I was greatly amused by this.

One of the ladies began to talk about the high principles of ECK as she knew them mentally, the same way I had once known them mentally, before I found the heart of the ECK teachings. She said, "I would like your opinion on this: The ECK really is the isness, isn't It?" And I said, "Yes, yes, ECK is the isness." She said, "Well, it's also seeing, knowing, and being, isn't it?" I said, "Yes, it's seeing, knowing, and being." And they continued to study me very carefully. I didn't know if I was dressed properly for a spiritual master; I hadn't bothered to wear a tie or jacket—just an ordinary sport shirt.

After a while one of the women became very quiet. Whatever the ECK was bringing to her was between the Inner Master and herself. I could see a change happening before my eyes, but her gabby friend never noticed. She kept chattering about isness and business, because they'd made a good deal: two for the price of one.

The woman who grew quiet was learning surrender to the Inner Master. It happened before my eyes; I could see it. I don't mean surrender to the physical self but to the Inner Master. I want to mention this again and again—there is no worship of the ECK Masters nor of the Living ECK Master. To have the attitude of worship toward any other being is to put one's self in spiritual slavery. My job is to lift you out of the bondage and into spiritual liberation.

By the time the meeting was over, it turned out that Spirit had given full value to one of the women; they didn't get a two-for-one special. One woman went away very quiet—she had met with something sacred and beautiful at the inner temple—and the other one left still chatting about this isness business.

To have the attitude of worship toward any other being is to put one's self in spiritual slavery.

LIVING IN THE PRESENCE OF GOD

We are all grateful for the writings that Paul Twitchell put out on Eckankar. All that the books can do is feed the mind, which is a step. It's a start. I like to read *The Shariyat-Ki-Sugmad* even today and spend a little time with *Stranger by the River*. It's a wonderful book of the dialogue between the great ECK Master Rebazar Tarzs as he's giving the spiritual works to Paul Twitchell back when Paul was just getting on the path, learning the beginning steps to mastership.

I had mentioned before that we must bring harmony into our lives, both inwardly and outwardly. To grow in Spirit, we must give up the old for the new. Soul is a complete entity. Before anything new can come in, we must give up something. If we are imprisoned by fear or doubts, this prevents us from giving up that little self to the Inner Master, the

Mahanta. And finally, as your faith in ECK is, so be
It unto you.

We must do the spiritual exercises with love for
God. It is not enough to sing the holy names of God
or do the sacred prayer song by rote, methodically or
without feeling. When the ECK comes into your
life—and many of you at times find the secret of the
power, the secret of the cosmic force working in your
life—It is working during those magical moments of
a day when no matter what you touch, it turns out
right. Everything you do seems to have the blessing
of God upon it. It's a day when you can't do anything
wrong; everything is right and you are aware of this.
This is living in the presence of God.

As ECKists, we want to learn the key, the secret
of this cosmic power, so that we can enter into harmony with all life and do it at will. When any situation, any obstacle, comes up in our life, we can chant
a name of God—HU, Sugmad, or your personal word—
and turn a negative situation into the spiritual. You
have this key. You must learn to work with it. You
must use the creative faculty within you.

*You must use
the creative
faculty within
you.*

OPENING THE DOOR OF SOUL

I experimented a lot with the Spiritual Exercises
of ECK. I was an adventurer, a traveler. I would do
a spiritual exercise the way it was described in the
ECK discourse, and if it didn't work after two weeks,
I'd do it a little bit differently. I wouldn't push against
the doors of Soul. Gradually, the awareness began to
open, first at one level of consciousness and then
another.

Sometimes you will find yourself working on the
inner planes in settings very much as we find here
at an ECK seminar. Maybe you are acting as an

usher, working in the higher worlds, carrying out some act of service to the ECK out of love for that Sound and Light of God which has filled you.

Another type of inner experience is completely different. It does not involve great adventures of the action kind. Rather, it's when you come into direct contact with the Sound and Light of God. This is direct communication with God.

The secret to this ECK power in your own life, to bring you what you must have for your spiritual unfoldment at that moment, or whatever Divine Spirit sees must be brought to you, will come. It happens very much like the apple coming down the aisle. My traveling companion was open to this cosmic power, the ECK; and because he was, It gave according to that which he had earned.

The gift from the ECK is an enjoyment of life—not running or hiding from it.

Enjoy yourself. The gift from the ECK is an enjoyment of life—not running or hiding from it, but living a life of responsibility to Sugmad, so that everything we do is done in the name of the Sugmad, the ECK, and the Mahanta.

Eckankar European Seminar, Amsterdam, The Netherlands, Friday, July 30, 1982

There's a lot we can do by talking with the children, telling them the stories of the ECK Masters in a very simple way.

17

QUESTIONS
AND ANSWERS

I'd like to answer some questions tonight. I figure with about sixteen hundred of us here, there ought to be at least somebody with a question. If not, then I'll just sit here.

Someone asked me just a few minutes ago, "Do you ever get nervous when you come out onstage?" Yes, sometimes. Even though I have an idea of what to say about the God Worlds of ECK, or Spirit, or the heavens that are hinted at in the Christian Bible, I'm not always sure how Spirit is going to bring the message, how It is going to say it. It may decide that I'll just come out here and there won't be a single word to be said. I'll just sit here for half an hour and look at you, and you'll look at me. At the end of that time, we'll wave to each other and leave.

ONE-ON-ONE

Before we start any questions tonight, I'd like to mention that the path of ECK is real, and the God Force, or Holy Spirit, really does work. It's not important whether It works in an organization, but whether It works in your life as an individual. The

The path of ECK is real, and the God Force, or Holy Spirit, really does work.

229

Living ECK Master is concerned with Soul—you as
the individual. Unlike some people who bring out
what they feel is the word of God and address themselves to the flock, we work with you, one-on-one,
through the inner planes, through the inner channels.

As you get more of this Sound and Light into your
life, there will be changes. I wrote the book *The Wind
of Change*, which is a testimony to the power of Spirit
working in everyday life. There may be more dramatic experiences of the Light and the Sound, but
the ECKists today are having greater experiences
than the mystics and saints of many of the religions.
A few of the religious leaders had these experiences,
but many ECKists today are having the same ones.

As you get more of this Sound and Light into your life, there will be changes.

Freedom for Soul

As these changes come, there will be one last
struggle before you're ready for the next stage of
unfoldment, to be lifted higher in the spiritual worlds.
Every obstacle will come up in front of you to try to
stop you from making that step.

There was a time in my own life when I had made
the decision to leave the Christian religion, because
I found life in the path of Eckankar. I knew that I
now had to go forward and listen to this Sound and
look at this Light in the presence of the Inner Master.
This brought a great reaction from my family and
friends who had never heard of Eckankar before. I
hadn't either, but I knew. When I made this decision
I was low on money, which seems to have been an
ongoing pattern in my life. Before each major change
in my spiritual unfoldment, a lack of money or the
desire for change would turn up.

To hold on to me, people with a certain background offered me a job as an insurance agent for

a Christian religion. ECKists make their living as insurance agents, as doctors, or in any other honorable profession. I thought it was interesting that there was an insurance organization affiliated with this particular religion. I thought to myself, *Don't they have any insurance in heaven?*

I had just canceled my insurance policy with them and got my premium back, which I was going to use to travel to another part of the United States where I could have my own life in ECK. Even though I gave up my insurance with them, they offered me a job. I went through with the interview but said, "No, thank you very much. It's a good profession, but I have another offer in the works, something else cooking in the pot." I had nothing, but I wasn't going to tell anybody.

Around that same time, I was hunting for an apartment. The first place I looked at was just perfect. If I had gotten that apartment, I probably would have stayed there for another six months or a year. But on that cold winter night, just as I got to the door, two other people came along hoping to rent the apartment. They were two young girls who were just beginning their business life; they wanted to room together, and this was a perfect apartment for them, as it was for me. The difference was, I had the deposit with me in cash and they didn't.

We all went inside with the landlady to view the apartment, and seeing how much they wanted it, I finally said, "OK, tell you what. If you want it, go back and get your money. I'll wait until you come back, and if no one rents it before then, it's yours." They got the money and returned, so I was out of an apartment.

I ended up staying in a house with a college friend of mine who was working for a social welfare

I said, "I have another offer in the works, something else cooking in the pot."

program. I helped him teach ex-convicts how to become responsible citizens so they wouldn't end up back in prison in another month or two. We had pickpockets and all kinds of interesting individuals in there, but I was perfectly safe there too.

Eventually one of the people with the religion I came from offered me an apartment. "It's just right for you," she said. It was in the same building as a friend of hers who would have made a monthly, weekly, and daily report on me. I wondered, *Where's the freedom for Soul?* The price was rock-bottom, everything about it was good, and I left, because Soul wants that freedom. A change in my life was coming, and the negative power put up every inducement for me to stay at that same level of consciousness. But I left—and it was hard. I'm not saying to leave your families; none of that is necessary. You get your change in your own way.

> A change in my life was coming, and the negative power put up every induce-ment for me to stay at that same level of consciousness.

I mentioned this to a lady who later became a Higher Initiate, which is someone who has reached Self-Realization. She just thought about it. I said, "In my life, I needed to move to express the change that was happening within myself." Later, when she got her higher state of awareness, she said, "Well, I never moved," and I said, "You didn't have to"—and she didn't. Most of us don't have to.

If you have any questions, we'll just hand the mike back to you so that everyone can hear.

SEX AND ECKANKAR

Q: Please, Harold, I would like to know the connection between sex and Eckankar.

HK: Well, that's an easy question!

You said *sex*, right? S-e-x? This is not to avoid the subject, but I was dictating an article the other day to be transcribed by a secretary back at the ECK office. I was talking about Eckankar and different religious sects, but I didn't say "religious." I said, "Eckankar and sects—that's spelled s-e-c-t-s." Just so we're talking about the same subject.

Many people look for Soul mates. At one time I did too. We've read in *The Tiger's Fang* about the positive and negative coming together, but it's the positive and negative within ourselves coming together. The loving relationship between a man and a woman can be—I won't say it always is—the highest and one of the most beautiful expressions of human love. By itself it won't lead you to states of consciousness beyond the Astral or the Mental worlds. The act of love itself won't lead you into the spiritual planes.

We're not a group that endorses sex for spiritual unfoldment, because it won't do it. But it's very good in a family for balance, and it's a form of communication. A truly loving relationship between a couple will be open and straightforward, without any guilt or shame, if everything is right between you and your mate. But as a form of lower communication, many things are done with the act of love which are actually a misuse of the psychic power, or black magic. Maybe the wife will say, "Well, if you won't respect my opinion or buy me that furniture, then it's going to be another week before we make love." This is a misuse, and it's done very often, frankly speaking.

Human love can be a high expression; the saying is, If you are not able to love your loved ones, how can you love God? The dirt and the guilt that has been put upon this act has been done by the priestcraft and the religions for control of their members, and this guilt has been instilled in us deeply over the centuries. In some religious organizations, it's a control factor. In New York a couple of weeks ago,

A truly loving relationship between a couple will be open and straightforward, without any guilt or shame.

two thousand individuals were married in one ceremony. But part of the marriage ceremony by this sect decreed that the couples have no relationship to express the unity of their marriage, that they have no relations for forty days. This is a control.

FINDING A BALANCE

It can be a beautiful expression between a man and woman. And it's your own business, your private business, of no concern to anyone else. It can be very good for balance too. There is nothing wrong with the act of making love, because this is part of the physical body. When we indulge in anything and overdo it, whether it's eating or drinking or making love or anything else, then we fall into lust. We have to find out what's right for us—something that doesn't pull us down to the common level of the animal.

When we indulge in anything and overdo it, then we fall into lust.

This relationship must be one of responsibility. It is not to be done lightly. The ECK Masters advocate virginity until marriage, but I am not going to come into your private life in any way or say that however you express your personal relationship is right or wrong. I won't do that, because you must know what is right for you as a couple.

ECK AND DRUGS DON'T MIX

Q: When one leaves the body by raising the consciousness, I believe it has a certain effect on the pituitary gland. When people take drugs does this do something similar? Could you tell me exactly what the physiological reaction is?

HK: Drugs and ECK do not mix, and the reaction on the body varies. People open themselves a little bit, with drugs, to the lower Astral Plane. Sometimes this happens before they come to ECK. Then when they step onto the path, they may give up drugs. But the drugs stick with you. Sometimes it takes years to work out.

You'll have a relapse of your drug experience. Some are good trips, some are not. If the person steps onto the path of ECK with this drug still in him, and there's a reaction where he runs into problems and becomes emotionally unbalanced, he'll write a letter to me and say, "What is wrong with ECK?"

There's nothing wrong with ECK. When the pure positive God Force comes in contact with that lower negative force, which is used merely to enslave the mind, there is a spark just like an electrical cord that shorts out.

VIOLATION OF THE SPIRITUAL LAW

People have been known to try to give someone the enlightenment at parties by putting some kind of drug in their drinks. This is a severe violation of spiritual law. The person could sometimes be driven to suicide or any degree of depravity. The one who gave that drug to the unsuspecting individual becomes responsible for that karma and must walk with that individual for however many lives it takes until that person is freed from the bondage of this drug experience. It's a long-term debt.

It's like a boomerang: For a while it flies out there and it goes high—and it might even do that for a number of years—but the law of life is that it must come back, and it will.

I feel very sad when I get a letter from someone who is being purified. As the ECK purifies Itself, the life of that individual goes through absolute hell. He'll blame ECK, but I have to stand back

When the pure positive God Force comes in contact with that lower negative force, there is a spark just like an electrical cord that shorts out.

and suggest he see a psychiatrist and get medical help. He has to dry out, in a way, and there's nothing I can do for him.

Drugs open you to entities that take control, and this is why violence has increased. Countries have karma with each other. The Romans went into lands that practiced the inner teachings and also drugs, and this is what destroyed the Roman Empire. This is what's undermining the United States today. The free use of drugs that are not prescribed by a medical doctor has infiltrated our law enforcement and judicial branches in the middle management area.

It has undermined our music. Rock is dead. They're trying to revive it; it was a child of the drug age and a product of the misuse of alcohol. It's interesting that when country singers would do their road tours, they kept themselves going on uppers and downers. It's reflected to a certain degree in country music. It's lower Astral. I used to love country music until I came farther along in ECK. Some of the classics are beautiful. But today we need something like the music of ECK. We're already seeing a change in the music in the world. There is a definite need for leadership in this area of music because of the healing it can bring to the spiritual bodies of man.

Now I know I took a long time to answer that question. You do go out of the body with drugs, but never very far. The natural way to leave the body is the way we do it in Eckankar, working with Soul. This is what Socrates spoke about—the releasing of Soul from the bondage of the physical body. He knew it then. In the tradition of the ECK Masters, this was the foundation of the teachings of Socrates and other great teachers of the past.

The natural way to leave the body is the way we do it in Eckankar, working with Soul. This is what Socrates spoke about— the releasing of Soul from the bondage of the physical body.

TEACHING SMALL CHILDREN ABOUT ECK

Q: Harold, how can we best teach our small children about ECK?

IIK: There are a number of ways to do it. We're developing the ECK culture. The small children enjoy some of the books we print for them. You can also chant *HU* or one of the names of God with your children. If they're a little older, you can read them a page or two at night from one of the books. They might like one of the adventure stories such as *The Drums of ECK*. You can also go to a library and get something colorful such as the "Tintin" series of books.

Explain the ECK principles that you find happening in the story, as you see them. You can talk about the principle of cause and effect, karma: The bad guy did this, and see what happened to him? If a character puts out a positive thought in the story, you can point out to the child how this thought was important to lead the character through the obstacles until he finally reached his goal.

As initiates, there's a lot we can do by talking with the children, telling them the stories of the ECK Masters in a very simple way. A small child of four might sit still for three sentences. That's enough. When they get to be six, maybe condense one of the ECK stories to two minutes. They'll find it helpful.

The duty of a parent is to show the child how to follow the path of ECK and to make his own way in this life. Because we're on the path of ECK, we do not allow our children to run undisciplined. In a restaurant you sometimes see a child seated behind you busily splashing his soup all over you, while the parents very proudly say, "Isn't he free?" We have to teach freedom with responsibility.

The duty of a parent is to show the child how to follow the path of ECK and to make his own way in this life.

Practicing Detachment

Q: Harold, which is the best exercise for practicing detachment in every situation in life, including very strange situations?

HK: Are you working with the Spiritual Exercises of ECK? Then use the ones that you find in the ECK discourse at the particular time the situation comes up. There are many exercises. It is important that you do the spiritual exercises and chant the name of God, your personal word.

There is the stream of consciousness from the mind that constantly goes through you, and chanting the word keeps this stream of consciousness pure. People who stop chanting or stop the spiritual exercises all of a sudden fall into depression and negativity, and they don't know why. It happens because that stream of consciousness, the play of the mind, has become polluted. The singing of this sacred prayer song or the name of God purifies the thoughts which lead to your actions. It makes for a happier, more harmonious life. You'll find the upliftment comes gradually as you are ready for it. But you will be uplifted.

The singing of this sacred prayer song or the name of God purifies the thoughts which lead to your actions.

Entering the Inner Temple

Q: What is the inner temple and how is it possible to gradually enter into it?

HK: The inner temple is that sacred place where Soul has communication with God, with the Sound and Light of God. This comes through the Spiritual Exercises of ECK. You may see the Light of God first in your Spiritual Eye; you may see It as a Blue Light or as a Blue Star, or as a globe of light—just a blob of light. This means that you have contact with this highest state of consciousness that is available. It can uplift you to that very same state, too, but not overnight—the shock would be too great.

After you see the Light in the Spiritual Eye or feel It in your heart center, then comes the Sound. The Sound may come first at times. The Sound may be that of the flute of God which comes from the Soul Plane, or you may hear the buzzing of bees or any number of different sounds. Later, as you move higher, it may be a very high peeping sound, a single peep, so high that it feels as if you can barely reach it. It's the Voice of God uplifting you.

YOUR KEY TO THE SPIRITUAL WORLDS

In the dream state you may see one of the ECK Masters coming to you; it may be Wah Z or Rebazar Tarzs or Peddar Zaskq. The presence of the Inner Master is both the Light and Sound, but you must be careful. The negative power can disguise itself with the face of the Inner Master, so you must test it.

You test it by singing the word of God, your personal word; or when you awaken, if the feeling of the visit from this Master leaves you with goodwill, love, and harmony, it was an ECK Master. If you test it using your personal word and you wake up feeling wrong, unsettled, and upset, it was the negative power in disguise to test you, to see if you would use your key to the spiritual worlds. The key, the word, will help you to see through the illusions. It will help you make spiritual decisions.

The key, the word, will help you to see through the illusions. It will help you make spiritual decisions.

Rebazar Tarzs, the great ECK Master, said to Paul Twitchell when Paul was beginning with the works of ECK: "As the Inner Master, that greater part of yourself, I am always with you; but are you always conscious that I am always with you?"

This is the challenge for you—to be creative with

*Know that the
presence of the
Master is
always with
you.*

your spiritual exercises, to try something new. If what you're trying doesn't work, try something new. Don't be frantic, don't push. Know that the presence of the Master is always with you.

The protection is there. All you have to do is remember to ask for help by singing the name of God or calling upon one of the ECK Masters.

In Spirit I am always with you.

*Eckankar European Seminar, Amsterdam,
The Netherlands, Saturday, July 31, 1982*

Why did we sit fogged in at the airport for five hours before we put our attention on the ECK?

18

The Practical Wisdom of ECK

*T*he practical wisdom of ECK is to open yourself to this Divine Spirit that comes down through the God Worlds of ECK, through all the different planes.

The ECK is here, and the Master's presence is always with you. The self-discipline comes in remembering to call upon this help. When an obstacle comes up, we so often forget and handle the daily situations the way we used to before we came into ECK—sometimes with anger, sometimes with fear, sometimes we just avoid it and shut our eyes.

Bringing Mastership into Our Life

As we walk on this path, we ought to be able to bring a degree of mastership into our own life. Whether it's in matters of health or wealth or anything else, begin using the spiritual principles that are given in *The Flute of God*, such as the Law of Attitudes and the Law of Harmony. Begin to use these.

There's a Higher Initiate who has traveled the world over for Eckankar. A number of years ago she went to Washington State with another lady for a training session on leadership in ECK. As they left

> As we walk on this path, we ought to be able to bring a degree of mastership into our own life.

243

to return home, fog came in and closed down the airport. They sat in the plane and waited and waited; five hours later they still hadn't taken off. Finally the lady with her began to crochet, and pretty soon this Higher Initiate said, "I'm going to read *The Shariyat-Ki-Sugmad.*"

Her companion asked, "Would you read it out loud while I crochet?" So she began to read from these sacred scriptures of Eckankar. Within three minutes the clouds parted, the sun broke through, and the pilot of the plane announced that due to a break in the weather, they were cleared to take off.

As soon as they took off, the weather behind them closed in again.

This Higher Initiate was talking about this last week, just before we came on this trip. She said, "Why did we sit there for five hours before we put our attention on the ECK?" I don't know why.

We were talking in the warehouse of the ECK office, when another ECKist came over. She just caught the last part of our conversation, about remembering to put your attention on the ECK when any problem or any danger threatens.

She said she had taken a vacation a few weeks earlier up to Wisconsin, which happens to be the state where I was raised. Rain was coming down steadily as she drove along with her brother and a friend. All of a sudden, right in front of her, she saw a tire that had fallen off someone's camper. She swung the wheel abruptly and swerved to the side to avoid this tire in the middle of the highway, but this caused the car to go into a skid. She went all over the road as she fought with the steering wheel to try to regain control, but it looked as though they were going over the side.

Then, at the last minute, she remembered to chant HU.

Then, at the last minute, she remembered to chant *HU*. She started to chant *HU-U-U-U*, and just like that, the car straightened itself out and headed smoothly down the highway. She said she must have spent several seconds fighting that wheel before she remembered to chant *HU*.

This ECK power will work in your life. It will work at the office, in your family, in traffic. It will give protection that you can tap into, if you will just remember to. This remembrance must be almost instantaneous—to become aware of the presence of the Master. I spoke about this last night: how Rebazar Tarzs said to Paul Twitchell, "I am always with you, but are you always conscious of my presence?"

SHINING THE LIGHT OF SOUL ON FEAR

As we bring ourselves close to this ECK, to this Spirit which sustains and supports all life—which we know from our previous backgrounds as the Holy Spirit, the Holy Ghost, the Comforter, Nam, and the Audible Life Current—we can become the master of our own ship, the captain of our destiny. And with this assurance that is with us, the fear and the dread and the loneliness begin to go away.

We can become the master of our own ship, the captain of our destiny.

THE POWER THAT FEAR CAN HAVE

I am going to keep it short, but I'd like to mention a final thing about fear and what power it has. On the plane from England to Amsterdam, we got to talking with a lady from the States. She said she loved to go camping and that she would park in the back of the campground where there were no people, where it was very quiet. She loved the peace and harmony that this contact with nature brought her. So on one camping trip, she took her two little dogs and parked way in the back.

After building a little campfire, she heated her food, and she and her little dogs ate their dinner. That night she slept out under the stars; she said she didn't even use a tent. Everything was quiet and peaceful, and as she fell asleep she could hear a brook babbling. It sounded like people talking, and it gave her company.

In the middle of the night, she was startled awake by what sounded like loud, heavy footsteps pounding through the forest where she was camped. She became absolutely terrified. The footsteps came closer and closer, making loud sounds of rustling leaves. She quickly grabbed her two little dogs to prevent them from going out and attacking this monster or doing some other foolish thing. She gathered both dogs in one arm, reached over and got her flashlight—and it was like the Light of ECK: If you can shine It into the unknown, sometimes just turning on the Light of Soul gives you enough information to take away the fear.

The insight from the ECK takes away ignorance, and with it, fear.

She shone the light in the direction of these giant footsteps, and the Light caught two flashing eyes, staring right at her. What she saw was a little field mouse walking through the dry leaves.

The insight from the ECK takes away ignorance, and with it, fear. Once these are taken from our life, then we enter into the freedom of Soul. We come to the states of being: wisdom, power, and freedom.

Eckankar European Seminar, Amsterdam, The Netherlands, Sunday, August 1, 1982

Along the side of the road I happened to see a big lighted billboard, and the message on it gave the answer I was looking for.

19
ECK
Consciousness Five

"ECK Consciousness Five" refers to the spiritual consciousness of the Fifth Plane. Paul Twitchell has said that this event is of great importance to the movement of Eckankar.

This event of Consciousness Five is the Self-Realization that occurs within each individual. We may fight and struggle against the tide of God, but someday the law of life will bring us to the high states of spiritual consciousness. It is the spiritual heritage of Soul.

Consciousness Five is the Self-Realization that occurs within each individual.

THE ECK SPIRITUAL AIDE PROGRAM

We now have what is called the ECK Spiritual Aide program. These are Higher Initiates in ECK who serve as vehicles for Spirit and listening posts for people who want someone to listen to their spiritual problems. The ECK Spiritual Aides can be reached through the Higher Initiates in your area.

There is a special flow of Spirit that occurs during the Spiritual Aide session. One of the ECK Spiritual Aides told of how, from his viewpoint, he saw the ECK give answers to a person who came with questions. The woman began to speak of all the troubles in her life while the ECK Spiritual Aide sat there quietly, just listening. As she talked, she began to answer her own questions. She'd ask another question and then give another answer. All of a sudden she noticed how the ECK was giving her the answers. Through the vehicle of the ECK Spiritual Aide, she was able to get her own answers from within.

THE SPIRITUAL HERITAGE OF SOUL

The whole point to the works of ECK is to lead Soul to the temple within you.

We first reach the state of self-knowledge, which we call Self-Realization. As we reach this Consciousness Five, we find that the wisdom of God comes into our life.

As we reach this Consciousness Five, we find that the wisdom of God comes into our life.

I have gotten answers in many ways. One particular time, I wanted to know how to get to a certain store, so I stopped to ask for directions. I went into a little shop to ask the man where to find the other store, but first I asked Spirit to give me the answer, for It will work in the smallest details of our everyday life. There was a customer in line ahead of me, and it just so happened that he asked about the same store I was looking for. In this instance, I found the location where I wished to go without any effort.

The question then is: How do I open myself to Spirit? We do this through the Spiritual Exercises of ECK and by chanting the sacred name of God.

Another time, while driving late at night, I was wondering how to bring the ECK message to all the people who wished news of Spirit. Along the side of the road I happened to see a big lighted billboard, a sign with a commercial message for a film company, and the message on it gave me the answer I was looking for. The front part of the message said, "Trust your stories to . . ."

Paul Twitchell wrote so many words on Eckankar that it could take lifetimes for Soul to learn all the lessons hidden in the writings. I like to work with stories that will show how to live ECK every day. The way to heaven lies in doing our daily duty and looking to the Mahanta.

SURRENDER TO GOD

During the training I received to take over the position of Living ECK Master, I was put through many disciplines by the ECK Masters. Many times I did not understand the reason for something, but each time I did as well as I could. At one point I was asked to do a particular job. I put my whole heart into doing it the best way that I could and was very proud of what I had accomplished.

Several hours later someone said, "We don't need that work." It was a test to see how attached I was to the fruits of my labor, whether I would say, "I have spent so much time on this; you must use this work." Instead, I took the work outside and threw it into the refuse bin, saying to myself, "The past is past," and I went about my work.

An hour later someone said, "Where is that work? We can use it." So I ran outside and climbed into this great big garbage bin and began searching for the work I had thrown away. Brushing the dirt off the papers, I was relieved to find that it was still OK.

The Master will give us duties and tests as the Inner Master. It is to teach us surrender to God. The Master does not want our money or possessions, but in attitude we give these possessions to the Mahanta. We remain the guardians and keepers

The way to heaven lies in doing our daily duty and looking to the Mahanta.

of our property, yet we use it wisely to benefit all life. With this attitude we are living the karmaless life, for all we have and all we do are in the name of the Mahanta. Our love for the Inner Master grows so strong that no evil force can harm us.

Our love for the Inner Master grows so strong that no evil force can harm us.

The Protection of the ECK

After the European Seminar last weekend in Amsterdam, someone told me how he had received the protection of the ECK. Not only did this protection surround him, but it also protected his family who were not ECKists. This protection involved the family car.

The ECKist and his wife had used this car to carry the ECK message to all parts of France. They often drove very fast at highway speeds, and the car always transported them faithfully. One day as his wife drove the car very slowly, she heard what sounded like a metal part fall from it. Unconcerned, she just kept driving and didn't even bother to mention it to her husband. She parked the car by the house, and later when her husband started to take it for a ride, he noticed that the steering wheel wouldn't turn. He got out to see what was wrong and found that one of the front wheels had broken loose! The ECKist said, "The ECK gave protection to my family too," and he wondered why. I told him, "Because you are carriers of the ECK message."

There is a great force of black magic in your country. I get your letters about this. For protection, you must put the image of the Inner Master at your Spiritual Eye and love the ECK with all your heart. Then go about your business with the assurance that the Mahanta never sleeps.

For protection, it is helpful to declare oneself a

vehicle for Spirit. This can be done every morning. Either quietly or aloud, we can say, "I declare myself a vehicle for the Sugmad, the ECK, and the Mahanta."

In some small way I would like to bring the power of ECK into your daily life. As your spiritual vision grows, you will see the greater power and you will rise in states of consciousness to reach Consciousness Five and go far beyond.

Look always to the inner, to the window of Soul. There you will find the Master within you. You may see Rebazar Tarzs or Wah Z or any one of the other ECK Masters.

To see one of the spiritual travelers is the greatest blessing in one's life.

Look always to the inner, to the window of Soul.

African Seminar, Lomé, Togo,
Friday, August 6, 1982

Anyone who can balance a basket like that would be a good ECKist.

20
CONSCIOUSNESS FIVE

There are some of you who are new to ECK and have just stepped from the Christian religion. Today, someone who was new to the ECK teachings wondered how Eckankar could fit in her life with her Christian religion. I will speak in a general way so that her identity is kept private.

FOLLOWING TWO PATHS

She wondered how to regard the idea of following two paths at the same time. The principle from the Christian Bible, which is also a spiritual principle, is: No man can follow two masters. This is true whether we look to the Catholic and Protestant religions at the same time, or to Eckankar and Christianity.

She felt it was not right for her to follow Christianity and Eckankar at the same time. When she spoke of Eckankar to her Christian family, the family became very upset. She did not feel ready to drop the Christian religion and take up Eckankar, and she asked what would be the right thing to do. The ECK does not separate families, and so I advised her to follow Christianity until she felt strong enough to embrace the path of ECK.

The first two years of Eckankar are for the purpose

of allowing the individual to look into the works to decide whether these are for him or not. The ECK Masters do not give the ECK initiation the moment a person expresses interest. During the first two years, the Inner Master or one of the ECK Masters will begin working with you. At the end of two years, the individual ought to have a good idea of whether or not he is ready for this direct path to God. If he is not ready, he is free to follow the path of his choice, whether it is Christianity or any other path.

The Outer and Inner Master

I spoke this morning about the Outer and Inner Master. In the teachings on the physical plane, we often encounter one type of teacher or another. It may be a minister or a priest, but his teachings are only from a written book. There are others who come to a teaching that follows an ascended master, and although this master may have power on the inner planes, the seeker of truth is looking for both the Outer and Inner Master in one being. And there is no one who can decide who your master is except you.

Very often the Inner Master will work with one in the dream state.

Very often the Inner Master will work with one in the dream state. This is a gentler way for Spirit to work with an individual who is opening himself for more of the Sound and Light of Spirit.

I received a letter from an ECKist who has had some success with the dream state and Soul Travel. He writes: "Lately the Soul Travel experiences have been more pronounced than they were in the past, especially in the dream state, in that twilight state just before sleep, or just before awakening in the physical." He has made an interesting observation: We are most aware of the inner worlds just before going into a deep sleep or before awakening.

He goes on to say, "In the past few dreams, I've been traveling around and have noticed that I seem to know everybody, and vice versa. I don't mean that I know them in the physical, because I don't, but we all seem to be old friends in the dream state. This shows me that I am indeed working on all levels all the time, only that the dream states open my attention to levels I wouldn't normally focus upon while working in the physical. I am becoming more aware of my involvement in these different areas and perhaps I'm helping the good of the whole in some way."

When someone says he cannot remember his dream travels and his experiences with the Light and Sound of ECK, I like to point out to him: Do you know that you are working in the inner planes as a vehicle for Sugmad? One may not remember his dreams yet still be serving in the other worlds.

My wife was saying before this trip that she had doubted the existence of some of the ECK Masters. She did not know of Towart Managi, and who could prove to her that Lai Tsi had been an ancient Chinese Master? The ones who could prove it to her were these ECK Masters—and they came to her in the dream state and gave proof. The question here is: If they were ECK Masters, what good does that do for her spiritual life? The duty of the ECK Masters, and especially the Living ECK Master, is to link Soul with the spiritual force.

Someone asked me this afternoon how he could learn to Soul Travel. Not everyone learns this aspect of Eckankar, because it is not necessary. Soul Travel works in the worlds of time and space. This includes the Astral, the Causal, the Mental, and the Etheric Planes. But when Soul reaches the state of Consciousness Five, It no longer lives, spiritually, in the worlds of time and space; It now exists with seeing,

The duty of the ECK Masters, and especially the Living ECK Master, is to link Soul with the spiritual force.

knowing, and being. While we are still living in this world, we can begin to work with the ECK and develop the creative power to meet our daily life. We begin to take responsibility for the conditions of our own life. We know that the troubles and sorrows of today were of our own making yesterday.

The Living ECK Master can help one break the karma of the past through the dream state.

The Living ECK Master can help one break the karma of the past through the dream state.

HELP FROM SPIRIT

Those individuals who give of themselves as carriers of the seed of ECK often find help from Spirit. Two ECKists, a young couple, left America and returned to France, but they did not know where they would stay because they had very little money. It just so happened that the gentleman's aunt owned a house. She offered to let them stay there for very little rent, and in the meantime she spent many thousands of francs remodeling this home. "I don't know why I'm doing this," she told them.

The ECK was preparing a home for them. The aunt had a serious illness, and shortly after they moved in, she translated from the physical body. Because they were vehicles for the ECK, the ECK let the aunt leave the physical body without great suffering. And as the woman observed, "It seems that the ECK benefits my family even though they are not ECKists." The rest of the family decided that this young couple could continue to rent the home at the same low rent that they had been paying before.

Someone told me this afternoon about the first time he read a book about the ECK Masters. The ECK Masters are leading him, in time, to that state of Consciousness Five. He works on a boat, and he took this book, given to him by a friend, aboard and read it before bedtime. After a while he put it aside and turned out the light. During the night he felt a great heat and jumped out of his bunk, afraid that the ship was on fire. But looking around the boat he saw there was no fire. The same thing happened a few nights later. I mentioned to him, "This is good, because it shows the power of the ECK, that ECK is real. It also shows that you are unfolding in your consciousness to have recognition of Its power."

I would like to mention one last instance of an ECKist who served as a vehicle for Spirit. When this ECK flows in, we must find a way to give It out. This was an ECKist who again had little money and was required to move out of his place. A mother and daughter of a branch of his family were going on a long vacation. They invited him to stay at their home without paying rent if he would help with the chores and take care of a sick dog that was a family friend.

This dog had been in the family for years and had lately become so sick that it could not walk. The woman had come to me and asked what she should do with the dog, and I suggested she see a doctor to put it to sleep. She said, "Oh, I could never do that," and I didn't say any more about the matter. Yet the dog was suffering, and it was Soul too. It had been ready to shed its physical body for many months. So during the time that this ECKist stayed in that home, a period of less than a month, in the middle of one afternoon the dog simply translated, or died, very quietly.

As we are vehicles for Spirit, it is done in such a quiet way that our neighbors never notice. You may find that your neighbors come to you to talk about their troubles without ever knowing that you are a member of Eckankar. Yet, you are serving as Its

As we are vehicles for Spirit, it is done in such a quiet way that our neighbors never notice.

vehicle by the mere act of listening to their troubles and turning them over to Spirit.

IN THE NEARNESS OF YOUR HEART

I have enjoyed this weekend and the opportunity to meet with many of you. The time is near an end, and we must soon leave, but we can be together in the nearness of your heart. If you wish to meet, go to that sacred temple within your heart. There you will find the ECK Master who can uplift you and break the bondage. This will lead to spiritual liberation.

There you will find the ECK Master who can uplift you and break the bondage. This will lead to spiritual liberation.

There are many things in your country which are as strange to us as things in our country would be to you. What I really like are the women who carry baskets on their heads, loaded with all kinds of things, and manage to keep a very good balance. Anyone who can balance a basket like that would be a good ECKist. I know that many of you can do it.

I would like to thank you for carrying the ECK message to your friends and neighbors. There is much work for all of us to do to carry the divine words to every part of our community.

I was able to visit the children's room for a short time this afternoon. Many of the children have great artistic talents. The children have clear vision, and when I asked how many of them had seen the Light or heard the Sound, several of them raised their hand. I saw among them many friends who travel on the inner planes.

Thank you for your devotion to Spirit. May the blessings be.

African Seminar, Lomé, Togo,
Saturday, August 7, 1982

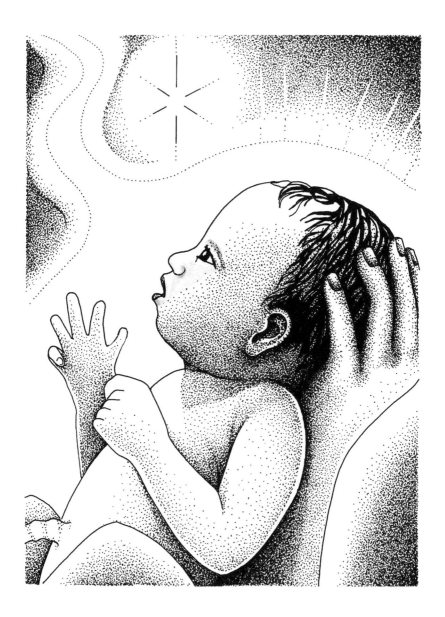

The breath of life is the ECK, or Spirit, coming into the body, and this is when Soul enters the temple of the baby.

21
THE BREATH OF LIFE

*I*n Eckankar we are concerned with the difference between the human state of consciousness and the God Consciousness. This is what we are looking toward.

First of all, to be in the human state of consciousness generally means a person is unhappy, nothing works right—they're not sure Soul goes beyond the body. In short, one's life is that of a slave. You're not quite sure where to look for the next step, or if indeed there is another step.

The person who has, through personal effort and discipline, worked into the higher states of realization—the spiritual realizations—very gradually ought to be able to come to a little happiness and joyfulness in their own life, and even have a bit of control over their material conditions.

The human consciousness looks for miracles. Letters come to me, as they did to Paul, asking for healings. And this is fine. Sometimes the Living ECK Master, as a vehicle, is able to take some of this karma away. But many times the quickest and surest way to get rid of this karma, this burden we have created, is just to go to a medical doctor, a dentist, a lawyer, or a banker. Approach life with common sense, and sometimes just with common courtesy.

Approach life with common sense, and sometimes just with common courtesy.

MOVING TOWARD SELF-MASTERY

In the spiritual life, too often we have been given the image of a saint: "This is a saint; this is how he lived. This is someone to really look up to." If we were to make a serious study of their lives, many times we would find an individual who was very erratic in his behavior. Often he didn't get along with the people of his time, and only when he was safely in the grave did someone make him a saint. He was allowed to roam free because he directed his erratic behavior into the field of religion.

A person who has a high degree of spiritual unfoldment will be balanced in his everyday life. He will use common sense and common courtesy with those people around him.

As we move on to this self-mastery, which is what we are looking for through experience with the Sound and Light of God—the twin aspects, the Voice of God—we become a bit more sensible about life. Our spiritual diet is as unique as our food diet. Some of you can eat ice cream, and more power to you. I believe I ate my full supply by the time I was about twenty-eight, and now I have to be a little careful. It's the same with the spiritual life. God has provided a way and a path for every Soul to come a little closer, to make one more step toward returning to God.

In the Christian faith there is one Bible and many different religions, and this is as it should be. The ECK Master does not come to destroy religions, but rather to enliven them.

THE PURPOSE OF THE NEGATIVE POWER

We have this little neighbor boy, Matthew, who's three years old and just now learning how to talk.

He talks like Donald Duck, and you really can't understand him. He's a cute little guy, but he's now getting to the stage where, if his mother says, "You stay in the yard," he'll figure a way to get out of the gate and wander around in the street. He's a little adventurer and he's getting into a lot of trouble with his mother.

The other day I saw little Matthew being pulled along by his mother. He looked very straightforward, as if he had just gotten some kind of enlightenment. He said a couple of things that I couldn't make out, and his mother decided to translate. "Do you know what Matthew said?" she asked. "No." "Matthew got lost," she said. "Oh?" "Mommy got scared." "Oh."

In the meantime, he's standing there real proud, the message is getting through. Then his mother leaned over and said, "And what happened to Matthew when Mommy found Matthew?" This is where he got his enlightenment, I guess. He stood there and didn't say one word but he got this sad expression on his face and started rubbing his seat with his hand. I left then, because a parent was disciplining her child.

Our spiritual life is very similar to this. Soul is sent into the lower worlds to get an education, to go to grade school, and to one day become a Co-worker with God. The negative force, which is known as Satan or whatever else, causes a big question that the Christians really can't understand: Why does God allow Satan in this world? The best answer they can come up with is that someday God is going to get even with Satan for causing all this trouble. But they misunderstand the purpose of the negative power.

The lower worlds, including earth, have been established by God as a training school with a very

Soul is sent into the lower worlds to get an education, to go to grade school, and to one day become a Co-worker with God.

stern teacher, a taskmaster, in charge. This is the negative power. The negative power is never allowed to let things get completely out of hand, because there are limitations. There are a number of workers who help to keep this world somewhat in balance. As we ECKists develop the spiritual consciousness, we learn how to live in this world yet not be of it.

In the human consciousness, one dreads the day that family members must leave, when the time comes to shed the body. This fear, and the lack of trust or knowledge about what happens in the other worlds, is the main reason that the people who are most afraid will go out and grab others by the lapels and say, "You believe my way or you're going to be damned!" It's a sad situation—they're so frantic, so uncertain of what's coming that they try to convince themselves by pulling on someone else's lapels.

We can live in peace and harmony with the various religions, and we can respect them.

God has allowed for all these different religions so that every Soul can find someplace to get religious or spiritual upliftment. This is as it should be. We can live in peace and harmony with the various religions, and we can respect them.

Working with Common Courtesy

I don't know how many of you are football fans, but the season is starting now. Bill Walsh of the San Francisco 49ers had a good season last year, and he went to the Super Bowl. No one expected him to do it. But he has a unique philosophy about how to work with people, and one of his strong rules is to work with common courtesy.

When he first began coaching the team, one of the players was constantly harassing the equipment manager, and he'd always do it in public. So the coach went and talked to this player, who had been an all-star pro a couple of years ago—a big man on the team—and he said, "Hey, listen. We've got too many important things to do here to be fighting among ourselves." But the man wouldn't quit.

Not too long after that this man, although he was a valuable player, was traded. The coach handled it very much like Matthew's mom when she warned him, "This is the gate. Don't go beyond it." If he does, the mother will spank the child, because she knows that the hurt from a spanking lasts a lot shorter time than if the child runs into the street and gets hit by a car. This is what the coach did, and this is often what the Inner Master does as we come onto the path of ECK.

THE DIVINE LAWS

We eventually come into full awareness of these divine laws, which operate whether we are aware of them or not. The only reason that we have had all our troubles is because we've been ignorant of these spiritual laws, and furthermore, we didn't have any idea where to learn them. They are scattered throughout the works of ECK.

We know some of the basic ones, such as: For every action there is an opposite and equal reaction. We call it karma. We do not have the concept of sin in Eckankar, but we do have the concept of total responsibility, which comes with total freedom. This is our goal: wisdom, power, and freedom, to work in the spiritual consciousness. When the time comes for our family members to leave this world, although we will feel sad since that comes with being in the physical body, we won't stay down for the rest of our life.

We eventually come into full awareness of these divine laws, which operate whether we are aware of them or not.

KEEPING IN SHAPE SPIRITUALLY

Being detached does not mean you put your emotions on a shelf and forget about them forever. The Emotional body also needs exercise, and there's a very valid time for it to cry. We have to cry. There are things we need to learn to keep our Mental body alert too. At work, for instance, when the boss says, "Technology's moving really fast; we'd like you to learn word processing," you learn word processing—and you stay flexible. Here on the physical plane we've got this body, and it also needs exercise. We call it physical exercise. Some of you like to jog, others like to swim.

The point of all this is that we also work in the Soul body, and this Soul body needs exercise in order to keep strong. We call these the Spiritual Exercises of ECK. In order to keep a physical muscle strong, we have to exercise it. In order to keep this contact with the Word of God open, we have to exercise the Soul body.

In order to keep this contact with the Word of God open, we have to exercise the Soul body.

Not much time is required for these contemplative exercises or these techniques of ECK—just twenty minutes a day.

Don't overdo it, don't go too fast. Take your time. As we go through the initiations—let's say the Second, for instance—you may not be aware of a single experience that's occurring. It's not important. The fact is that you have a greater flow of Sound and Light that is coming into your being, into your presence.

I gave the example the other day that if you were working in a warehouse and someone asked you, "Did you get a lot of orders of ECK books out today?" you might say yes, you did. You started out with a whole stack of orders and now they're gone. But would you remember every order you filled? Every book you pulled? A lot of times when we are doing things by rote and routine, we actually are in another state of consciousness. We set the body in motion and then we daydream. When the day is done we know we've finished the work, but if somebody were to ask how many times your arm moved out to pick up a book, you couldn't tell them. Furthermore, is it important? The fact is, the job got done and you know it got done, and even though you don't remember all the details, they really aren't that important.

THE BALANCE OF THE SOUND

You get more of the Sound and Light coming in at each initiation in ECK. We take them very slowly. You want It to come in at a gradual pace. The saints mostly had the Light of God, and that's all they had. As It would pour in, they didn't know how to work with It.

You get more of the Sound and Light coming in at each initiation in ECK.

The role of the Sound of God is greater than the Light—It comes in and balances the Light so that it doesn't burn us.

When I say that the Light comes in, and It can burn us, that doesn't mean we burn to a crisp or turn brown or something like this; it means we can become erratic, do strange things, pester people. We might do something that society frowns on and soon find ourselves in a hospital, put there because we're a danger to ourselves and to those around us. We haven't learned balance.

This is the protection we have on the path of ECK— the balance of this Sound. What makes Eckankar unique and sets it off from most of the religious teachings is that we have the twin aspects of God, which are the Light and Sound. Many of the religions speak of the Light; very few are even aware of the Sound. They have absolutely no idea of what this means.

It is spoken of in the Bible, in the Gospel of John: "In the beginning was the Word. . . . And the Word was made flesh and dwelt among us." This Word, of course, refers to the Sound, the Voice of God manifested in the physical. At Pentecost, the disciples who gathered together were visited by this Holy Spirit, which is the ECK, and It sounded like a wind rushing through the room. Little tongues of fire appeared on their heads, and they were able to speak in tongues. The two manifestations, the Sound and Light, were there, but hardly anyone in the church understands what this means.

This doesn't mean that the experiences of Sound and Light are limited to Eckankar. They are not.

This doesn't mean that the experiences of Sound and Light are limited to Eckankar. They are not. In many of the religions in the East, in Africa and in Pakistan, the people are taught about the sound of HU, which is a sacred name of God, as children. When they come in contact with the ECK teachings and are told that there is a sacred word which can bring upliftment, and they find that it is HU, they say, "Ah! I know that; my mother taught me as a child."

Meeting the ECK Masters

My eight-year-old daughter wants to meet the ECK Masters, but she doesn't really want to say she's afraid, so she'll hem and haw about it. One day while I was working at my desk, she came in, walked around, and fiddled with the paper clips. Finally she said, "Could I see Rebazar Tarzs and Paulji if I wanted to?" I said, "Yes, you can." She said, "Sometimes I can feel somebody behind me." I said, "What about it?" She said, "Can they get in a very small space?" I asked her what she meant.

She said, "Well, one day I was standing with my back against the door—it was right up against the wall, and I felt somebody behind me." I said, "They're working in the Soul body, and Soul can take up any space; It can stand anywhere It wants to, even half in the wall." Then I got kind of firm with her because she was fiddling around, and I said, "Do you want to see the ECK Masters or don't you?" She said, "I don't know. If I have a choice, I'd rather not, because I don't want them sitting there watching me." I said, "That's your choice. They aren't going to butt in on you; they're not going to come in and just stand around when you don't want them, so don't worry about it. Just say you don't want them here right now, and they'll stand back. They won't get in your space."

A couple of days later, she got up in the morning and said, "I met some of the ECK Masters when I was dreaming." Then she said, "It's OK if I meet the ECK Masters when I'm laying down and asleep, but I just don't want to meet them when I'm standing up and awake." She doesn't want Rebazar Tarzs appearing in the room on her.

What Makes ECK Real?

Some people had experiences with these ECK Masters even before 1965, when the modern teachings of ECK came out. There will be times when someone is going to say that the outer writings of ECK are not true for this or that reason. We must never rely on the outer too much. Go to the temple within you. My purpose as the Living ECK Master is to provide the ECK books and discourses so that you can make this actual contact with the Sound and Light of God. If you can do this, you will be far ahead of a follower of any orthodox religion.

This is what makes ECK real, and it's done at a slow pace. If you pay attention to the Inner Master,

Some people had experiences with these ECK Masters even before 1965, when the modern teachings of ECK came out.

you will not get out of balance. When the greater amount of Light and Sound comes in, we must give out greater service. It has to come out in some form of service. If you take too much ECK in and you don't have enough going out, you're going to become unbalanced. You're going to make erratic decisions. We don't want that.

THE CONTROVERSY OVER ABORTION

There is another point I wanted to make before leaving. Today there is a very big controversy about whether abortion is right or wrong. To me, that is a personal choice for the individual. If in your heart you feel you don't want abortion, may you have that choice. The same applies if a woman feels, as a personal choice, that she does not want the responsibility of raising a child, preparing for its education, and so on. Understand that Soul does not come into the body until the first breath of life, and sometimes later. This is exactly as it is spoken of in the Bible too.

A statement was made by President Reagan around the beginning of September at Kansas State University. It sounds very logical on the surface. I took it out of the newspaper. Speaking about the proposed constitutional amendment to ban abortions, he said, "But out of all the debate on this subject has come one disputed fact: the uncertainty of when life begins." In his very persuasive way, he went on to say: "Simple morality dictates that unless and until someone can prove the unborn human is not alive, we must give it the benefit of the doubt and assume it is." The fact is, there is no uncertainty about when life begins. What proof will one accept as to whether the unborn human is alive or not? Certainly, if I were a Christian, I would look to the Bible.

I sat down one Sunday morning and looked through the Bible again. I had studied it for years in the past, and though I'm on the path of ECK and have found a greater truth for myself, I realize this Bible is a great help for other people. Paul Twitchell had many times made references back to the Bible so that there would be a bridge for those of you who were coming from the Christian background—you were between paths and were searching—so that you could have some kind of a step to help you gain confidence in the Sound and Light of God.

I would like to quote something about the source of human life. It's from Genesis 2:7, which tells from the biblical point of view the progression of creation and how life comes into the body. The ECK Masters support the statement as it is given in Genesis 2:7. Notice the three parts to it: "And the Lord God formed man of the dust of the ground, and breathed into his nostrils the breath of life; and man became a living soul."

"And the Lord God formed man of the dust of the ground." We know that when Soul leaves this temple, the body decays and turns to dust. Whatever is left of the dust has the same mineral composition as does the earth, and this is why man was formed of the dust of the ground. It is not the physical body we are interested in. The spiritual liberation we speak of is not for the body; it's spiritual liberation of Soul—to shake Itself loose from the law of karma.

The first step, then, is that the Lord God formed man of the dust of the ground, and secondly, "breathed into his nostrils the breath of life." This is the ECK, or Spirit, coming in. This is when Soul enters the temple of the baby. Thirdly, "and man became a living soul." So in answer to the president, who wanted proof of when life comes into the

This is the ECK, or Spirit, coming in. This is when Soul enters the temple of the baby.

human body, I would just say to read the Bible.

I don't like to get into the position of saying to people to read your own Bible, but sometimes it's necessary. I did want to make this point today, though, because there is such a controversy. Man actually wants to keep woman in slavery, and he almost succeeded except he botched up the finances so badly that she had to go out and work. He hated it like fury when she left the heat of the kitchen and went out to bring home the bacon—but there's no way he could get along without her help in bringing home some of the bacon. It takes two people in most cases today. It makes men mad that they've lost this control.

LIVING THE GOLDEN RULE

In Soul there is no higher, no lower. I'm not higher than you.

In Soul there is no higher, no lower. I'm not higher than you. A Fifth Initiate is no higher than a First. I am no higher than a Christian; a Christian is no higher than an ECKist—because we are Soul.

This is something that has been overlooked by those who bring out these statements about abortion. They are not interested in truth; they're interested in political power. I hate to say it, but it's true—that if they are looking for authority, if they are looking for a final word, they can look in their own Bible. It's sufficient for everything they need to know.

If these people would spend a little more time living the Golden Rule—Do unto others as you would have them first do unto you—we could live together in peace and harmony. We could allow other Souls the freedom to choose their own way of life, to choose the path of God they want to walk.

We don't have to revert to the time of the Crusades where man in his arrogance and vanity said, The way

I believe in God is right; therefore, I will go out and convert everyone I can in the name of God, in the name of Christ. Anyone who does not accept my belief will be put to torture. We have records of the Inquisition, which was a terrible time in our history, and many other things like the Crusades. There is no need for man, if he has really reached any degree of spiritual unfoldment, to go back to the dark ages of spiritual ignorance. We can take a big step this time, or we can fall back.

I'm going to another seminar in Florida this weekend, so we're leaving right away. I've had a good time here, and though I won't be able to shake hands with you, it's not necessary.

You make the contact here, and you go within yourself. This is where you meet the Inner Master. This is where you develop that spiritual foundation so that you will be strong as you go, step-by-step, through the initiations, and you will never be pushed over by the psychic waves that come.

You make the contact here, and you go within yourself. This is where you meet the Inner Master.

Whenever there is a question about anything, you don't take it to an authority such as myself or anyone else. You go to that inner temple, and you check it: Do I hear the Sound? Do I see the Light? Or your answer may come in a different way: you may get it as a feeling or an impression of knowing what is right. And if this is how it works for you, it is because of your peculiar, unique approach. We choose how we want to go through life, the techniques and the ways.

The Darshan can be given at a meeting such as this where there are relatively few of us, just visiting with each other as I sit here and talk for a while. It enlivens Soul, and this is the function of the Light Giver: to give Soul a few more extra watts. With a little bit of help, it will come.

I'm looking to have you move toward self-mastery so that, at some time, you no longer lean on me. You can now, as you have to—but make your own decisions.

I'm looking to have you move toward self-mastery so that, at some time, you no longer lean on me.

Many of the things that come up as problems in your life can be handled by plain old common sense. Sometimes we dig a hole, but we haven't thought to leave ourselves some way to get out, so we hope for a miracle. Sometimes we just have to learn in our own way.

I would like to thank you for coming. I enjoyed meeting some of you physically, but inwardly is more important. Enjoy yourself, enjoy each other's company; learn what you can on the physical here, but most of your learning will come with the Inner Master.

Greensboro Regional Seminar, Greensboro, North Carolina, September 18, 1982

As you work toward self-mastery, this Master power—the ECK—flows through you in greater degrees. You are responsible for the disciplines that keep this line open between yourself and Spirit. The key is simple: the Spiritual Exercises of ECK.

22
THE MASTER POWER

*I*n a marriage, when you think you know how the other person is thinking and you begin to take them for granted, then things start to go wrong. It's simply because the communication has broken down. There is a way to open this back up.

It's difficult sometimes, after you've stopped talking, to get the communication going again. You may feel that your spouse doesn't love you or doesn't care about you. Before the wife opens her mouth, the husband may think he knows exactly what she's going to say, but actually he doesn't.

Sometimes you can do little things to work this out. For instance, you can take a little time to interview each other, just for enjoyment. Act like you're a reporter for a newspaper.

If you are the one interviewing your spouse, though you can't defend yourself—you just have to sit there and take the answers—you can ask all kinds of fun questions. Your spouse may or may not decide to answer. You ask things such as, What is the happiest time you ever had? In other words, you stretch from the most positive to the most negative, and you do it with each other's permission. Then you switch roles after a while. This helps to open communication, and if it doesn't work, counseling is a good idea too.

Marriage is hard today. Times are fast, the karma

> *When things start to go wrong, it's simply because the communication has broken down.*

is fast; husband and wife both have to go out and work, take a beating all day long, and somewhere along the way you might wonder, *How can I keep things together?* Sometimes we panic as we run into problems with our family. But as we contact that Master power within us, we learn that for every problem, for every situation that comes into our life, there is an answer, there is a solution, or at least a way to control what's happening.

We have to learn how to actually work with this Master power.

ECK, THE MASTER POWER

The Antarctic explorers found an unusual occurrence when they were way down at the South Pole. They had government stations scattered a mile or two apart to conduct studies on petroleum or weather. People would have to travel quite a distance across the snow to visit each other's huts. Many times it was reported that when they would see a group of people approaching for a visit, they would often see one more person than the number that finally arrived. For instance, a person would casually count six people coming, but when the group got there, all of a sudden he'd notice that there were only five. Such incidents have been reported before too. This is sometimes the ECK, which is the Master power, or Spirit.

The Holy Spirit spoken of in the Bible is the ECK. This ECK can be heard as Sound and seen as Light.

What separates, or differentiates, Eckankar from most other religious teachings is the fact that it has these two aspects within its teachings: the Sound and the Light. Most other religious paths do not. There are a few that have it, but at a lower level. The purpose of the Living ECK Master is to show you how to contact the Sound and Light.

You might ask: Why contact the Sound and Light? Because Spirit, or ECK, is the Voice of God, and when you have contact with either the Light or the Sound or the Inner Master, then you have contact with God, with the Voice of God; you have this communication.

THE PROTECTION OF SPIRIT

For those of you who were raised in the Christian tradition, as I was, you may remember the story of the three men in the fiery furnace, which actually should be the story of four men in the fiery furnace.

This took place during the time of the Babylonian captivity of the Jewish nation, when Nebuchadnezzar was the king of Babylon. Daniel was one of the giants of those biblical times. He had interpreted a dream for the king, and being the only one who gave an interpretation that satisfied the king, he was promoted to an honored position and taken into the king's house.

Daniel was pretty shrewd, and he said to the king, "I have three friends, and I'd like for them to be in charge of the affairs of the province of Babylon, if that would be all right." The king was open to this, so he said, "Sure." The three men were Shadrach, Meshach, and Abednego.

The Chaldeans, who were also interspersed throughout the ruling government of Nebuchadnezzar's kingdom, were jealous of the important positions that the three Jewish men had gotten, and they wanted to get them out. To accomplish this, they convinced the king, very cleverly, that it would be a good idea to put up a golden image and then call the princes, governors, captains, sheriffs, and rulers

Spirit, or ECK, is the Voice of God, and when you have contact with either the Light or the Sound or the Inner Master, then you have contact with God.

of all the provinces together to come worship this statue. This, they said, would be an indication that these people accepted the gods of Babylon and also Nebuchadnezzar as the king.

The plot moved along very nicely. The golden image was made and put up, and the word went out throughout the whole kingdom to come for the dedication of this statue.

When all the people arrived, it was announced that as soon as the music started to play—the flutes and other instruments—they were to bow down before Nebuchadnezzar's golden statue, and anyone who didn't do it would be thrown into the furnace. They drew the people there under false pretenses, letting them believe it was to dedicate this image, but they arrived there to find out they had to fall flat on the ground in front of it.

These three men—Shadrach, Meshach, and Abednego—had such a firm belief in their own Inner Master, their own religion, that when everyone else bowed down, they remained standing. Of course, the Chaldeans who were jealous of them immediately went and reported this to the king, and he was furious.

These three men had such a firm belief in their own Inner Master, their own religion, that when everyone else bowed down, they remained standing.

Why would anyone disobey his command? This was a threat to his kingdom. So he called for the three men to be brought to him and he said, "Unless you bow down, I'm going to throw you into the flaming furnace." They said, "You might as well do it, because we're never going to bow down." I guess they had a pretty strong sense of independence and were willing to back it up.

To make sure the furnace was going to be hot enough for them, the king had it heated seven times hotter than usual. The three men were tied up and thrown into the flames. It was so hot that the soldiers died as they threw the men in there. Then everyone stood back and waited for the punishment to be fulfilled, but the men didn't burn.

As Nebuchadnezzar watched the furnace, he said to his aides and counselors, "Did we not cast three men bound into the midst of the fire?" They had been tied up and thrown to the bottom of the furnace, yet not only were there four men in there, but they were unbound and walking around. The king couldn't understand it, but he let them come out of the fire.

This was the Master principle. It may have manifested in a form that is called an angel in the Bible, it may have been an ECK Master; it may have been anything. What happened was that this Divine Spirit formed a matrix, and the vibrations of those who were in the furnace were raised beyond the point where the fire could touch them. Their hair wasn't singed and their clothes didn't even smell of smoke— and after all that, they got a promotion!

CONTACTING THE MASTER POWER

We are trying to make contact with this Master power, by whatever name you want to call it. What I try to do with each of you is to somehow make this contact, so that you learn to work with the Inner Master, to listen and learn to trust It in your own way.

You learn to work with the Inner Master, to listen and learn to trust It in your own way.

The Inner Master has his own conversations with each individual. To some of us he's gentle, or maybe gentle sometimes and a little more firm at other times—whatever it takes for us to learn the laws of Spirit, these divine laws. The ignorance of these laws causes all of our health problems, sadness, and unhappiness.

The Inner Master leads us to an awareness—you might call it an enlightenment—of this power that is already here and is already working every moment in our lives. What sets an ECKist apart from someone who has never contacted the Sound and Light is the fact that he's aware of Its presence and can call upon It; he knows the technique through his inner word. The inward linkup of the Inner Master and the Outer Master is where the teachings really come from.

How the Secret Word Works

The path of ECK and the spiritual exercises give us the tools to experiment with, to figure out ways to work with situations that come up in our lives. At the Second Initiation, for example, you get a secret word. This word unlocks that Master power. It doesn't control a situation.

If something is not going very well at work, you don't begin singing this word to yourself in order to control your boss so he'll get off your back. Maybe the guy wants to fire you, and you're trying to figure out how to stay there because you need the paycheck to eat and live. So you work with it in a different way. You say: I turn this situation over to Spirit so that when I have learned the lessons that are necessary for me to understand another divine principle, then this burden can be taken from me.

This is how one's secret word works.

This is how one's secret word works.

Each person has his own. At a certain time, even during an initiation such as the Second, all of a sudden you may say, It doesn't work for me anymore; what's wrong? At this point, begin experimenting, like the chemist in his lab. Try combinations—try this word, that word, try different words. Or use the same word that you were given but try it in different combinations and see if that works. You begin experimenting.

As you work toward self-mastery, as this Master power—the ECK—flows through you in greater and greater degrees, you've got to make this contact, yourself. You are responsible for the disciplines that keep this line open between yourself and Spirit. The key is simple: the Spiritual Exercises of ECK. And if a word works for you, keep going with it. The proof, of course, is if you can see the Light or hear the Sound, or if in the dream state or in contemplation you can see the Inner Master.

WHO IS MY INNER MASTER?

The question may be, Who is my Inner Master? Only you can answer that. At the inner temple, the Holy Spirit, the ECK, forms a matrix that will take the appearance of either myself, Peddar Zaskq, or Rebazar Tarzs. It may even take the appearance of Christ. Each Master will take you and then pass you on to the next one when you are ready. There is no jealousy between the Masters of a high spiritual order. When the time is right, one Master passes you to the next. These jealousies and divisions are generally created by the followers of one path or another down here who will say to others, My Master is greater than yours. They don't understand that all the Outer Master can do is lead you to that Inner Master. This doesn't mean that your life is going to be happy and joyful from moment to moment, but you ought to be able to find at least a few minutes each day where you are working in that survival state of consciousness. This is working in the spiritual consciousness.

WHAT TO SEEK FIRST

In the nonsurvival state we have unhappiness, lethargy, melancholy, poverty, you name it. This is the human state of consciousness. The human consciousness wants me to do miracles—such as healings or

Keep this line open between yourself and Spirit. The key is simple: the Spiritual Exercises of ECK.

making the money come in—and there's nothing wrong with this. You can ask the Inner Master for these things, but it's the human state of consciousness doing the asking. Even in the Christian Bible, Christ said to his followers, "But seek ye first the kingdom of God,...and all these things shall be added unto you."

Don't seek the attributes of God first—wisdom, knowledge, understanding—because those are only the attributes. Seek ye first God-Realization, which is the kingdom of heaven, the Kingdom of God, and all things shall be added unto you.

Contact with the Light and Sound

I saw a lady at the seminar who has been in Eckankar since 1965. Though she's getting along in years now, her eyes are crystal clear. I asked her, "Still got contact with the Light and Sound of God?" and she said, "Oh, yes!" This contact with the twin pillars of God is important. When the psychic waves blow across the world bringing attacks of one kind or another, someone might say the writings of Paul Twitchell are this and that. Remember, we don't look at the writings of any of the ECK Masters as the final word. Their purpose is to take us within. If we build a firm spiritual foundation at that inner temple, no one will ever be able to move us from it.

If we build a firm spiritual foundation at that inner temple, no one will ever be able to move us from it.

You won't look to me as an authority to tell you that Eckankar is right, because you're going to check it out for yourself. If it works for you, it's right for you. If it doesn't work for you, it's not right for you. You might want to give it a trial period of a certain time; you might not. The choice is totally yours.

WHY CAN'T A WOMAN BECOME THE LIVING ECK MASTER?

I had an interesting conversation a little while ago with a lady who had a real good question for me. She asked, "Why can't a woman become the Living ECK Master?" It was early this morning, I was still a little groggy, and this was quite a question to have to face right off. I had to recommend that she go within to ask the Inner Master.

As far as the spiritual law goes, women and men can become ECK Masters. At any one time there is just one Living ECK Master.

So in answer to the question of why a woman can't become the Living ECK Master, it's a matter of the atoms and how they are arranged. All I could say was: Keep unfolding and opening yourself more as a clear vehicle for God, and as you do, your values will change.

It's very much the same way as when we first come on the path of ECK—we want to Soul Travel or read the future, the ECK-Vidya. These things are very enjoyable, but yet we want to keep in mind to "seek ye first the kingdom of God." That's what we want to do, and this is where I have to put your attention again and again. It's my responsibility to those of you who follow the path of ECK to see that you keep up with the spiritual exercises.

Keep unfolding and opening yourself more as a clear vehicle for God, and as you do, your values will change.

THE IMPORTANCE OF THE MONTHLY INITIATE REPORT

That is why it's also important to write a monthly report. If you have this inner contact, you don't have to mail it to me, but you may if you want to. The importance of the monthly report is so that you can make a personal assessment: Do I have contact with Spirit? Am I faced with big problems in my life that I'm not able to handle? Write them down.

Spirit knows our problems and our situations, but It won't heal or cure them until we have come to an understanding of what they are and can put our finger on exactly what is wrong in our life. As soon as we can do that, the ECK begins to work. One good way of formulating our problem or situation is in the monthly report. It can be a very good spiritual aid.

Spirit knows our problems but It won't heal them until we have come to an understanding of what is wrong in our life.

REQUESTS FOR HEALING

Sometimes I receive letters that say, "My husband needs a healing," and my question is always, "Has he asked for one? Did he ask you to ask me?" The individual must ask for himself, unless he is completely incapacitated. A child, for instance, may not be able to ask, so one of the parents may.

You might see someone else's condition or illness and feel that the person should be healed—but we don't know that. I turn it over to Spirit if the individual asks for himself. If there is an indication that he has sought out all the help available, Divine Spirit then heals—through the doctor, the dentist, the lawyer, the banker, or the financial adviser.

This is how the ECK works down here. We look for the best medical help we can find, and when we've tried everything and it hasn't worked, that is when the ECK steps in. The ECK doesn't lead or live your life for you; It helps when you've made every effort for yourself. Self-mastery means living 100 percent of your own life and expecting no one else to do it for you. Then if you need a little bit of help, you get a little bit of help.

If we are tempted to ask that another person be healed, we should realize that maybe the person doesn't want the healing. Maybe he or she is perfectly happy with the illness because it serves some purpose of self-preservation in their own mind, and when we step in, we violate this.

During the Vietnam and Korean and other wars, there was a lot of combat fatigue that made peculiar things happen. One soldier had a condition whose medical name I won't attempt, but it translates from Greek to *bent back*. The person walks around with his back at a forty-five-degree angle. The situation was a little bit like in *M*A*S*H* on TV, where one of the characters dressed up in women's clothes, trying to get himself discharged. Whenever a general or somebody in authority would come through, he'd quickly get into a dress and hope to get himself kicked out of the service.

This man who walked around at a forty-five-degree angle was put in the psychiatric ward. The psychiatrist told him, "I'm going to give you sodium pentothal, and when you wake up, you're going to be cured." When the soldier woke up, he found he could stand up straight—and he was absolutely furious. The first thing he tried to do was slug the psychiatrist, because being cured meant he had to go back into combat. Although there was no physical cause for this condition, it had been his form of self-preservation.

TURNING IT OVER TO SPIRIT

We don't know what another person needs. I won't interfere; I turn it over to Spirit. If someone comes to you and wants a healing, whether they're an ECKist or not, the best thing to do is suggest

We don't know what another person needs. I won't interfere; I turn it over to Spirit.

they go see a doctor. If it's incurable or if they have sought a lot of medical aid without any relief, then you might simply suggest that they write to the Living ECK Master. It's the best way. This is how you can act and do everything in the name of Spirit, where you don't pick up karma yourself.

In the training for an individual to become the Living ECK Master, you learn how to turn things like this over to Spirit.

Psychic healers don't always have this ability. They can take on the karma, and maybe their physical stamina is such that they can go on for many years. A friend was telling me that in the frontier times, her grandfather had this ability. The family lived in Utah, way out in the country where there was no doctor, and often there was serious illness. The head of the family had this power to heal, and many times he was able to cure them. But as he got to be middle-aged he came down with a very serious illness, and he never understood he was paying off the karma of all the people that he had helped cure.

I turn it over to Spirit. Spirit may bring a healing; It may bring an understanding or a source of help.

I don't cure anyone myself. I turn it over to Spirit. Spirit may bring a healing; It may bring an understanding. It may lead the person to a doctor or a source of help that he's never considered before. But of myself, I don't do anything. The quicker I can pass this off into the Audible Life Stream, into the ECK, into Spirit, the quicker I do it. If I think about it, or if any part of it stays with me, then I get a health problem. If that happens, I have to get right at it and get myself straightened out. This is a real art, and it's part of the discipline and the training that you will receive on your way to self-mastery as you come in contact with this Master power.

FIXING IT YOURSELF

As you come in contact with this Master power, the Master does less and less for you. He'll put the wrench in your hands; you fix things yourself. He doesn't do this unless he knows you can handle it; and when you need the help, you'll be given the help.

We have a backyard about the size of a postage stamp, and it needs mowing too. I had told my wife and daughter, "Listen, if you want the lawn, you take care of it." Then, of course, we had to go to Sears and buy one of these little reel lawn mowers, since it doesn't pay to get a better kind for such a little patch of grass. I had to push the heavy kind when I was a kid, and we had a lot more lawn then, so I figured my daughter could push that small thing.

You know how kids are at that age; they think everything is made of steel, iron, stone, or granite. The back of the lawn mower has a little roller on it so that when you push forward and cut the grass, you can draw it back smoothly. If this roller breaks, the mower gets stuck in the ground and you can only mow forward.

After working in the yard for a while one day, all of a sudden my daughter runs into the house, pleased as punch, and says, "The lawn mower broke!" Of course, I was a kid once, too, and I know how these things happen. I would use something the way it wasn't supposed to be used, and it would break. So I asked, "How did it break?" She said she was just mowing the lawn and this little brace for the roller on one side, which was made of plastic, "just broke." She said, "I'll get some Elmer's Glue and fix it. It'll be OK." Kids of that age believe Elmer's Glue will fix anything.

I came outside later and saw she had Elmer's

As you come in contact with this Master power, the Master does less and less for you.

Glue smeared all over it. "When it dries, it'll be OK," she said. I decided to go and try to find some new braces for it, but in the meantime, I asked her exactly how it had broken.

She explained that she had tried to get the lawn mower off the lawn and onto the sidewalk at the place where the sidewalk was too high. Instead of finding a spot where it was more level with the lawn, she just pulled it over the edge and forced it until it broke. I said, "Yeah, that's what I figured. You think everything in the world is made of steel and granite, but I have news for you: Parts of it are made of feathers."

So I bought four of these little parts at a quarter each and decided to let her fix it. I knew she could do it if she sat down and thought about it. I said, "Now go out to the garage and get two wrenches."

She got them and then sat down on the grass looking at the lawn mower with a puzzled expression. I said, "I'll give you a hint. Put it on the same way as the one that isn't broken. When you get all the rollers on, put all the spacers in between too." But as she took the lawn mower apart in the backyard, she scattered the rollers all over. Thus I took that opportunity to show her how to keep things together so when you're ready to reach for something, you don't have to go hunting in the weeds and underneath the rosebushes.

A little while later she came upstairs and said, "It's fixed! Do you want to come down and look?"

I said, "Sure do."

And you know, she'd actually fixed the thing! She was so proud, as if now this was her lawn mower; she had helped manufacture it, and now she had the pride of ownership.

This is how the Master power works: It will let you start fixing things yourself.

This is how the Master power works: It will let you start fixing things yourself. You go to the dentist, who says you need to have a tooth drilled; and you figure out maybe it was because you ate too much sugar. You start learning to avoid the things that hurt you, that cause you pain; and you look for the things that help you and make your life more positive, happier, and cheerful.

Orlando Regional Seminar, Orlando, Florida,
September 19, 1982

About the Author

Award-winning author, teacher, and spiritual guide Sri Harold Klemp helps seekers reach their full potential. He is the Mahanta, the Living ECK Master and spiritual leader of Eckankar, the Path of Spiritual Freedom. He is the latest in a long line of spiritual Adepts who have served throughout history in every culture of the world.

Sri Harold teaches creative spiritual practices that enable anyone to achieve life mastery and gain inner peace and contentment. His messages are relevant to today's spiritual needs and resonate with every generation. *Kirkus Reviews* comments, "The powerful optimism of these teachings should resonate with all readers, even those unacquainted with ECK."

Sri Harold's body of work includes more than one hundred books, which have been translated into eighteen languages and won multiple awards. The miraculous, true-life stories he shares lift the veil between heaven and earth.

In his groundbreaking memoir, *Autobiography of a Modern Prophet*, he reveals secrets to spiritual success gleaned from his personal journey into the heart of God. Find your own path to true happiness, wisdom, and love in Sri Harold Klemp's inspired writings.

Next Steps in Spiritual Exploration

- **Browse our website: www.Eckankar.org.**
  Watch videos; get free books, answers to FAQs, and more info.
- **Attend an Eckankar event** in your area.
  Visit "Eckankar around the World" on our website.
- **Explore advanced spiritual study** with the Eckankar discourses that come with membership.
- **Read additional books** about the ECK teachings.
- See "Contact Eckankar" page 300.

Advanced Spiritual Living

Go higher, further, deeper with your spiritual exploration!

ECK membership brings many unique benefits and a focus on the ECK discourses. These are dynamic spiritual courses you study at home, one per month.

The first year of study brings *The Easy Way Discourses* by Harold Klemp, with uplifting spiritual exercises, audio excerpts from his seminar talks, and activities to personalize your spiritual journey. Classes are available in many areas.

Each year you choose to continue with ECK membership can bring new levels of divine freedom, inner strength to meet the challenges of life, and direct experience with the love and power of God.

Here's a sampling of titles from *The Easy Way Discourses*:

- In Soul You Are Free
- Reincarnation—Why You Came to Earth Again
- The Master Principle
- The God Worlds—Where No One Has Gone Before?

Books

You may find these books by Harold Klemp to be of special interest. They are available at bookstores, online booksellers, or directly from Eckankar.

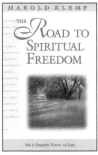

Book 17

The Mahanta Transcripts Series

The Mahanta Transcripts, books 1–17, are from Harold Klemp's talks at Eckankar seminars. He has taught thousands how to have a natural, direct relationship with the Holy Spirit. The stories and wonderful insights contained in these talks will lead you to deeper spiritual understanding.

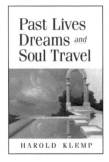

Past Lives, Dreams, and Soul Travel

These stories and exercises help you find your true purpose, discover greater love than you've ever known, and learn that spiritual freedom is within reach.

The Spiritual Exercises of ECK

This book is a staircase with 131 steps leading to the doorway to spiritual freedom, self-mastery, wisdom, and love. A comprehensive volume of spiritual exercises for every need.

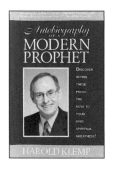

Autobiography of a Modern Prophet

This riveting story of Harold Klemp's climb up the Mountain of God will help you discover the keys to your own spiritual greatness.

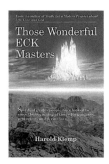

Those Wonderful ECK Masters

Would you like to have *personal* experience with spiritual masters that people all over the world—since the beginning of time—have looked to for guidance, protection, and divine love? This book includes real-life stories and spiritual exercises to meet eleven ECK Masters.

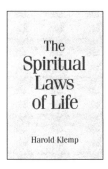

The Spiritual Laws of Life

Learn how to keep in tune with your true spiritual nature. Spiritual laws reveal the behind-the-scenes forces at work in your daily life.

CONTACT ECKANKAR

For more information about ECK, to order ECK books, or to enroll in ECK membership, you may

- visit www.ECKBooks.org;

- enroll online at "Membership" at www.Eckankar.org (click on "Online Membership Application");

- call Eckankar (952) 380-2222;

- write to
  ECKANKAR, Dept. BK 64
  PO Box 2000
  Chanhassen, MN 55317-2000 USA.

GLOSSARY

Words set in SMALL CAPS are defined elsewhere in this glossary.

Arahata An experienced and qualified teacher of ECKANKAR classes.

Blue Light How the MAHANTA often appears in the inner worlds to the CHELA or seeker.

chela A spiritual student, often a member of ECKANKAR.

ECK The Life Force, Holy Spirit, or Audible Life Current which sustains all life.

Eckankar *EHK-ahn-kahr* The Path of Spiritual Freedom. Also known as the Ancient Science of SOUL TRAVEL. A truly spiritual way of life for the individual in modern times. The teachings provide a framework for anyone to explore their own spiritual experiences. Established by PAUL TWITCHELL, the modern-day founder, in 1965. The word means Co-worker with God.

ECK Masters Spiritual Masters who can assist and protect people in their spiritual studies and travels. The ECK Masters are from a long line of God-Realized SOULS who know the responsibility that goes with spiritual freedom.

Fubbi Quantz The guardian of the SHARIYAT-KI-SUGMAD at the Katsupari Monastery in northern Tibet. He was the MAHANTA, the LIVING ECK MASTER during the time of Buddha, about 500 BC.

God-Realization The state of God Consciousness. Complete and conscious awareness of God.

Gopal Das The guardian of the SHARIYAT-KI-SUGMAD at the Temple of Askleposis on the Astral PLANE. He was the MAHANTA, the LIVING ECK MASTER in Egypt, about 3000 BC.

HU *HYOO* The most ancient, secret name for God. It can be sung as a love song to God aloud or silently to oneself to align with God's love.

initiation   Earned by a member of ECKANKAR through spiritual unfoldment and service to God. The initiation is a private ceremony in which the individual is linked to the Sound and Light of God.

Kal Niranjan   The Kal; the negative power, also known as Satan or the devil.

Karma, Law of   The Law of Cause and Effect, action and reaction, justice, retribution, and reward, which applies to the lower or psychic worlds: the Physical, Astral, Causal, Mental, and Etheric PLANES.

Klemp, Harold   The present MAHANTA, the LIVING ECK MASTER. SRI Harold Klemp became the Mahanta, the Living ECK Master in 1981. His spiritual name is WAH Z.

Lai Tsi   An ancient Chinese ECK MASTER.

Living ECK Master   The spiritual leader of ECKANKAR. He leads SOUL back to God. He teaches in the physical world as the Outer Master, in the dream state as the Dream Master, and in the spiritual worlds as the Inner Master. SRI HAROLD KLEMP became the MAHANTA, the Living ECK Master in 1981.

Mahanta   An expression of the Spirit of God that is always with you. Sometimes seen as a BLUE LIGHT or Blue Star or in the form of the Mahanta, the LIVING ECK MASTER. The highest state of God Consciousness on earth, only embodied in the Living ECK Master. He is the Living Word.

Mahdis *MAH-dees*   The initiate of the Fifth Circle (SOUL PLANE); often used as a generic term for all High Initiates in ECK.

Peddar Zaskq   The spiritual name for PAUL TWITCHELL, the modern-day founder of ECKANKAR and the MAHANTA, the LIVING ECK MASTER from 1965 to 1971.

planes   Levels of existence, such as the Physical, Astral, Causal, Mental, Etheric, and SOUL Planes.

Rami Nuri   The guardian of the SHARIYAT-KI-SUGMAD at the House of Moksha in the city of Retz, Venus. He served as the MAHANTA, the LIVING ECK MASTER. The letter *M* appears on his forehead.

Rebazar Tarzs   A Tibetan ECK MASTER known as the Torchbearer of ECKANKAR in the lower worlds.

Satsang   A class in which students of ECK discuss a monthly lesson from ECKANKAR.

Self-Realization   SOUL recognition. The entering of Soul into the Soul PLANE and there beholding Itself as pure Spirit. A state of seeing, knowing, and being.

Shamus-i-Tabriz   Guardian of the SHARIYAT-KI-SUGMAD on the Causal PLANE. He was the MAHANTA, the LIVING ECK MASTER in ancient Persia.

Shariyat-Ki-Sugmad   The sacred scriptures of ECKANKAR. The scriptures are comprised of twelve volumes in the spiritual worlds. The first two were transcribed from the inner PLANES by PAUL TWITCHELL, modern-day founder of Eckankar.

Soul   The True Self, an individual, eternal spark of God. The inner, most sacred part of each person. Soul can see, know, and perceive all things. It is the creative center of Its own world.

Soul Travel   The expansion of consciousness. The ability of SOUL to transcend the physical body and travel into the spiritual worlds of God. Soul Travel is taught only by the LIVING ECK MASTER. It helps people unfold spiritually and can provide proof of the existence of God and life after death.

Sound and Light of ECK   The Holy Spirit. The two aspects through which God appears in the lower worlds. People can experience them by looking and listening within themselves and through SOUL TRAVEL.

Spiritual Exercises of ECK   Daily practices for direct, personal experience with the Sound Current. Creative techniques using contemplation and the singing of sacred words to bring the higher awareness of SOUL into daily life.

Sri   A title of spiritual respect, similar to reverend or pastor, used for those who have attained the Kingdom of God. In ECKANKAR, it is reserved for the MAHANTA, the LIVING ECK MASTER.

Sugmad *SOOG-mahd*   A sacred name for God. It is the source of all life, neither male nor female, the Ocean of Love and Mercy.

Temples of Golden Wisdom   Golden Wisdom Temples found on the various PLANES—from the Physical to the Anami Lok; CHELAS of ECKANKAR are taken to these temples in the SOUL body to be educated in the divine knowledge; sections of the SHARIYAT-KI-SUGMAD, the sacred teachings of ECK, are kept at these temples.

Towart Managi   The ECK MASTER in charge of the SHARIYAT-KI-SUGMAD in the TEMPLE OF GOLDEN WISDOM on the Mental PLANE. He was the MAHANTA, the LIVING ECK MASTER in ancient Abyssinia (now Ethiopia).

Twitchell, Paul   An American ECK MASTER who brought the modern teachings of ECKANKAR to the world through his writings and lectures. His spiritual name is PEDDAR ZASKQ.

Vahana   The ECK missionary; a carrier of ECK or the message of ECK.

vairag   The spiritual virtue of detachment.

Vajra Manjushri *VAHJ-rah Mahn-JOO-shree*   The LIVING ECK MASTER in Persia who was executed by King Hakhamanish I in about 700 BC through the instigation of a priest of Mithra; He now teaches in the Causal PLANE.

Wah Z *WAH zee*   The spiritual name of SRI HAROLD KLEMP. It means the secret doctrine. It is his name in the spiritual worlds.

Yaubl Sacabi   Guardian of the SHARIYAT-KI-SUGMAD in the spiritual city of Agam Des. He was the MAHANTA, the LIVING ECK MASTER in ancient Greece.

For more explanations of ECKANKAR terms, see *A Cosmic Sea of Words: The ECKANKAR Lexicon*, by Harold Klemp.

INDEX

abortion, 272–74
acorn planter, the. See *Man Who Planted Trees, The*
act(ion)
  karmaless, 104, 252
  life of, 127, 134
advice, 121, 208
Africa, 207
agnostic, 62, 187
Alexander the Great, 194–95
Alphabet for Young ECKists, 206
altar of Blinding Light, 2, 3, 7
Anami, 8, 10
anger, 46, 93–94, 102, 149, 243, 265
animals, 259
attachment, 44, 46, 102, 149
attention, 183, 201
attitude(s), 3, 125, 191
Audible Life Stream, 1, 8, 219, 222, 245, 290
awareness, 69, 80, 134, 179, 226, 267, 283

balance, 233, 264, 269
belief, 71
black magic, 188, 233, 252
blessing(s), 12, 191, 226
Blue Light, 47, 68, 80, 110, 131, 132, 133, 180, 192, 205, 214, 238. *See also* Mahanta
Blue Star, 80, 133, 154, 174, 238
body
  emotional, 122, 130
  Mental, 113, 129
  physical, 130, 135
Böhme, Jakob, 100, 204
Brother Lawrence, 27, 49

changes, 17, 230
charity, 106, 108
Cheyenne Indians, 67
child in the wilderness, 91, 92, 93, 96
children
  and discipline, 161–62, 178, 265
  and ECK, 7, 35, 174–77, 237
  having, 137
  spiritual consciousness of, 175, 178–79, 197
  spiritual exercises with, 161, 185
Children's Day, 160
Christ, 65, 89, 285
Christ consciousness, 65
Christian
  Bible, 30, 62, 192, 196, 229, 264, 270, 272–74, 280, 286
  religion, 54, 115, 230, 255, 281
  stories, 281–83
cleanliness, 144
Columbus, Christopher, 147
commitment, 1
common sense, 197, 263, 264
communication, 164, 180, 205, 209, 227, 238, 279
compassion, 3, 83

confidence, 107, 149, 197
Consciousness
    change(s) in, 119, 230
    Five, 249, 250, 253, 255, 257,
        258
    human, 66, 91, 118, 127, 163,
        263, 266, 286
    state of, 53
contemplation, 2, 10. *See also*
    Spiritual Exercises of ECK
control
    of another, 188, 274, 284
    over material conditions, 263
    by religions, 65, 122, 233
courage, 53
courtesy, 266
Co-worker(s), 19, 38, 45, 83, 85,
    213, 214, 265
creation, story of, 273
creative
    faculty, 226
    flow, 152, 184
    force, 99, 156 *See also* ECK
    imagination, 21, 68
creativity, 47, 80, 190, 220, 239
crusades, 275
cycles, 62, 140

dark night of Soul, 62
Darshan, 56, 275
death
    of family member, 83–85, 266
    fear of, 52, 107
    of physical body, 156
    survive, 117
declaration, 104
depression, 238
detachment, 129, 196, 238, 268
diet, 209, 220, 264
disaster, 122
disciple, 12
discipline, 73, 79, 96, 161, 163,
    178, 237, 243, 251, 263, 285
dream(s)
    healing in, 126
    interpretation of, 112
    recall, 257

state, 105, 110, 112, 132, 156,
    197, 216, 256, 285
symbols, 121–22
work off karma in, 137, 258
drugs, 114, 234–36
Drums of ECK, The (Twitchell),
    237

Easy Way technique, 26, 52, 114,
    140
ECK
    books, 13, 38, 41, 71, 99, 120,
        154, 182, 211–12, 214, 268
        (see also *Alphabet for Young
        ECKists; Drums of ECK,
        The; ECKANKAR—The Key
        to Secret Worlds; Flute of
        God, The; In My Soul I Am
        Free; Key to ECKANKAR,
        The; Spiritual Notebook,
        The; Stranger by the River;
        Tiger's Fang, The; Wind of
        Change, The*)
    culture, 17, 146, 148, 237
    discourses, 47, 68, 131, 138,
        182, 238
    doctrines, 221
    flow of, 17
    force, 63, 146, 221
    gospel of, 13
    initiates, 13
    key to, 223
    Masters, *See* ECK Masters
    message of, 8, 12, 13, 23, 34,
        41, 58, 104, 120, 229
    power, 227, 259
    presence of, 283
    principles of, 179, 206
    seminar(s), 150
    as Spirit, 99
    Spiritual Aide, *See* ECK
        Spiritual Aide
    step aside from, 24
    talking about, 221
    teachings of, 36, 154, 189, 224
    working in everyday life, 132
Eckankar

International Office, 4
path of, 9, 17, 37, 47, 54, 82, 99,
  117, 118, 132, 179, 229, 284
*ECKANKAR—The Key to Secret
  Worlds* (Twitchell), 26, 41,
  140, 222, 223
ECK Masters, 19, 56, 108, 257,
  270–71. *See also* Fubbi
  Quantz; Gopal Das; Lai Tsi;
  Milarepa; Peddar Zaskq
  (Paul Twitchell); Rebazar
  Tarzs; Shamus-i-Tabriz;
  Towart Managi; Vajra
  Manjushri; Wah Z; Yaubl
  Sacabi
ECK Spiritual Aide, 56–57,
  249–50
ECK-Vidya, 10, 104, 193
  classes, 193
  readings, 47, 135, 156, 287
Egypt, 48
EK symbol, 143, 148
emotion(s), 62, 138. *See also*
  body: emotional
energy, 18, 58
entities, 236
eternity, rest points in, 68
exercise, 129–30, 138
existentialism, 187
experience(s)
  astral, 110
  direct, 108, 132
  inner, 12, 132
  spiritual, 66, 71, 131, 204–5

faith, 71, 81, 83, 226
family, 103, 255
fasting, 163, 210
fate, 140
fear, 3, 108, 197, 243, 245
finances, 112, 137, 149, 191
fire, spiritual, 147
Flute of God, The (Twitchell), 29,
  109, 191, 212, 213, 243
foundation, 13, 82, 113, 161, 164,
  169–70, 179, 286
freedom

as attribute of Spirit, 100, 164,
  246, 267
attribute of spiritual exercises,
  106
of choice, 37, 74–75, 91, 274
levels of, 164
for others, 21
and responsibility, 237
for Soul, 206, 232
Fubbi Quantz, 4, 9, 10, 12, 19, 79,
  147
future, 47, 135. *See also* ECK-
  Vidya

Gionesco, Jean, 38
  Man Who Planted Trees, The,
  38
give, learning to, 28
gluttony, spiritual, 138
goal(s)
  of God-Realization, 28, 37, 43
  in life, 152
  spiritual, 17, 110
God. *See also* Sugmad
  attributes of, 286
  belief in, 187
  Consciousness, 263
  experience of, 10
  heart of, 3, 8, 92
  interest in, 62
  love for, 226
  names of, 178, 250
  need for, 62
  presence of, 226
  relationship with, 96
  spark of, 160
God-Realization, 9, 17, 26, 80, 96,
  106, 121, 157, 286
God Worlds
  chart, 80
  of ECK, 7–8, 10, 31, 69, 229
  pure positive, 9, 51, 96, 156
Golden Age, 148, 164
Golden Rule, 196, 274
goodwill, 19, 134, 152, 209, 239
Gopal Das, 12, 19, 207
gossip, 77–78, 93–94

Greece, 146
greed, 46, 102, 149
guilt, 104, 122, 196, 233

habits, 17
happiness, 76, 83, 127, 134, 135, 263
harmony
  between ECK Masters, 19
  between Souls, 53, 160, 209
  creating, 21, 222
  from ECK Master, 239
  laws of, 151, 243
  working in, 19
Harold and the Purple Crayon (Johnson), 173–74
healer(s), 102
  psychic, 51, 290
healing(s)
  psychic, 285
  spiritual, 51–52, 125–26, 138, 157, 288
health, 13, 121, 127, 149
  problem, 101, 137, 283
heart
  of God, 3, 8, 80, 114
  openness of, 207
heaven
  finding, 65
  path to, 61
  of religions, 206
  third, 65
Higher Initiates, 132, 135
  as example, 17
  experiences of, 145, 198, 232, 243
  worship of, 139
Himalayas, 12
Hinduism, 54
Holy Ghost, 55
Holy Spirit, 2
HU, 70, 76, 81, 164, 177, 226, 244–45, 270
Hubbard, Elbert
  A Message to Garcia, 28–29

illusion, 102–3

imagination, 4, 47, 80
immortality, 194–96
incarnation(s), 92
individuality, 38, 130
Ingersoll, Robert, 62
initiate report, 132–33, 287–88
initiation
  earning, 11
  fragrance during, 155
  hardships around, 58
  Light and Sound in, 269
Initiation
  Fifth, 11, 274
  First, 11, 58, 274
  Second, 11, 58, 127, 155, 284
  Third, 155
In My Soul I Am Free (Steiger), 26, 52, 114, 140
Inner Master
  as Blue Light, 68
  chela works with, 156, 283
  connection with, 56
  gives assistance, 14, 70, 86, 125
  gives Darshan, 56
  knowing of, 81
  learning from, 275
  love for, 252
  meeting with, 47, 73, 74, 107, 182, 194, 224
  presence of, 75, 230, 239–40
  relationship with chela, 24, 27, 131
  surrender to, 225
  tests from, 251
inspiration, 47

jealousy, 285
Jesus. *See* Christ
Jivatma, 45
Job, 62–63
John, 30, 270
Johnson, Crockett
  Harold and the Purple Crayon, 173–74
justice, 2

Kal Niranjan 45, 46, 66. *See also*

Satan
karma, 17, 45, 150–51
  beyond, 164
  cause of, 102, 149
  and healing, 101, 263, 290
  initial, 92
  law of, 78
  negative, 123
  past, 258
  positive, 123
  responsibility for, 235
  work through, 63, 78, 137
Katsupari Monastery, 4
Key to ECKANKAR, The
  (Twitchell), 223
Klemp, Harold
  Wind of Change, The, 55, 211,
  230
knowingness, 11, 68, 74
knowledge, 36, 224, 286
Krishna, 89

Lai Tsi, 12, 19, 95–96, 257
  contemplation seed, 96
  law(s), spiritual, 55, 101, 102,
  149, 157, 164, 267, 283
Law(s)
  of Attitudes, 29, 243
  of cause and effect, 123
  of ECK, 94
  of Harmony, 243
  of Karma, 78
  of Silence, 74, 75, 79, 86
leadership, 166
lessons, 17, 45, 95, 104
liberation, spiritual, 8–9, 99, 140,
  141, 225, 260
lifetime(s), 3, 141
Light and Sound, 1, 14, 99, 110.
  See also ECK
  aware of, 75, 222
  contact, 18, 195, 227, 286
  as experience of God, 119
  experiences of, 24, 105–6, 110,
  112, 161, 204–5, 230
  flow of, 268
  in God Worlds, 68, 80

in initiation, 58
learn about, 8, 12, 36, 90, 190
love for, 227
open to, 256
seek, 162
seen and heard, 30, 71, 73
and spiritual exercises, 140
as Spirit, 55, 85, 100, 131, 143,
  280
at temple within oneself, 127
two pillars of, 82
light, pink, 100, 204
Light
  Blue. (*see* Blue Light)
  of ECK, 35, 246
  of God, 3, 7, 9
  as knowledge, 36
Living ECK Master. *See also*
  Mahanta
  acceptance of, 69, 133
  becoming, 287
  example of, 17
  gives liberation, 99
  gives spiritual exercises, 9
  helps chela, 56, 230
  meets with chela on inner
    planes, 25–26, 140
  opportunity to meet, 28, 54, 92
  responsibilities of, 10, 149
  and spiritual healings, 51, 263
  will not influence, 13
  worship of, 139
  writing to, 101
loneliness, 52, 83, 245
loyalty, 1, 3
love
  from chelas to Master, 18
  of children, 35
  comes from ECK, 14, 239
  of ECK Masters, 20
  human, 161, 233
  of Master, 69, 75
  on path of ECK, 9
  for others, 160
  receiving, 111
  of self, 3
  of Soul, 53
  world of, 2

lust, 46, 102, 149
Luther, Martin, 129, 147

Magellan, Ferdinand, 147
Mahanta. *See also* Living ECK
    Master
    contact, 80
    gives direction, 11
    name of, 104
    presence of, 52, 243
    responsibilities of, 10
Mahdis, Area, 21
Man Who Planted Trees, The
    (Gionesco), 38
Marpa, 12
marriage, 137, 156, 213, 279
Master(s), ECK. *See* ECK
    Masters
Message to Garcia, A (Hubbard),
    28–29
Middle Ages, 146
Milarepa, 12
mind
    five passions of the, 44, 46,
        102, 149 (*see also* anger;
        attachment; greed; lust;
        vanity)
    functions of, 135
miracles, 263, 285
mission, 4, 9, 10, 85
Mithraism, 89
monastery, 9, 10. *See also*
    Katsupari Monastery
music
    country, 236
    of ECK, 2, 17
mystery school(s), 48
Mystic World, The, 131

negative power. *See* Kal Niran-
    jan; Satan
new year, spiritual, 9, 31

Ocean of Love and Mercy, 3, 10,
    91, 143, 206

October 9, 20, 31
Oracle of Delphi, 193
order, 144
Outer Master, 256, 284
outflow, 137, 272

Pac-Man, 162–63
painting, 34
past, 135
    life/lives, 90, 118
Paul. *See* Saul of Tarsus
peace, 135
Peddar Zaskq, 12, 19, 79, 156,
    216, 239, 285. *See also*
    Twitchell, Paul
Pentecost, 30, 192, 270
phenomena, 110
plane(s)
    colors of, 30
    inner, 26
    sounds of (*see* Sound: of ECK)
Plane(s)
    Astral, 45, 66, 92, 100
    Causal, 45, 66, 92
    Etheric, 92
    Fifth, 106, 157, 249
    Mental, 45, 92
    Ninth, 106
    Physical, 4, 9, 45, 92
    Soul, 18, 55, 157
plus factor, 27, 165
poverty, of Spirit, 50
power
    as attribute of Spirit, 164, 230,
        246, 267
    ECK, (*see* ECK: power)
    Master, 280, 284
    misuse of, 53
prayer, 130, 188
principle, Master, 283
problem(s), 280, 288
    answers to, 213, 250, 276
procrastination, 44
protection, 204, 215, 252, 269
psychic
    waves, 169, 286
    worlds, 68, 149

purification, by Spirit, 101
purpose
    of ECK, 55, 191
    of life, 118, 127
    of Living ECK Master, 280–81
    of Soul, 213
Rebazar Tarzs, 7–8, 12, 19, 40,
    73, 79, 147, 156, 225, 239,
    245, 253, 270, 285
religion, orthodox, 9, 28, 140,
    206, 271
Renaissance, 147
resistance, to Spirit, 132
responsibility(ies)
    of chela, 24, 100, 123, 135, 136,
        201, 237, 267
    to life, 196
    of Mahanta, 10
    to Sugmad, 227
ritual(s), 66
Rod of ECK Power, 31
routines, 17

saint, 264
Satan, 45, 265. See also Kal
    Niranjan
Satsang, 23, 44, 215
Saul of Tarsus, 30, 65, 100, 123,
    196, 204
security, 2
seeker, of truth, 17, 146–47
self-identity, 184
self-mastery, 31, 69, 156, 191,
    200–1, 264, 276, 284, 288,
    290
self-preservation, 289
Self-Realization, 9, 17, 26, 80, 96,
    157, 223, 232, 249, 250
self-reliance, 149, 165
self-righteousness, 3
serenity, 135, 198
service, 3, 57, 136, 157, 165, 272
sex, 232–33
Shamus-i-Tabriz, 8, 19
Shariyat-Ki-Sugmad, The, 20,
    30, 131, 225, 244
Shariyat-Ki-Sugmad, 79, 138

Silent Ones, Nine, 1, 12
sin, 196, 267
singing, 33–34, 148
Socrates, 18
Soul
    call of, 91, 114, 152, 219
    creativity of, 163
    doors of, 226
    existence of, 181–82
    experience of, 46, 92
    heritage of, 249
    home of, 74
    journey of, 45
    lives beyond physical body, 83
    mates (see Soul mates)
    nature of, 173, 181–82
    Plane (see Plane(s): Soul)
    rejuvenation of, 89
    speaking directly to, 7
    Travel, See Soul Travel
    vision of, 46
Soul mates, 233
Soul Travel, 68–69, 256, 257, 287
sound(s)
    of buzzing of bees, 31, 55, 75,
        110, 127, 222, 239
    of flute, 31, 55, 75, 127, 222,
        239
    of humming, 35
    in singing, 34
    of stringed orchestra, 75
    sustains life, 36
    of thunder, 222
    of water, 127
    of whirlpool, 75
    of wind, 30
Sound
    Current (see Sound Current)
    of ECK, 31, 35, 37, 110
    neutralizes Light, 100, 180,
        203, 269
    Wave (see Sound Wave)
Sound Current, 114, 219
Sound Wave, 99
space
    feeling of, 134
    giving, 21, 53
Spiritual Exercises of ECK

Spiritual Exercises of ECK
(*continued*)
attributes from, 106, 238
with children, 161
and consciousness, 50, 69, 94, 96
creative, 21, 47, 105
and death, 52
discipline of, 96
and dreams, 285
experimenting with, 26, 226
and karma, 63
as key, 120
practice of, 107, 154, 164, 222
raises consciousness, 9, 103
for spiritual body, 129, 268
take us into inner worlds, 61,
66, 91, 140, 166
taking time for, 212
as way to heaven, 71, 206
Spiritual Eye, 177, 222, 239, 252
spiritual hunger, 219, 223
Spiritual Notebook, The
(Twitchell), 20, 41, 80, 89,
183, 211
spiritual traveler(s), 8, 107, 253
Steiger, Brad, 26, 114
In My Soul I Am Free, 26, 52,
114, 140
Stranger by the River (Twitchell),
225
strength, 12, 13, 53, 82
success
material, 52, 136, 191
spiritual, 191, 200
sugar, 126
Sugmad. *See also* God
experience of, 10
heart of, 3, 7, 8
learn about, 41
loyalty to, 1, 3
service to, 3, 74, 136
way to, 27
support, 11
surrender, 3, 196, 225, 251, 284

techniques. *See* Easy Way
technique; Spiritual Exercises of ECK

teenagers, 184
television, 183
temple
of clay, 90
within oneself, 12, 13, 20, 37,
47, 74, 127, 194, 238
Temple of Golden Wisdom, 182
test(s), 26, 251
Third Eye, 133
Tiger's Fang, The (Twitchell), 7,
8, 9, 40, 55, 211, 233
time, 44, 215
Tisra Til, 133, 222
tolerance, 3
tools, 8
Towart Managi, 257
translation, 83, 161. *See also*
Death
traps, 163
trust, 77
truth
expression of, 146, 164
self-recognition of, 106
shadow of, 179
Spirit leads to, 17
world of, 2
Turkey, 160
Twitchell, Paul. *See also* Peddar
Zaskq
brought out ECK writings, 13,
110, 138
Drums of ECK, The, 237
*ECKANKAR—The Key to
Secret Worlds*, 26, 41, 140,
222, 223
experiences of, 55, 245
Flute of God, The, 29, 109, 191,
212, 213, 243
as healer, 51
and his family, 103
humor of, 17
journeys of, 7–8
Key to ECKANKAR, The, 223
looked for God Consciousness,
95
as Mahanta, 8, 10
opportunities of, 27
as spiritual Master, 8, 127

Spiritual Notebook, The, 20,
    41, 80, 89, 183, 211
  as storyteller, 68
Stranger by the River, 225
Tiger's Fang, The, 7, 8, 9, 40,
    55, 211, 233
  writings of, 40, 73, 223, 225,
    251, 286

Understanding, 286
  of our actions, 94
  of troubles, 63
unfoldment
  of chela, 24, 56
  different levels of, 53, 80
  Soul's, 28, 92
  spiritual, 110, 122, 197, 209,
    227, 233, 264
uninitiated, 8, 12, 13
upliftment, 104, 156, 157, 238

vairag. *See* detachment
Vairagi, Order of, 1, 8, 11–12, 19,
    199
Vajra Manjushri, 89
vanity, 46, 102, 149
vehicle
  declare oneself a, 13
  for ECK, 41, 57, 104, 125, 203,
    249
  ECKist as a, 85, 146, 259
  for God, 257
  silent, 104
violence, 236
virginity, 234
vision, inner, 2, 144
voice, still small, 26
Voice of God, 71, 99, 114, 127,
    143, 192, 222, 239, 264, 270,
    281. *See also* ECK

Wah Z, 156, 239, 253
Wandering Jew, 51
wars, religious, 153
waters of immortality, 194–95

Wayshower, 10, 24, 96
Wheel of the Eighty-Four, 206
Wind of Change, The (Klemp),
    55, 211, 230
wisdom, 106, 164, 243, 246, 250,
    267, 286
word, secret, 73, 80, 226, 239,
    284
Word, the, 30, 204, 219, 270. *See
    also* ECK
worlds, lower, 92
worship
  attitude of, 225
  in ECK, 139
  of God, 24, 61, 66, 91, 139
  of Living ECK Master, 66

Yaubl Sacabi, 19